أصول اللغة العربية القرآنية

ESSENTIALS OF QURANIC ARABIC

Volume 1

Masood Aḥmed Ranginwala

Edited by
Dr. Abū Zayd Obaidullah Choudry
Director of the Quranic Literacy Institute
and
Sami Shamma
Professor of Qur'ānic Arabic, Hartford Seminary

ISLAMIC LEARNING FOUNDATION

Second Edition August 2013

Third Edition February 2015

ISBN 978-1-257-64498-8

Published by:
ILF- Islamic Learning Foundation (NY)
ICNA (Islamic Circle of North America)
166-26 89th Ave
Jamaica, NY 04262

masoodar@gmail.com
@MasoodAhmedR

Ordering information:

Special discounts are available on quantity purchases in the US by bookstores, institutions, mosques, educators, and others. For details, contact the publisher at the email above. This is a non-profit work, and neither the author, nor the publisher seek any profit. Please note that all profits go towards advancing Qur'ānic Studies. Additional copies of this 2-Volume Series softcover textbook or e-book can be purchased at: http://www.lulu.com/spotlight/MasoodR

Cover design by Adam Ranginwala and Omar Ranginwala.

Any mistakes or shortcomings in this book are due to errors of the author, and all that is correct and true solely are due to Allah ﷻ. Please feel free to contact the author at the email listed above to notify him of any errors present.

بسم الله الرحمن الرحيم

الحمد لله ربّ العالمين و الصّلاة و السّلام على نبينا محمّد

و على آله و صحبه أجمعين و من استنّ بسنّته إلى يوم الدين

القرآن شافع مشفع و ماحل مصدق من جعله أمامه

قاده إلى الجنة و من جعله خلف ظهره ساقه إلى النار

"The Qur'ān is an intercessor, something given permission to intercede, and it is rightfully believed in. Whoever puts it in front of him, it will lead him to Paradise; whoever puts it behind him, it will steer him to the Hellfire."

(An authentic Ḥadīth found in [المعجم الكبير] by At-Ṭabarānī, on the authority of 'Abdullāh ibn Mas'ūd verified as Ṣaḥīḥ in [السلسلة الصحيحة] by Sheikh al-Albāni)

Acknowledgements

All Praise is to Allah ﷻ for His Help and Guidance in allowing this Book to be manifest. I would also like to thank my many teachers who have guided me and imparted me knowledge in this sacred language. I am even more indebted to my parents who have raised me on the Religion, and who continue to advise and guide me. I am also grateful to my wife and children who have been very patient with this effort, and whose precious time I have sacrificed. I also give sincere thanks to the editors of this book, Dr. Abū Zayd, founder of the Quranic Literacy Institute and Professor Sami Shamma from the Hartford Seminary. Both gave excellent suggestions, corrected mistakes, and improved on its format and readability.

One special note of thanks also goes to one of my early teachers, Ustādh Noumān 'Alī Khān, founder of the Bayyinah Arabic Institute. He was my initial inspiration to teach what I learned of Qur'ānic Arabic and make it accessible to those who wish to learn from its treasures. I also thank my teachers at the Qibla Institute (formerly the Sunnipath Institute) namely Sheikh Hamza Karamāli and Sheikh Farīd Dingle. I also thank Sheikh Shakiel Humayun from the Foundation of Knowledge and Development. The individuals involved with websites "The Qur'ānic Arabic Corpus", "Zekr", and "OpenBurhan" also deserve recognition as their resources were used extensively for this work. May Allah ﷻ reward all these special people, and others not mentioned here who contributed to this book.

The journey of learning this sacred language has been an arduous one for me and has come with its challenges. It is my hope that this book series can facilitate this journey for other students, enabling them to understand the lofty and majestic words of the Qur'ān.

Transliteration Key

ئ/ؤ/أ/ء	'	ر	r	ف	f
ا	ā	ز	z	ق	q
ب	b	س	s	ك/ک	k
ت	t	ش	sh	ل	l
ث	th	ص	ṣ	م	m
ج	j	ض	ḍ	ن	n
ح	ḥ	ط	ṭ	ه/ة	h
خ	kh	ظ	ẓ	و	w, ū, u
د	d	ع	'	ي	y, i, ī
ذ	dh	غ	gh		

This transliteration key is provided to help bridge the gap between Arabic and English letters. There are several letters that are specific to the Arabic language, and do not have an English equivalent. We have chosen to capitalize many of the Arabic terms mentioned in this book, especially those of a grammatical context. Furthermore, Arabic terms written in English have been pluralized in English to facilitate the reader.

Reviews of "Essentials of Quranic Arabic"

★★★★★ **"I highly recommend Essentials of Qur'anic Arabic Volume 1"**

If your intention is to learn the grammatical functions of the language of The Qur'ān, then you find this book to be indispensable. The author has effectively organized the lessons to assist the student in being able to make the connections between the grammatical concepts and how they function in sentences or phrases within sentences. As a student of Qur'ānic Arabic, you will begin to see that the language has many nuances serving as a stimulus to further appreciate the depth, breadth, scope of the language as revealed and articulated in The Qur'ān.

As an added bonus, free of charge, the author has made available video instructional lessons of the chapters in volume one. To access the video lessons go to the following website *www.islamiconlineuniversity.com*. Go to the section Diploma in Islamic Studies-set up your account. Then, after you set up your account, go to Under the featured courses section, select Introduction To Qur'ānic Arabic Level 1. I highly recommend Essentials of Qur'ānic Arabic Volume 1 it will give you the necessary foundation to continue on at the intermediate and advanced levels of studying Qur'ānic Arabic grammar. (by JMC, Amazon.com, 8/14)

★★★★★ **"An amazing two volume set"**

An amazing two volume set, an enormous amount of time and care was put into the preparation of these 2 volumes. Fantastic resource....and it really helps to see how the various verbal and noun forms fit together to give a complete view..... (by David Martin, www.lulu.com, 11/13)

★★★★★ **"Beautiful book for learning Qur'anic Arabic"**

This is a beautiful book for anyone who desires to learn Qur'ānic Arabic. I am a serious student of the Arabic language and I bought this book for a friend of mine who wishes to be able to read the Qur'ān in Arabic. The book is very detailed, explains grammar points clearly, and includes a large amount of vocabulary found in the Qur'ān. The book itself is glossy and beautifully illustrated. I was very happy to find this book and it makes a beautiful gift for anyone who desires to learn the Arabic of the Qur'an. (by Student, Amazon.com, 7/14)

★★★★★ **"Quranic Arabic Grammar book - One of a Kind"**

Very well written and only book I have come across that has chapters on Qur'ānic Grammar Analysis and the Balāgha [Volume 2]. The summary tables of different grammatical topics are also very helpful for readers to comprehend the topic. Last but not the least, the appendix and the answers to review question sections are very thoughtful. (Muḥammad Ḥamid, Amazon.com, 10/14)

★★★★★ **"If you want to learn Arabic, then first read the Qur'an"**

This book was intended to be for my father, and he is always looking at it. I appreciate this offer! (Sebastian Garcia, Amazon.com, 4/13)

★★★★★ **"Great book at good price"**

This book makes Qur'ānic Arabic grammar easy. It needs no teacher. Lots of examples from the Qur'ān. But, one thing, though. You must have some basic knowledge about the Qur'ān and Arabic language before you can read it by yourself. Otherwise, read with someone else who possess that knowledge. I am happy and a regular user of this book. Finally, the price is so affordable! (by 'Abdullah Noman, Amazon.com, 2/14)

★★★★★ **"The focus on the Quran here is key..."**

The book goes at a nice pace to try to organize all the different constructs, rules and patterns in the mind so that one can get comfortable with the Qur'ān quickly. The focus on the Qur'ān here is key as the strategy and methodology used is to enable fast ascension to being able to analyze, understand and be familiar with any verse where references can be used for the very infrequent vocabulary while the principles are already understood. There is a lot of details, clear charts, terminology, and the diacritics are used on even the grammatical terms to make it consistent and easy to follow. The examples help instill the knowledge firmly as there is ultimately a lot to grasp if just reading but if by reciting, writing, listening and utilizing the linguistic faculties of our mind fully, the book gives you the ability to learn what you need at a fast pace without leaving one with any feelings of incompleteness or that anything is missing. I would hope more people would become fluent in the Qur'ānic Arabic, as it is a significant step towards being firm in knowledge and embodiment of Islam. (by Gregory Morse, www.lulu.com, 8/14)

✧✧✧✧✧ **"may Allah ﷻ reward you immensely for writing your book"**

I really appreciate a book that is concise, written in simplified English. I studied an intensive Arabic Qur'ānic grammar course a couple of years ago and the book we were going through. "Journey Through The Qur'ān", by Alan Jones, was one of the most complicated books I've ever had to study. It often left me frustrated and saddened. I have since, bought various books to understand and consolidate my understanding, as I like to compare how different authors explain the same concept with varied examples. Alḥamdulillah, I am studying your book and I can tell you that it is so easy to understand, Alḥamdulillah. (Umm Emaan, IOU Student, 1/14).

✧✧✧✧✧ **"I am teaching from your book"**

I am teaching from your book at the Hartford Seminary as well as the Cheshire Correctional Institution. It is the only book I found that is organized in the way I have been teaching for some years. Actually, I stopped writing my own textbook after I found yours.... .
(Sami Shamma, Adjunct Professor, Hartford Seminary, Chaplain CT Department of Corrections, 8/14)

✧✧✧✧✧ **"this struck me as the one"**
I am a big fan of that book; I've seen many different Arabic books and this struck me as the one.
(@calling2creator, twitter.com, 7/14)

Table of Contents

Foreword

Arabic grammar deals with principles by which the states of the endings of the words are known regarding declension (I'rāb) and construction (Binā'), and the manner of constructing one word with another. It is highly essential for the students of Arabic to learn this science in order to be proficient in the language. Acquiring an understanding of word patterns (Ṣarf) is also of prime importance in learning the language. "Essentials of Qur'ānic Arabic" is a book compiled for easy understanding of Qur'ānic Arabic with focus on its grammar rules. There are many books on Arabic grammar on the market today. For example, Hidāyatun Naḥw is one classical book that has been used in teaching Arabic grammar for generations.

The goal of this book is to enable the student to read, translate, and understand the Āyāt of the Qur'ān, Aḥādīth, and Arabic sentences without difficulty. Emphasis is also placed on learning the vocabulary with the help of standard dictionaries. Chapters in "Essentials of Qur'ānic Arabic" are organized in a simple way that can easily be understood by the students of this Subject. Review questions at the end of this book are very useful to practice and revise the concepts learned during the study. This is a comprehensive book dealing with all the important aspects of the Subject of Qur'ānic Arabic grammar. I am confident that when a student studies this book thoroughly with the guidance of a teacher or engages in self-study, they would develop a very good foundation in this science, and it would absolve them of the need to study similar books on the Subject.

I pray to Allah﷾ that He may make this book beneficial for the students of Arabic grammar and simplify the path to understanding the Qur'ān, and the Sunnah of the Prophet Muḥammadﷺ. I also pray that Allah﷾ bestow rewards for the compiler and everyone who contributed to its completion and publication. آمِين

Dr. Moḥammad Yūnus,
Director of the Tarbiyah Department (and Former Amīr) of ICNA
Imām, Masjid Da'wah, Bonifay, Fl.

Preface

I. The Importance of the Arabic Language

There are numerous benefits of learning the Arabic language. The primary benefit is to understand the Qur'ān, the final message of Allahﷻ that was revealed only in Arabic. By learning Arabic, the Final Revelation can be better comprehended, pondered upon, and used as a means of guidance. It is guidance, which is the most important benefit that one can obtain from this. The Qur'ān itself reminds us of these benefits as well.

﴿ إِنَّا أَنزَلْنَاهُ قُرْآنًا عَرَبِيًّا لَّعَلَّكُمْ تَعْقِلُونَ ﴾

Indeed, We have sent it, an Arabic Qur'ān so that you all may understand. (12:3)

﴿ قُرآنًا عَرَبِيًّا غَيْرَ ذِي عِوَجٍ لَّعَلَّهُمْ يَتَّقُونَ ﴾

It is a Qur'ān in Arabic, without any crookedness, in order that they may have Taqwah. (39:28)

Knowledge of the Arabic language is a means by which belief and awareness in Allahﷻ can be strengthened and elevated. It is through this language that Allahﷻ speaks to us. Translations are often inaccurate and cannot equal the beauty of the actual Arabic language. Translations are important but we need to know Arabic in "real" time. We cannot take out our translations during Ṣalāh, Jumu'ah Khutbah, or Tarāwīḥ in Ramaḍān. It is also through this language that the Messenger of Allahﷺ speaks to us. His living example and teachings are the best course of guidance for us, and a direct reflection from the Qur'ān.

Many scholars of Islam have stressed the importance of learning the language. Imām Shāf'īe said:

> "Every Muslim is obligated to learn the Arabic tongue to the utmost of his power in order to profess through it "There is no God but Allah and Muḥammad is His Messenger" and to utter what is mandated upon him...."[1]

Sheikh Ibn Taymīyah said:

> "The Arabic language is part of the religion, and knowing it is obligatory. This is because the ability to understand the Qur'ān and Sunnah is obligatory on every Muslim, and yet they cannot be understood without knowing Arabic, and (the general Islamic principle is that) every act that is an essential prerequisite to perform an obligatory act is also obligatory".[2]

1 Ar-Risāla [الرِّسالة], Imām Shāf'īe, pg. 93.

2 Iqtidā Ṣirātul Mustaqīm [اقتضاء الصراط المستقيم] pg. 469.

Islam has been preserved through the medium of Arabic, primarily through the Qur'ān and the Sunnah. In addition, it has been preserved through the numerous classical books on Islam written by scholars over the past 1400 years or so. These are some of the most important benefits of learning Arabic among others.

II. Text Goals and Objectives

The ultimate goal of this text is to enable the student to understand of the fundamentals of Qur'ānic grammar. Specifically, to understand the Qur'ān in terms of reading comprehension (i.e. understand the Qur'ān that you read). Our goal here is not to develop fluency in speaking the language. Instead, our first focus is on understanding the written words. From this, there is a direct progression to listening comprehension. Many think that speaking Arabic is the most important aspect of learning the language. However, we do not hold this sentiment, particularly in the context that the majority of today's Muslims do not understand basic spoken Arabic. However, since they have some basic ability to read the Qur'ān, a more realistic and relevant goal is to focus on Qur'ānic reading comprehension. Fluency in the language should be prioritized after gaining a solid foundation in reading and listening comprehension. Thus, our goal here is to gain reading and listening comprehension of the Divine words of Allah ﷻ. All other goals relative to learning Arabic should be secondary. Nonetheless, by learning Qur'ānic Arabic alone, the Ḥadīth of His Messenger ﷺ and other Islamic and contemporary Arabic literature can also be traversed.

III. Methodology of this Book

This book begins with the study of the three types of Arabic words, namely nouns, particles, and verbs. Then, it looks at various types of "Word Constructions" and compound words. This is followed by the study of "Noun Sentences", or Nominal Arabic sentences. The second half of the book focuses on verbs, verbal sentences, and verb derivatives. All throughout this book, a firm emphasis is placed on grammar. The vocabulary that is emphasized is specific to that of the Qur'ān, and taken from the collection "80% of Qur'ānic Vocabulary".[3] Each Lesson from this textbook comes with a list of vocabulary that needs to be learned and memorized.[4] More depth in vocabulary will Inshā-Allah allow the student to better utilize and apply grammar principles. Much of the technical Arabic terminology[5] found in Arabic grammar study is not emphasized to provide ease for the novice student. Each lesson covers specific fundamental rules of Arabic that are presented in a simplified and condensed manner, so that Qur'ānic Arabic can be learned in a most efficient way. Lastly, review questions are included in the back of the book

---

3 This excellent compilation of "high-yield" Qur'ānic vocabulary by 'Abdul-Raḥeem 'Abdul-'Azeez is available online for free download at http://emuslim.com/Qur'ān/English80.asp. Memorizing this booklet is a fundamental component of learning the basic essential vocabulary of Qur'ānic Arabic. It has been incorporated into this textbook for ease.

4 Refer to Required Vocabulary List for "Essentials of Qur'ānic Arabic" on pg. 151. This also includes "Supplemental Qur'ānic Vocabulary" as well.

5 A Glossary of Arabic Grammar Terminology is provided on pages 184-186 near the end of this book for reference if needed for important or commonly used Arabic grammar terms.

for every lesson so that the student can appropriately review the material. Without appropriate review and practicing examples from the Qur'ān, Qur'ānic Arabic cannot be properly learned.

There are several topics in Arabic Grammar that may be difficult. This will require effort and persistence. Inshā-Allah with time these concepts will be mastered. As the student embarks forward, concepts should start coming together like pieces of a puzzle. The goal of this First Volume is to develop the ability to translate a typical Āyah from the Qur'ān, Ḥadīth, or an Arabic sentence with the aid of an Arabic dictionary. The Second Volume builds on the core Arabic grammar principles found in this First Volume, in addition to other topics in intermediate grammar.

IV. Advice for the Student

It is essential to start with a righteous intention, and not to let this go. The Prophet ﷺ said in one well-known Ḥadīth central to Islam:

﴿إِنَّمَا الْأَعْمالُ بِالنِّيَاتِ وَ إِنَّما لِكُلِّ ٱمْرِئٍ ما نَوَى...﴾

"Indeed actions are by intention, and each person will have what he intends..."[6]

Keep in mind that when you are learning Arabic, you are in fact learning the Qur'ān, and developing the keys to understanding the Lofty Words of Allah ﷻ. Furthermore, you are also learning to understand the comprehensive speech of His Messenger ﷺ. The key to learning Arabic is being constant and consistent. This is not an endeavor of a few months. It takes persistence of several years to truly learn the language.[7] Most students give up after the first few weeks. However, the purpose of this book is to equip students with the necessary skills and fundamentals by which the Qur'ān, Ḥadīth, and other Arabic literature can be properly understood and utilized. The first step is the hardest: other steps become easier once that first step has been taken successfully.

Realize that the Qur'ān is weighty. Allah ﷻ tells His Messenger ﷺ:

﴿إِنَّا سَنُلْقِي عَلَيْكَ قَوْلًا ثَقِيلًا﴾

"Indeed, We will soon send upon you a weighty word" (73:4).

One final caveat is that the student should increase his/her connection with the Qur'ān. The Prophet ﷺ said: "The Book of Allah is the Rope of Allah which is dangling from the Heavens down to the Earth"[8]. It is of no benefit to learn the Arabic Grammar but not have a regular connection with the Qur'ān. This connection with the Qur'ān is

6 Ṣaḥīḥ al-Bukhāri, Chapter on Beginning of Revelation: كتاب بدء العحي, Ḥadīth #1.

7 This does not mean that students cannot learn the basics of Qur'ānic Arabic in less time. In a few months and with some dedication, students should be able to learn basic Qur'ānic Arabic بِإِذْنِ الله.

8 Musnad of Imām Aḥmed, [كتاب الله حبل ممدود من السماء إلى الأرض] Ḥadīth Classified as Ḥasan Ṣaḥīḥ by Sheikh Albāni.

essential and keeps our goal in focus. We need to continuously ask Allah ﷻ to help us succeed in this important journey. We also need to remain steadfast since Shayṭān will try to deter us from this great endeavor, and so will many commitments from our everyday lives.

The material presented in this textbook is ideally learned in a classroom setting with a teacher proficient in Qur'ānic Arabic Grammar. Nonetheless, dedicated students who can read the Qur'ān and do not have access to a teacher can Inshā-Allah benefit from the material presented here. Please note that we have collaborated with Islamic Online University in offering a free 3-level video course on "Introduction to Qur'ānic Arabic"[9]. This 3-level course series in the Diploma section of IOU is based on this textbook and would be helpful to all students. Additionally, for students who have taken an Introductory Arabic course, it should be very useful for review and advancement in the language. Students who are weak in Arabic reading and/or writing should devote the necessary time to enhance their skills prior to starting this course[10].

The gauge for successfully learning the material is successfully completing the assigned lessons and memorizing the required vocabulary. One major reason why students are not able to go forward in Arabic studies is that they simply do not study the material. Other similar reasons are not completing enough practice assignments and questions, or not memorizing enough vocabulary. When the material presented here has been mastered, the student will Inshā-Allah be able to translate a typical Āyah from the Qur'ān.

[9] You can register for this and other excellent free IOU courses at **www.islamiconlineuniversity.com/diploma.**

[10] An excellent free resource is the IOU Diploma course titled "Arabic Reading and Writing Made Easy".

History of Arabic Grammar

I. Arabic at the time of the Prophet ﷺ

Arabic had evolved to a very high level as a language when the Qur'ān was revealed. In terms of writing, Arabic words at the time did not have any dots on its letters besides not having any Ḥarakāt (diacritical vowel marks). The Arabs prided their language to such a degree that they would call non-Arabs [عجمي] or "one who is illiterate in language". The Arabs knew their language so well that illiteracy only made them better in mastering their native tongue. It was at this time that the lofty and imitable words of the Qur'ān were revealed to them through Prophet Muḥammad ﷺ. In fact, the Qur'ān directly challenged the Arabs in their own language to produce something like it. In Sūrah Baqarah, the following is stated:

﴿ وَإِن كُنتُمْ فِي رَيْبٍ مِّمَّا نَزَّلْنَا عَلَىٰ عَبْدِنَا فَأْتُوا۟ بِسُورَةٍ مِّن مِّثْلِهِۦ
وَٱدْعُوا۟ شُهَدَآءَكُم مِّن دُونِ ٱللَّهِ إِن كُنتُمْ صَٰدِقِينَ ﴾

"And if you are in doubt concerning that which We have sent down to Our slave, then produce a chapter of the like thereof and call your witnesses besides Allah, if you are truthful" (2:23).

The people of Makkah were well acquainted with Muḥammad ﷺ and his place in society. They all recognized him as the most exemplary and trustworthy among them. Further, it was known that he ﷺ had no ability to read or write. Muḥammad ﷺ was commanded to say:

﴿ قُلْ يَٰٓأَيُّهَا ٱلنَّاسُ إِنِّي رَسُولُ ٱللَّهِ إِلَيْكُمْ جَمِيعًا ٱلَّذِي لَهُۥ مُلْكُ ٱلسَّمَٰوَٰتِ وَٱلْأَرْضِ لَآ إِلَٰهَ إِلَّا هُوَ يُحْيِۦ وَيُمِيتُ
فَـَٔامِنُوا۟ بِٱللَّهِ وَرَسُولِهِ ٱلنَّبِيِّ ٱلْأُمِّيِّ ٱلَّذِي يُؤْمِنُ بِٱللَّهِ وَكَلِمَٰتِهِۦ وَٱتَّبِعُوهُ لَعَلَّكُمْ تَهْتَدُونَ ﴾

"Say: "O mankind! Verily, I am sent to you all as the Messenger of Allah, to Whom belongs the dominion of the heavens and the earth. None has the right to be worshiped but He; it is He Who gives life and causes death. So believe in Allah and His Messenger, the Prophet who can neither read nor write, who believes in Allah and His Words, and follow him so that you may be guided" (7:158).

Despite his lack of ability in reading and writing, which was a sign of his prophethood mentioned in the prior Scriptures[11], the Messenger of Allah ﷺ had been given the gift of eloquence by Allah ﷻ, and was the most eloquent

11 "Those who follow the Messenger, the Prophet who can neither read nor write whom they find written with them in the Torah and the Injīl (Gospel), who enjoins upon them what is right and forbids them what is wrong and makes lawful for them the good things and prohibits for them the evil and relieves them of their burden and the shackles which were upon them. So they who have believed in him, honored him, supported him and followed the light which was sent down with him it is those who will be the successful (7:157)."

of the Arabs. The Prophet ﷺ said:

﴿ بُعِثْتُ بِجَوامِعِ الْكَلِمِ ﴾

"I have been sent with Comprehensive speech."[12]

II. Evolution of Arabic Grammar

The earliest attempt to write the Arabic grammar began when ʻAli commissioned one of his students Abu al-Aswad ad-Du'ali (69 AH[13]) to codify Arabic grammar. During the time of the caliphate of ʻAli, it was apparent that Arabic grammar needed to be systemized. This was because many of the non-Arabs who had embraced Islam were making critical errors in the language. Here is an excerpt from Ad-Du'ali:[14]

> "I came to the Leader of the Believers, ʻAli ibn Abī Ṭālib, and found that he was holding a note in his hand. I asked, "What is this, O Leader of the Believers?" He said, "I have been thinking of the language of the Arabs, and I came to find out that it has been corrupted through contacts with these foreigners. Therefore, I have decided to put something that they (the Arabs) refer to and rely on." Then, he gave me the note and on it, he wrote:
>
> > "Speech is made of nouns, verbs, and particles. Nouns are names of things, verbs provide information, and particles complete the meaning." Then he said to me, "Follow this approach and add to it what comes to your mind."
>
> Ad-Du'ali continued to say, "I wrote two chapters on conjunctions and attributes then two chapters on exclamation and interrogatives. Then I wrote about [إِنَّ وَ أَخَوَاتِهَا] and I skipped [لَكِنَّ]. When I showed that to him, he ordered me to add [لَكِنَّ]. Therefore, every time I finished a chapter I showed it to him, until I covered what I thought to be enough. He said, "How beautiful is the approach you have taken!""

At this point in history, the science of grammar called [النَّحْو] started to evolve and blossom. Following Ad-Du'ali came many other grammarians, who studied and developed the science of the language. *The period between 750 and 1500 AD saw more than 4000 grammarians* who have been recorded in history.[15] Of these, the most famous was Sībaway (180 AH), who compiled the work, "Al-Kitāb", which became the standard reference for Arabic grammar. The teacher of Sībaway, al-Khalīl (75 AH) compiled the first complete Arabic dictionary [كِتَابُ الْعَيْنِ] based on Arabic root letters. The work of these grammarians and their counterparts set the paradigm for subsequent generations

12 Ṣaḥīḥ al-Bukhāri, Chapter on Holding Fast to the Book and Sunnah: كتاب الاعتصام بالكتاب و السنة, Ḥadīth # 6845.

13 AH refers to "After Hijri", is also the reference point for the Muslim calendar. The first year AH corresponds to 622 CE (Gregorian Calendar).

14 Adapted from Ibn al-Anbari in his book [نُزْهة الالباء في طبقات الأدباء].

15 Jiyad, Mohammed. *A Hundred and One Rules!*

of grammarians. These grammarians studied the Arabic of the Qur'ān, pre-Islamic poetry, and other literature from Bedouin Arabs as the ideal standard of the language. Interestingly, the pure, unadulterated language of the Bedouin Arabs became regarded as what we now know as Classical Arabic or Fuṣḥā [اَلْفُصْحى]. This pure Arabic was spoken for the first 300 years AH. Even though Classical Arabic is spoken rarely in today's time, the rules of Classical Arabic have been preserved in the voluminous classical works from Islamic scholarship. We hope that Inshā-Allah our Ummah will once again be able to understand and speak the original language that was spoken by the Prophet ﷺ, his companions رضي الله عنهم, and the early successors. آمين!

Lesson 1: Introduction to Arabic Grammar: The Arabic Word [الكلمة]

'Ali ﷺ said: "Speech is made of nouns, verbs, and particles. Nouns are names of things, verbs provide information, and particles complete the meaning." Then he ﷺ said to Abu al-Aswad ad-Du'ali ﷺ "Follow this approach and add to it what comes to your mind." We will Inshā Allah start in this same manner as A'li ﷺ, beginning with the study of the basic unit of speech, the word.

I. Pre-Grammar Review of Arabic

A. The Arabic Letters

These following letters comprise the complete Arabic alphabet and they are written from right to left.

ا ب ت ث ج ح خ د ذ ر ز س ش ص ض ط ظ ع غ ف ق ك ل م ن ه و ي

B. Tajwīd[16]

We need to know the correct pronunciation (Tajwīd) of each letter in a word. If we speak it wrong, there can sometimes be a drastic change in its meaning. Each letter should be pronounced according to its proper articulation (Makhraj). Please note the subtle difference between the hard Qāf and the light Kāf in the first example below. Short and long vowels also need to be pronounced correctly; else, the improper meaning can be ascribed. In the second example, look at the vowel placed on the last Nūn letter on each of the two words. If the vowel is not appropriately elongated or shorted, the incorrect word will be articulated, and the meaning drastically altered.

- كَلْبٌ (dog) vs. قَلْبٌ (heart)
- جَعَلْنَا (We made) vs. جَعَلْنَ (the women made)

Appropriate Tajwīd prevents the listener from confusing between similar letters. This is important especially for letters that sound similar. The letters shown on the following page are often difficult to distinguish and frequently pronounced incorrectly. This is commonplace particularly for those from Southeast Asia.

16 There are many resources to learn and review Tajwīd. We recommend the excellent online lectures of Tajwīd on www.youtube.com by Sheikh Yāsir Qādhi or Ustādh Wisām Sharief.

➢ س vs. ص vs. ث

➢ ز vs. ظ vs. ذ

➢ ق vs. ك

➢ أ vs. ع

➢ ح vs. ه

C. Vowels and Diacritical marks in Arabic: A Quick Review

1. There are three vowels (حَرَكات) in Arabic: Ḍammah, Fatḥah, and Kasrah.

- Ḍammah (ـُ)
- Fatḥah (ـَ)
- Kasrah (ـِ)

2. The **Sukūn** (ـْ) is a symbol that represents a necessary silence on a letter.

Arabic cannot have two consecutive Sukūn because this causes no pronunciation between letters. When there is the potential of two consecutive Sukūn occurring during sentence construction, a Kasrah is added between those letters so that "flow" is maintained between words. Let us look at the example below to get clarity on this concept.

➢ قالَتْ ٱلْأَعْرابُ *becomes written as* قالَتِ ٱلْأَعْرابُ

You will note that a silent Alif is between two Sākin letters of Tā and Lām. If there is no addition vowel added to one of the underlined letters, none of the three letters would be articulated properly. Thus, by adding a Kasrah to the first Sākin letter Tā, the letters are articulated with the middle Alif being silent.

3. **Tanwīn** refers to doubling of one of the three short vowels represented by the following [ـً ـٌ ـٍ].

Tanwīn has a Nūn sound at the end. Tanwīn Ḍammah can also be represented by the symbol [ـٌ]. It has a Nūn sound at the end. One detail to note is that Double Fatḥah is directly followed by an Alif. Examples of this are seen in the following words: [رَجُلًا/مَسْجِدًا/بَيْتًا]. Omitting the last Alif in each of these three words would render the word as being incorrectly written. This Alif is pronounced if there is a pause or end at the letter, which ends in Fatḥah.

One exception to these rules is when a word ending with a Tā Marbūṭah has Fatḥah Tanwīn. For example, the word [آيَةً] is pronounced as "Ayah". Here, there is no Alif afterwards, nor is there an Alif sound after a pause or stop. Instead, the sound at the pause or stop is that of a light "ah". Essentially, the Tā Marbūṭah letter phonetically sounds like the letter [ه]. This phonetic occurrence is irrespective of which vowel is placed, and occurs even if the Definite article "Al" is affixed to the word. For example, all of the following words are spoken with the same ending of the [ه] letter: [مُسْلِمَةٌ/البَقَرَة/آيَةٍ]. So, the word [آيَةً] is pronounced as "Āyah" and this is the same whether the ending is Ḍammah, Kasrah, or Fatḥah. Another exception to this rule of Alif following a Fatḥah Tanwīn is that of words ending in Alif Hamza. Words such as [ماءً] or [نساءً] do not end with an Alif.

4. Shadda [ـَّـ ـِّـ ـُّـ ـٌّـ ـٍّـ ـًّـ] is a symbol placed above a letter and causes a doubling of the letter. For example, in the word [قَلَّ], the root letters are [قلل], where the Shadda Lām represents two Lāms[17].

D. Distinction of the Alif [ا] and Hamzah [أ]

Alif [ا] is a letter, which is pronounced only when it starts a sentence or when, is present directly after a pause within a sentence. The letter Hamzah [ء], on the other hand, is always pronounced. If Alif is the first letter at the initiation of a sentence, or after a pause, a Hamzah al-Waṣl is added so that it can be pronounced. This essentially is an Alif with a vowel, most cases being the Fatḥah. This is because Alif by itself is a silent letter, when not used as a vowel. In general, the Hamzah al-Waṣl is represented as an Alif with a small Ṣād on top [ٱ]. Please note that the actual use of the Hamzah al-Waṣl despite its presence is dictated by the rules described above. There are times when it is silent, and there are times when the Hamzah al-Waṣl (Alif) is vocalized.

In example (i) on the next page, the Alif is pronounced because it starts the sentence. In example (ii) however, Alif remains silent **if the sentence is articulated to its end without a pause**. The letter Hamzah on the other hand is pronounced even though it comes in the middle of a sentence, as we see in (ii). Please note that in (ii), if there is a spoken pause after [يَا أَيُّهَا ٱلَّذِينَ آمَنُوا], the Alif in [ٱدْخُلوا] will have to be pronounced. In this case, there is a Ḍammah on the Alif. If there is no pause, the Alif is silent.

---

[17] In case of the letter with a Shadda, the first letter grammatically contains a Sukūn which is not apparent.

(i) ٱدْخُلُوا فِي ٱلسِّلْمِ كَافَّةً

(ii)[18] ﴿ يَا أَيُّهَا ٱلَّذِينَ آمَنُوا ٱدْخُلُوا فِي ٱلسِّلْمِ كَافَّةً ﴾

In the following example from Sūrah Fātiḥah below, the first Alif takes a Fatḥah, as is the typical case of sentences that begin with [ال]. As for the second Alif, it remains silent since there is already a preceding vowel before it (Kasrah).

﴿ ٱلْحَمْدُ لِلَّهِ رَبِّ ٱلْعَٰلَمِينَ ﴾

The Hamzah needs to be "seated" on one of three letters. The "seat" of the Hamzah can be Alif, Wāw, or Yā, depending on the preceding vowel[19]. Please note that in the first example below [سَأَلَ], the seat of the Hamzah is an Alif because its preceding vowel is a Fatḥah. In the second example, the seat is a Wāw, since its preceding vowel is a Ḍammah.

سَأَلَ رُؤُوسٌ بَرِيءٌ

E. Difference between Tā [ت] and Tā Marbūṭah [ة]

Tā Marbūṭah is pronounced as a Tā [ت]. However, if it is the last word in a sentence, or if there is a pause ending with this letter, it is pronounced as a [ه] as was mentioned in Section C. A general rule that occurs in Arabic reading is the following: when there is a stop at the end of a sentence, or a pause in the middle, the last vowel is **not** spoken. The exception to this principle is that of words ending with **double Fatḥah vowels**.

F. Tashkīl

Most written Arabic including Classical Islamic texts do not have Tashkīl (short vowels and diacritical markings). The main exception to this is the Qur'ān and Ḥadīth collections. Being able to read Arabic without Tashkīl requires a thorough knowledge of both grammar and vocabulary. For Qur'ān reading, we generally recommend using the Naskhī[20] Muṣḥaf (the mint green Saudi Muṣḥaf) instead of the Farsi Muṣḥaf to learn Arabic since it emphasizes the Hamzah and excludes extra Tashkīl. Please note both are authentic Muṣḥafs. Most written Arabic today in Islamic literature and beyond follow this Naskhī Muṣḥaf style.

[18] "O you who believe, Enter into Islām completely" (2:208).

[19] Please note that there are exceptions to this rule when it comes to the Hamza being preceded by the Alif for some words. You have for example the following words, which do not follow this rule: [صَائِم/سائِل/جاؤُوا].

[20] This cursive style of Arabic writing originated in the 4th century AH, and was widely used for copying the Qur'ān. Since the 5th century AH, the Naskhī script gradually replaced Kūfic for copying of the Qur'ān due to its beauty and legibility. It is perhaps the most popular script today in the Arabic world. Furthermore, most Arabic today has diacritical marks from this style.

II. The Arabic Word [الكَلِمَة]

A. Arabic Word Categories

Words in Arabic are usually associated with a "Root Verb" composed of three "root" letters. Its meaning is typically related to the root word, either directly or indirectly. The vast majority of Arabic nouns are based on a single three-letter root verb. For example, the word [عِلْمٌ] that means "knowledge" comes from the verb [عَلِمَ], "to know". The word [فِتْنَةٌ], which means "tribulation" or "trial" is derived from the verb [فَتَنَ], "to test".

- The Arabic Word is one of three categories of words.

  i. Fi'l [فِعْلٌ] (verb)

  ii. Ism [اِسْمٌ] (noun)

  iii. Ḥarf [حَرْفٌ] (particle)

B. Ism - The Arabic Noun [اَلْاِسْم]

i. The Arabic noun includes the following categories of words:

- noun
- pronoun
- adjective
- verbal noun (denotes action not confined to a specific time period (past, present, or future)

ii. Only nouns carry Tanwīn [ـً ـٌ ـٍ]

iii. Only nouns carry Tā Marbūṭah [ة]

iv. Only nouns contain "Al" [ال-]

v. Most words beginning with the letter [م] are nouns.

vi. When we mention the Name "Allah" linguistically, we avoid saying "the word Allah" or "the name Allah" in order to give proper respect to Allahﷻ, and to prevent using His name in a casual way. Instead, we say [لَفْظُ الْجَلَالَة], the Grand Word.

vii. Nouns can have several different plural patterns, and thus are more challenging to learn than English plurals. *It is essential to memorize the plural of a noun along with its single form.*

C. F'il - The Arabic Verb [اَلْفِعل]

The Arabic verb or "F'il" refers to an action confined to a specific time. Thus, the action is confined to the Past, Present, or Future Tense.

- **e.g.** He killed ≠ he is killing, He went ≠ he is going

i. It does not have Tā Marbūṭah [ة].

ii. It does not have Tanwīn [ـً ـٌ ـٍ].

iii. It does not carry the particle "Al" [الـ].

iv. Numerous nouns and verb-like entities can be derived from verbs.

v. Verbs are conjugated in the Past Tense, the Future/Present Tense, or the Command Tense.

vi. Most words that begin with the letter Yā [يَـ] are verbs. On a similar note, many words that also begin the letter Tā [تَـ] also are verbs.

D. Ḥarf - The Arabic Particle [اَلْحَرْف]

The third category of words in Arabic is particles or [حُرُوف]. A particle associates with a word directly following it to result in a useful meaning (in speech). The associated word is either a verb or a noun. A particle itself is composed of one, two, or three letters. There are several particles in Arabic that have diverse grammatical functions. In this Volume, we will focus on particles that cause a change in I'rāb. Specifically, they are those that cause a change in inflection or case of the word that they are associated. Particles that do not cause a change in I'rāb are termed [حُرُوف غَيْرُ عامِلَة]. Those will also be reviewed.

➢ Particles include the following categories of words among others:

- Prepositions
- Words indicating Emphasis
- Conjunctions
- Particles of Negation
- Conditional Particles
- Particles of Interrogation
- Connectors

III. The Four Characteristics of Arabic Nouns [اَلأَسْماء]

An Ism is defined as an Arabic noun. In this text, the term "noun" will be synonymous with "Ism". It can be a person, place, object, adjective, verbal noun, or action (e.g. murder, anger).

➢ **Every Arabic Noun has four characteristics**

i. **I'rāb [إِعْراب] - Case or inflection** (grammatically known as nominative, accusative, or genitive).

a) [رَفْع] Raf' (nominative)

b) [نَصْب] Naṣb (accusative)

c) [جَرّ] Jarr (genitive)

ii. **[اَلْعَدَد] Number/plurality (single, dual, or plural)**

iii. **[اَلْجِنْس] Gender (masculine or feminine)**

iv. **[اَلْقِسْم] Definiteness (Indefinite or Definite)**

Only nouns carry all these four characteristics mentioned above. **Verbs and Particles have different rules, and are discussed later.** Knowing the four characteristics of nouns allows one to determine the inflection or "grammatical state" of the word in an Āyah of the Qur'ān, or in a typical Arabic sentence. This is known as I'rāb.

IV. I'rāb [إِعْراب]

The I'rāb of a noun points to the specific grammatical role that it has in a sentence. For example, in a Verbal Sentence, the word that takes the I'rāb of Raf' is identified as the Doer, or the subject, which does the action. A word in the Naṣb case, on the other hand, in the same sentence will be identified as the Direct Object of the verb. A word with the I'rāb of Jarr is either associated with a preposition or functions in a role of possession.

To determine the I'rāb of a noun, we need to examine the inflection on its last letter. In order to do this, we first need to determine the other three qualities of the respective word, such as its gender, plurality, and definiteness. We then examine the noun's ending vowel, and then lastly determine its I'rāb. Please note that verbs can also have I'rāb, and are discussed later in Lesson 10 in more detail. One will better understand I'rāb and inflection of Arabic words by looking at the following principles and examples presented here in this Lesson.

A. The Three Types of I'rāb (for Nouns)

i. رَفْع Raf' (Nominative)

- Subject in a Verbal Sentence.
- Subject in a Nominal sentence.
- Predicate in a Nominal sentence.
- In Arabic, there are up to eight conditions in which a noun can take the Raf' case. Some of these conditions are discussed in this First Volume, while the rest are discussed in Volume 2.

ii. نَصْب Naṣb (Accusative)

- Object in a Verbal Sentence.
- Objects of certain particles [إنّ و أخواتها].
- Adverbs [مَفْعُول] denoting detail of an action (of a verb).
- In Arabic, please note that there are up to twelve conditions where a noun can take the Naṣb case. Some of these conditions are examined in this First Volume, while the remaining are discussed in Volume 2.

iii. جرّ Jarr (Genitive)

- Can denote possession, typically the word after "of" [إضافة].
- Objects of preposition [حُروف الجَرّ]
- In Arabic, only one of the two conditions above causes a noun to be Jarr.

B. Determining I'rāb of Nouns

Determining the I'rāb of nouns is done by examining the vowel ending on the last letter. The Ḍammah vowel typically denotes the case of Raf'. The Fatḥah vowel denotes the Naṣb case whereas the Kasrah vowel denotes the Jarr case. Please note that nouns that are Indefinite typically carry Tanwīn, whereas nouns that are Definite (with "Al") do not carry Tanwīn. Even though identifying the last vowel usually allows one to successfully determine the I'rāb, this is sometimes not the case. There are several exceptions, particularly if the noun is not singular. At this point, we are only beginning to analyze the Arabic noun and the concept of I'rāb. It is important to focus on the main principles rather to dwell on the exceptions.

i. **Ḍammah** [ـُ ـٌ] at the end of a noun denotes **Raf'.**

ii. **Fatḥah** [ـَ ـً] at the end on a noun **typically denotes Naṣb.**

- (Exceptions are the Partially Flexible nouns like [مَرْيَمَ] and [إبْرَاهِيمَ].

iii. **Kasrah** [ـِـ ـٍـ] at the end of a noun denotes **Jarr.**

- Exceptions are <u>rare</u> such as words like [قاضٍ] and [ماضٍ] both of which are Raf'.

C. <u>Identifying Singularity, Plurality and Duality of Nouns</u>

Arabic nouns come in the singular, dual, or plural tense. The specific number that is reflected by any word depends on its morphology, and/or its ending. Unlike English, Arabic words are also found in the dual form. Furthermore, words in the plural form (more than two) come in one of several different plural patterns.

1. <u>Dual Nouns and their Structure</u> [ـَانِ / ـَيْنِ]

A dual noun can be readily identified by looking at its ending. It typically carries one of two endings, [ـَانِ] or [ـَيْنِ]. Any noun in the single form can be converted to the dual form by simply adding one of the two endings above at its end. The specific dual ending chosen is based on the I'rāb of the respective word. The ending [ـَانِ] denotes Raf', while the [ـَيْنِ] ending denotes either Jarr or Naṣb.

a. [ـَانِ] Raf'

b. [ـَيْنِ] Naṣb or Jarr

Table 1: I'rāb of Singular and Dual Nouns				
Singular (Raf')	Singular (Naṣb)[21]	Singular (Jarr)	Dual (Raf')	Dual (Naṣb/Jarr)
كَلِمَةٌ word	كَلِمَةً	كَلِمَةٍ	كَلِمَتَانِ	كَلِمَتَيْنِ
حَبِيبٌ beloved	حَبِيبًا	حَبِيبٍ	حَبِيبَانِ	حَبِيبَيْنِ
مُسْلِمٌ Muslim	مُسْلِمًا	مُسْلِمٍ	مُسْلِمَانِ	مُسْلِمَيْنِ
عَيْنٌ eye	عَيْنًا	عَيْنٍ	عَيْنَانِ	عَيْنَيْنِ

﴿كَلِمَتَانِ حَبِيبَتَانِ إلى الرَّحْمٰنِ خَفِيفَتَانِ عَلٰى اللِّسانِ ثَقِيلَتَانِ فِي الْمِيزَانِ سُبحانَ اللهِ وبِحَمدِهِ سُبحانَ اللهِ الْعَظِيمِ﴾

"Two words beloved words to Ar-Raḥmān, that are light on the tongue, heavy on the scales,

[سُبحانَ اللهِ وبِحَمدِهِ سُبحان اللهِ الْعَظِيمِ][22]".

[21] For Indefinite nouns which have a double Fatḥah ending (Fatḥah with Tanwīn), an extra Alif is placed at the ending letter. The exception is the Tā Marbūṭah. For example, for the word [مُسْلِمٌ] in Naṣb is [مُسْلِمًا] and not [مُسْلِمً]. This Alif denotes a Fatḥah Tanwīn if Tashkīl is not present. It also indicates that the Alif be pronounced if a stop is made at that letter, as opposed to no pronunciation of the last vowel if it is a Ḍammah or Kasrah Tanwīn.

In looking at this Ḥadīth, the underlined words are all dual. However, we also see that some words with the [ـَانِ] ending in the Ḥadīth are not dual. For example, the words [سُبْحان / الرَّحمان / اللِّسان / ميزان] are all single. This shows that there are several words in Arabic with an [ـَان] ending that are not dual. It is important to note that this occurrence is yet another exception, which sometimes may occur. However, these words can end in either Ḍammah, Fatḥah, or Kasrah, whereas dual ending is always with a Kasrah.

2. <u>Sound Masculine Plural</u> [جَمْعُ المُذَكَّرِ السَّالِم]

The "Sound Masculine Plural" is the plural pattern found on nouns that act as "Doer Nouns" [اِسْمُ الْفاعِل] or "Passive Nouns" [اِسْمُ الْمَفْعول]. Nouns that depict a person or persons doing a particular action take this pattern. Similar to the dual inflection on nouns, there are two possible endings. The [ـُونَ] ending is placed on sound masculine plural that take Raf', while the [ـِينَ] ending is placed on plurals taking either Naṣb or Jarr.

Table 2: I'rāb of Sound Masculine Plural					
Singular (Raf')		Singular (Naṣb)	Singular (Jarr)	Plural (Raf')	Plural (Naṣb/Jarr)
مُسْلِمٌ	Muslim	مُسْلِمًا	مُسْلِمٍ	مُسْلِمُونَ	مُسْلِمِينَ
نَاصِرٌ	helper	نَاصِرًا	نَاصِرٍ	نَاصِرُونَ	نَاصِرِينَ
مُعَلَّمٌ	student	مُعَلَّمًا	مُعَلَّمٍ	مُعَلَّمُونَ	مُعَلَّمِينَ

3. <u>Sound Feminine Plural</u> [جَمْعُ المُؤَنَّثِ السَّالِم]

This plural pattern only applies to words that have the feminine Tā Marbūṭah letter [ة]. Most nouns that end with this letter take this Sound Feminine Plural even if they are nonhuman objects. The [ـَات] ending replaces the Tā Marbūṭah. The ending in Raf' is [ـَاتٌ], while the ending in Naṣb/Jarr is [ـَاتٍ].

22 Ṣaḥīḥ al-Bukhāri, Chapter on Tawhīd: كتاب التَّوحيد, Ḥadīth #7124. This is the Last Ḥadīth of Ṣaḥīḥ al-Bukhāri

Table 3: I'rāb of Sound Feminine Plurals					
Singular (Raf')		Singular (Naṣb)	Singular (Jarr)	Plural (Raf')	Plural (Naṣb/Jarr)
مُسْلِمَةٌ	Muslimah	مُسْلِمَةً	مُسْلِمَةٍ	مُسْلِماتٌ	مُسْلِماتٍ
كَلِمَةٌ	word	كَلِمَةً	كَلِمَةٍ	كَلِمَاتٌ	كَلِمَاتٍ
آيَةٌ	sign	آيَةً	آيَةٍ	آيَاتٌ	آيَاتٍ

4. Broken Plurals [جَمْعُ التَّكْسِير]

Broken Plurals are by far the most common plural pattern type for nouns. There are several different patterns possible. As we go forward in later lessons, we will discuss these patterns in detail. Also for ease and clarity, we will assume that any specific noun takes only one respective Broken Plural pattern.[23] Unlike dual nouns and Sound Plurals, the I'rāb of Broken Plurals is determined simply by looking at the vowel endings (just like in single nouns).

Table 4: I'rāb of Broken Plurals					
Singular[24] (Raf')	Singular (Naṣb)	Singular (Jarr)	Plural (Raf')	Plural (Naṣb)	Plural (Jarr)
قَلَمٌ	قَلَمًا	قَلَمٍ	أَقْلَامٌ	أَقْلَامًا	أَقْلَامٍ
قَلْبٌ	قَلْبًا	قَلْبٍ	قُلُوبٌ	قُلُوبًا	قُلُوبٍ
رَسُولٌ	رَسُولًا	رَسُولٍ	رُسُلٌ	رُسُلًا	رُسُلٍ

23 Most nouns in Arabic take a Broken Plural, which consists of one of several different morphological patterns that are discussed later. Some nouns take more than one type of Broken Plural pattern. For example, the word بَحْر can take two plural patterns, بُحُور and بِحَار. In the Qur'ān we only find the pattern بِحَار mentioned. Thus this is the most prominent pattern for this word, and should be memorized and focused upon and not the other for ease and clarity.

24 The meaning of the following words is the following: [قَلَمٌ] is pen, [قَلْبٌ] is heart, and [رَسُولٌ] is messenger.

Lesson 2: I'rāb and Flexibility

I. The Three Categories of Arabic Words: Revisited

1. **Noun** [أَسْماءٌ / اِسْمٌ]

   - [اِسْمٌ] can be a noun, pronoun, adjective, adverb, or infinitive verb (verbal noun). In this text, the term noun will be synonymous with Ism.

2. **Verb** [أَفْعَالٌ / فِعْلٌ]

   - It is defined as action connected to a specific time (past, present, or future). It does not carry Tā Marbūṭah or Tanwīn[25].

3. **Particle** [حُرُوفٌ / حَرْفٌ]

   - A particle needs to join to a corresponding word to yield a meaning. It always comes before the word that it links with. It is often composed of less than three letters.

II. The Noun [الاسْم] and Its Four Characteristics

A. Gender [اَلجِنْس]

Every noun has a gender, either masculine or feminine. The gender of the noun will require other words referring to it (pronouns, pointing nouns, adjectives, and verbs) to adapt to its respective gender. For example, when an adjective describes "a girl", it needs to be modified to the feminine morphology. This same principle holds true for a pronoun or a Pointing Noun (that, this, etc.) that refers to a respective noun.

All Arabic nouns can be assumed masculine unless proven otherwise. This is because feminine nouns usually contain a sign within their word structure that points to their femininity. The most common sign is the Tā Marbūṭah [ة]. Please note that words that are universally feminine (mother, daughter, female names, etc.) do not need such a sign in their word structure.

[25] In rare cases, verbs can have Tanwīn. In the Qur'ān (96:15) ﴿كَلَّا لَئِن لَّم يَنتَهِ لَنَسفَعاً بِالنَّاصِيَةِ﴾, the underlined word is a verb with an apparent Tanwīn. This situation however has more to do with morphology than grammar. The suffixed emphatic particle is known as the Nūn of emphasis (نون التوكيد), and is indicated by Tanwīn.

➢ Common Feminine Signs on Nouns

- ending with: Tā Marbūṭah [ة] as in [كَلِمَةٌ]
- ending with Alif Mamdūdah [ـاء] as in [سَماءٌ][26]
- body parts in pairs: [عَيْنٌ / رِجْلٌ / يَدٌ][27]
- names of countries or lands: [الرُّومُ / مِصْرُ][28]
- **Special feminine nouns:** the feminine nouns shown below do not possess a feminine sign in their word structure.

Table 5: Special Feminine Nouns											
سُوقٌ	نارٌ	خَمْرٌ	نَفْسٌ	رِيحٌ	شَمْسٌ	حَرْبٌ	سَبِيلٌ	عَصا	كَأْسٌ	بِئْرٌ	دارٌ
market	fire	wine	self; soul	wind	sun	war	path	stick	cup	well	house

➢ **Exceptions:**

- Masculine names with a feminine sign [طَلْحَةٌ].
- Masculine Broken Plurals such as the following: [رِجالٌ/ملائِكَةٌ/رُسُلٌ]. Please see discussion on Broken Plurals in the next section.

B. Number/Plurality [اَلْعَدَد]

i. Singular

ii. Dual - add [ـَانِ] or [ـَيْنِ] to its end.

a) [ـَانِ] : Raf'

b) [ـَيْنِ] : Naṣb or Jarr

iii. Plural (more than 2)

a) **Broken Plural** [جَمْعُ التَّكْسِير] - most common plural

The most common types of Broken Plurals are listed on the next page. Please note that Broken Plurals in Arabic are considered feminine single. This is grammatically the case even if the respective noun is masculine. If the noun is a "male person", then there are two correct grammatical possibilities being either male or female. This point is being mentioned since both these two variations are found in the Qur'ān.

26 Translated as "sky" or "heaven".

27 Translated from left to right as " eye, foot, and hand".

28 Translated from left to right as "Rome and Egypt".

Broken Plural Pattern[29]	Single Noun	Plural Noun
أَفْعَالٌ	قَلَمٌ pen	أَقْلَامٌ
فُعُولٌ	دَرْسٌ lesson	دُرُوسٌ
فِعَالٌ	جَبَلٌ mountain	جِبالٌ
فَعاعِلُ	مَسْجِدٌ mosque	مَساجِدُ

b) **Sound Feminine Plural** [جَمْعُ المُؤَنَّثِ السَّالِمِ] ending with Tā Marbūṭah [ة].

- [اتٌ] **replaces** [ة] **in** Raf' I'rāb.
- [اتٍ] **replaces** [ة] **in** Jarr or Naṣb I'rāb.

c) **Sound Masculine Plural** [جَمْعُ المُذَكَّرِ السَّالِمِ].

These plurals are found on "Doers" or persons involved in doing a certain action, or task. They can also be found on persons receiving the action termed "Passive Nouns". These two categories of nouns are discussed in detail in Lesson 11, sections II and III.

- [ونَ] is added to the **end** of the single noun in Raf' I'rāb.
- [ينَ] is added to the **end** of the single noun in Jarr or Naṣb I'rāb.

C. Definiteness [المَعْرِفَة/النَّكِرَة]

i. Definiteness [اَلْمَعْرِفَة]

A Definite or proper noun is a noun that is specific, defined, and more than ordinary. It may also be a noun that is specified by a relationship (e.g. my pen, his mother, etc.). Any noun that begins with the particle [ال-] is Definite since this particle denotes "the" on that particular noun. Any noun that is given a name also becomes Definite by default. In this case, an [ال-] does not need to be added. For example, the following nouns are all Definite: [مُحَمَّدٌ/عَائِشَةُ/مَنْصُورٌ/مِصْرُ/مَكَّةُ]. In these cases, an [ال-] does not need to be added. Please also note that most Definite nouns do not carry Tanwīn since nouns with [ال-] cannot carry Tanwīn. This is also the case with many names that are Partially Flexible. Flexibility is discussed later on in Section III of this lesson.

29 The letters [فعل] represent a stem in Arabic grammar that denote various patterns of words, whether nouns or verbs. These letters are used to teach morphological derivations and conjugation patterns of several different classes of words in Arabic. We will revisit this [فعل] stem frequently in this Volume and later as well Inshā-Allah.

a) Adding [ال-] adds the particle "the" to any Indefinite noun making it Definite. Words with [ال-] do not take Tanwīn and end in a single vowel.

مَسْجِدٌ ⇨ اَلْمَسْجِدُ

Mosque → **the** mosque

b) Any proper name of a person or place is Definite: [مُحَمَّدٌ / مَكَّةُ /مُوسَى]

c) Any possession relationship is Definite. Examples are the following:

my house / your town / Messenger of Allah

[رَسولُ اللهِ / بَلَدُكَ / بَيْتِي]

ii. Indefiniteness [اَلنَّكِرَة]

Nouns that do not have [ال-] are typically Indefinite and take Tanwīn by default[30]. Please note the following examples [قَلَمٌ / مَسْجِدٌ / رَجُلٌ][31].

D. I'rāb [إِعْراب] - Case/Inflection

The term I'rāb reflects a specific case that every noun carries. Specifically, it is a characteristic that imparts the noun to have certain grammatical function(s). Every noun carries one of three cases. The default case of a noun is the Raf' state. For example, only nouns in the Raf' I'rāb can function as the Subject in a Nominal Sentence. Likewise, the "Doer" can only be Raf' in a Verbal Sentence. By contrast, only a noun in the "Naṣb" I'rāb can function as an "object" of a verb in a Verbal Sentence. The specific I'rāb is reflected on nouns by the varying vowels at their ends.

i. The Three Cases

- [رَفْع] Raf' - Nominative
- [نَصْب] Naṣb - Accusative
- [جَرّ] Jarr - Genitive

30 Please note that certain proper names take Tanwīn and include the following [مُحَمَّدٌ / نُوحٌ / مَنْصُورٌ].

31 Translations of the words from left to right are the following "a man, a masjid, a pen".

ii. How to Distinguish the Three Different I'rābs

a. By the Ending Vowel on a Noun

1. **Ḍammah** [ـُ ـٌ] at the end of a noun denotes **Raf'**.

2. **Fatḥah** [ـَ ـً] at the end on a noun **typically denotes Naṣb.**
   - Exceptions are the Partially Flexible nouns like [مَرْيَمَ] and [إِبْرَاهِيْمَ].

3. **Kasrah** [ـِ ـٍ] at the end of a noun denotes **Jarr.**
   - Exceptions are rare such as words like [قَاضٍ] and [مَاضٍ], both of which are Raf' here.

b. By the Dual Ending on a Noun (revisited)

- [ـَانِ] for Raf'
- [ـَيْنِ] for Naṣb or Jarr

c. By the Endings on Sound Masculine Plurals (revisited)

- [ـُوْنَ] for Raf'
- [ـِيْنَ]for Naṣb or Jarr

d. By the Endings on Sound Feminine Plurals

- [ـَاتٌ] for Raf'
- [ـَاتٍ] for Naṣb or Jarr

Table 6: Inflection of "Noun Endings" by I'rāb and Flexibility[32]			
[جَرّ] Jarr	[نَصْب] Naṣb	[رَفع] Raf'	**Type of Noun**
Kasrah	Fatḥah	Ḍammah	Singular
Kasrah	Fatḥah	Ḍammah	Broken Plural
ـَيْنِ	ـَيْنِ	ـَانِ	Dual
ـِينَ	ـِينَ	ـُونَ	Sound Masculine Plural
ـَاتٍ	ـَاتٍ	ـَاتٌ	Sound Feminine Plural[33]
Kasrah	Fatḥah	Ḍammah	Flexible Noun [مُعْرَب]
Fatḥah	Fatḥah	Ḍammah	Partially Flexible [غير مُنْصَرِف]
no change	no change	no change	Inflexible [مَبْنِي]

Analyzing Nouns from the Qur'ān			
Qur'ānic Āyāt	**Selected Noun in *single form***	**Gender, Plurality, and Definiteness**	**I'rāb**
﴿رَبُّ ٱلْمَشْرِقَيْنِ وَرَبُّ ٱلمَغْرِبَيْنِ﴾ "Lord of the two easts and wests" (55:17)	مَغْرِب [west]	Male, Dual, and Definite	Naṣb or Jarr
﴿ أَلَآ إِنَّهُم هُمُ ٱلْمُفْسِدُونَ وَلَٰكِن لَّا يَشْعُرُونَ﴾ "Unquestionably, it is they who are the corrupters, but they perceive it not."(2:12)	مُفْسِد[corrupter]	Male, Plural (proper), and Definite	Raf'
﴿ وَبَشِّرِ ٱلَّذِين آمَنُواْ وَعَمِلُواْ ٱلصَّالِحَاتِ أَنَّ لَهُمْ جَنَّاتٍ تَجْرِي مِن تَحْتِهَا ٱلأَنْهَارُ...﴾ "And give good tidings to those who believe and do righteous deeds that they will have gardens beneath which rivers flow..."(2:25)	جَنَّة [garden]	Female, plural (proper), Indefinite	Naṣb here (not Jarr)
	نَهَر [river]	Female (Broken Plural), plural, Definite	Raf'

[32] This is discussed in the next section in detail.

[33] Please note that non-human nouns with "Sound Feminine Plurals" can behave like Broken Plurals, and thus can be "feminine singular". They can also be treated as "feminine plural" as well grammatically.

Analyzing Nouns from the Qur'ān (Contd.)			
Qur'ānic Āyat	**Selected Noun in *single form***	**Gender, Plurality, and Definiteness**	**I'rāb**
﴿ وَإِذْ وَاعَدْنَا مُوسَى أَرْبَعِينَ لَيْلَةً ثُمَّ ٱتَّخَذْتُمُ ٱلْعِجْلَ مِن بَعْدِهِ وَأَنتُمْ ظَالِمُونَ ﴾ "And [recall] when We made an appointment with Mūsa for forty nights. Then you took [for worship] the calf after him, while you were wrongdoers."(2:51)	لَيْلَة [night]	Female, single, Indefinite	Naṣb
	عِجْل [calf]	Male, single, Indefinite	Naṣb
﴿ أَلَمْ نَجْعَلِ ٱلْأَرْضَ مِهَادًا ۞ وَٱلْجِبَالَ أَوْتَادًا ﴾ "Have We not made the earth a resting place?, And the mountains as pegs?"(78:6-7)	أَرْض [earth]	Female, single, Definite	Naṣb
	جَبَل [mountain]	Female single (Broken Plural), Definite	Naṣb

III. Flexibility and I'rāb

What do we mean by flexibility? Flexibility is the ability of a noun to adapt its ending appropriately (inflect) to one of the three I'rāb states. A noun that is fully Flexible perfectly adapts its endings to a particular I'rāb as per the rules discussed earlier in this chapter. Please note that most nouns in Arabic are (fully) Flexible. However, many nouns in Arabic are Partially Flexible, and thus change their endings "partially". Other nouns in Arabic are completely Inflexible, and cannot change their endings at all. Despite this, every noun takes an I'rāb, even if its ending does not change appropriately. The I'rāb of Inflexible words is based on their context in the respective sentence. In one sense, one may say that flexibility is a fifth characteristic that each noun inherently has. The difference with respect to the other characteristics of nouns (gender, plurality, definiteness, and I'rāb) however is that the Flexibility of any respective noun cannot change, and is fixed.

A. The Concept of Flexibility

All Muslims are required to pray the obligatory Ṣalāh daily, even if they have a physical impairment that limits their ability to do Rukū', Sujūd, or to stand. If a Muslim has these impairments, they should pray the Ṣalāh to the best of their ability and Inshā Allah they will be complying with the rules of Ṣalāh like the Muslim who stands, does proper Rukū', and Sujūd etc.

This concept of Flexibility perhaps can be better understood by using a simile. Let us take the example of three Muslim individuals. The first is Muḥammad who is healthy and "fully flexible". He does Ṣalāh according to full rules and proper motions (of doing Rukū' and Sujūd). Then we have a second individual, Zaid who has a bad back. He is able to stand, but cannot flex properly and do proper Rukū' and Sujūd. Unlike Muḥammad, Zaid needs to use a chair during Ṣalāh, but his Ṣalāh is accepted and valid since he followed the rules to the utmost of his ability (or in this case flexibility). We then have a third, Manṣūr who is unfortunately crippled. Despite being unable to stand or bend, he performs Ṣalāh in bed using hand gestures. Even though neither Manṣūr nor Zaid can perform the appropriate actions of Ṣalāh like Muḥammad, their Ṣalāh is accepted Inshā Allah. Altogether, the prayer of all three Muslims is accepted. This is because they all performed the actions of Ṣalāh as much as they were capable of despite their varying degrees of Flexibility.

B. <u>The Three Degrees of Flexibility of Nouns</u>

Similar to the preceding simile, nouns also can have one of three degrees of flexibility. Specifically, this flexibility is in terms of how their endings adapt appropriately to the respective I'rāb that they have. Flexibility has no effect on I'rāb, and is a specific attribute of the particular noun in question. It is divided into three categories:

(i) Flexible- the normal noun [مُعْرَب]

(ii) Inflexible noun [مَبْنى]

(iii) Partially Flexible noun [غَيرُ مُنْصَرِف]

1. <u>Flexible Nouns</u> [مُعْرَب]

The normal noun in terms of Flexibility is one whose ending fully conforms to express its respective I'rāb.

<u>**e.g.**</u> [رَبٌّ / مُسْلِمٌ / قَلَمٌ / مَسْجِدٌ / بَيْتٌ / اَلقُرآنُ]

2. <u>Inflexible Nouns</u> [مَبْنى]

Inflexible Nouns do not change structurally, but still carry one of three I'rāb. The I'rāb that it carries depends on its context in the sentence. For example, if the noun is an owner or possessor, then it is Jarr. Please note that the term [مَبْنى] is also used for verbs that do not inflect an I'rāb. Inflexible Nouns include Pronouns [هُوَ/هِيَ/هُم], Pointing nouns [هٰذا/ذٰلِكَ], Relative Pronouns [اَلَّذِي], and names such as [عِيسٰى] or [مُوسٰى].

I'rāb of Inflexible Nouns		
Raf'	**Naṣb**	**Raf'**
﴾ وَإِذْ قَالَ مُوسَىٰ لِقَوْمِهِ ... ﴿	﴾ وَكَلَّمَ ٱللَّهُ مُوسَىٰ تَكْلِيمًا ﴿	﴾ وَأَوْحَيْنَا إِلَىٰ مُوسَىٰ.. ﴿
And when Mūsa said to his people...(2:54) (Mūsaﷺ is the Subject)	And when Allah talked to Mūsa directly (4:163) (Mūsaﷺ is the direct object)	And when We revealed to Mūsa...(7:117) (Ḥarf causes Mūsaﷺ to be Jarr)
﴾...وَأَنْتُمْ لِبَاسٌ لَهُنَّ ﴿	﴾ ٱعْبُدُوا رَبَّكُمُ ٱلَّذِي خَلَقَكُمْ ﴿	﴾ لَكُمْ دِينُكُمْ وَلِيَ دِينِ ﴿
...and you are a garment to them (2:187).	...worship your Lord the One Who created you... (2:21).	To you is your religion, and to me in my religion (109:6).

3. <u>Partially Flexible Nouns</u> [غَيْرُ مُنْصَرِفٍ]

These nouns follow all the rules of fully flexible nouns except the following:

- They <u>do not</u> take Kasrah.
- They <u>do not</u> take Tanwīn (no double vowel).
- They <u>do not</u> take [ال-] nor are they Muḍāf[34].

➤ <u>Categories of Nouns that are Partially Flexible</u>

(i) <u>Non-Arabic Names</u>: e.g. [فِرْعَوْنُ] and [إِبْرَهِيمَ]

Raf'	**Naṣb**	**Jarr**
فِرْعَوْنُ	فِرْعَوْنَ	فِرْعَوْنَ
إبراهيمُ	إبراهيمَ	إبراهيمَ

(ii) **Feminine names** in Arabic that have no masculine counterpart.
(i) e.g. [عَائِشَةُ]

(iii) **Names of places** (these are grammatically feminine).
(ii) e.g. [مَكَّةُ /مِصْرُ/ أَمْرِيكَةُ]

(iv) **Certain three-letter Arab names**
(iii) e.g. [عُمَرُ]

(v) **Comparative and superlative adjectives and colors.**
(iv) e.g.[35] [أَسْوَدُ] **and** [أَكْبَرُ]

---

34 See Lesson 5 on the section on Possession Constructions.

(vi) Attributes occurring in the pattern of [فَعْلان]

(v) e.g.[36] [كَسْلانُ] and [غَضْبانُ]

(vii) Broken Plural Patterns on patterns [مَفاعِل] and [فُعَلاء].

Table 7: Broken Plurals on patterns [مَفاعِل] and [فُعَلاء]		
Stem	**Plural Pattern**	**Example**
فُعَلاءُ	فُعَلاءُ	غُرَباءُ
	أَفْعِلاءُ	أَغْنِياءُ
مَفاعِلُ	فَعالِلُ	كَواكِبُ
	فَعالِيلُ	سَكَاكِينُ
	مَفاعِلُ	مَساجِدُ

Please note when these two Broken Plural patterns are **only** Partially Flexible when they do not contain [ال-] or are not part of an Iḍāfa Construction. So, when they have [ال-], or they are part of an Iḍāfa, they are Flexible. Let us take a few examples from the Qur'ān to illustrate this point.

i. ﴿...وَلَوْلَا دَفْعُ اللَّهِ النَّاسَ بَعْضَهُم بِبَعْضٍ لَّهُدِّمَتْ صَوَامِعُ وَبِيَعٌ وَصَلَوَاتٌ وَمَسَاجِدُ يُذْكَرُ فِيهَا اسْمُ اللَّهِ كَثِيرًا...﴾

"..And were it not that Allah checks the people, some by means of others, there would have been demolished monasteries, churches, synagogues, and mosques in which the name of Allah is much mentioned..."(22:40)

ii. ﴿لَّوْلَا جَاءُوا عَلَيْهِ بِأَرْبَعَةِ شُهَدَاءَ ۚ فَإِذْ لَمْ يَأْتُوا بِالشُّهَدَاءِ فَأُولَٰئِكَ عِندَ اللَّهِ هُمُ الْكَاذِبُونَ﴾

"Why did they [who slandered] not produce for it four witnesses? And when they do not produce the witnesses, then it is they, in the sight of Allah, who are the liars." (24:13)

In example (i), the underlined nouns are all Indefinite and Rafʿ. If these nouns were Flexible, they are each expected to take two Ḍammahs. The nouns that are shaded do not take Tanwīn because they are Partially Flexible and have the stem of [مَفاعِل]. In Āyah (ii), the word [شُهَداء] on the pattern of [فُعَلاء] is mentioned twice both in Jarr case. When [شُهَداء] has the Definite Article, it is Flexible, and takes Kasrah. However without the Definite Article, [شُهَداء] cannot take the Kasrah since it is Partially Flexible.

35 Translation from left to right is "black" and "greater".

36 Translation from left to right is "lazy" and "angry". Words on the pattern on [فَعْلان] are Partially Flexible when they have a feminine equivalent on the pattern of [فَعْلى]. The word [الرَّحْمٰن] being one of the attributes of Allah does not have a feminine equivalent. It therefore is not Partially Flexible despite it being on the forementioned pattern.

Lesson 3: The Pronouns [الضَّمائِر] and the Pointing Nouns [أَسماءُ الإشارَة]

I. Pronouns [ضَمائِر / ضَمِير]

Arabic pronouns are of two types, Attached and Detached. Please note that the Detached Pronouns are typically Raf'[37]. Attached Pronouns on the other hand, cannot take Raf', but instead take either the Jarr or Naṣb case. All pronouns are completely Inflexible [مَبْنِي]. Sometimes, the Attached Pronouns can modify one of its vowels for the purpose of better phonation or sound as per Arabic Morphology. As we saw in the previous chapter, minor changes in the structure of a word due to phonation [الصَّرف] do not affect I'rāb. A pronoun is inherently tied to the gender and the plurality of the noun that it refers to. Singular inanimate objects are referred to by the Third Person pronouns [هُوَ] or [هِيَ] depending on the gender. Inanimate plurals are usually referred to by the pronoun [هِيَ] since they are usually grammatically feminine singular. This is discussed later on in Lesson 4, Section IV.

A. The Detached Pronouns [اَلضَّمائِرُ الْمُنْفَصِلَة]

Table 8: Detached Pronouns [الضَّمائِر المُنفَصِلَة]

Plural	Dual	Single	
هُمْ	هُما	هُوَ	3rd Person masculine
هُنَّ	هُما	هِيَ	3rd Person feminine
أَنْتُمْ	أَنْتُما	أَنْتَ	2nd Person masculine
أَنْتُنَّ	أَنْتُما	أَنْتِ	2nd Person feminine
نَحْنُ	نَحْنُ	أَنا	1st Person

[37] Exception to this is the particle [إِيَّا], which is always Naṣb. Please see the following page for a discussion on [إِيَّا].

1. Detached Pronoun Structure

- i. All Third Person pronouns begin with letter [ه].
- ii. All Second Person pronouns begin with letters [أَنْتَ].
- iii. All dual pronouns end with letters [ما].
- iv. All masculine Second/Third Persons plural end with letter [مْ].
- v. All feminine Second/Third Person plurals end with letter [نَّ].
- vi. It is easiest to remember these phonetically from the far right [هُوَ هُما هُمْ].

2. Detached Pronouns in Naṣb: [إِيَّا]

The particle [إِيَّا] allows a Detached Pronoun to function as a Direct Object for verbs. [إِيَّا] is the only Detached Pronoun in the Naṣb state, functioning as a Direct Object, and preceding a verb for meaning of exclusivity[38]. In a normal Verbal Sentence pattern, the Direct Object follows the verb. Examples of these pronouns are the following: [إِيَّاكَ / إِيَّايَ / إِيَّاكُمْ / إِيَّانا].

﴿ إِيَّاكَ نَعْبُدُ وَإِيَّاكَ نَسْتَعِينُ ﴾

"To You alone we worship and to You alone we ask for help." (1:5)

﴿ يا بَنِي إِسْرَائِيلَ ٱذْكُرُوا۟ نِعْمَتِيَ ٱلَّتِي أَنْعَمْتُ عَلَيْكُمْ وَأَوْفُوا۟ بِعَهْدِي أُوفِ بِعَهْدِكُمْ وَإِيَّايَ فَٱرْهَبُونِ ﴾

"O Children of Israel, remember My favor which I have bestowed upon you and fulfill My covenant that I will fulfill your covenant [from Me], and be afraid of only Me." (2:40)

B. The Attached Pronouns [اَلضَّمائِرُ الْمُتَّصِلَة]

Attached Pronouns attach to the ends of nouns, verbs, and certain particles. An Attached Pronoun joins a noun with no [ال-] at its end, and becomes a Possession Construction or [إِضافَة]. The pronoun takes the case of Jarr while being Inflexible [مَبْنِي].

[38] This is related to the advanced grammar principle called تقديم و تأخير. In this case, placing the Direct Object before the verb causes exclusivity and places emphasis on the word that has an abnormal sentence structure in terms of sequence.

When a pronoun is attached to a verb at its end, the pronoun becomes a "Direct Object" of that verb. In this case, the pronoun always takes the Naṣb I'rāb. Attached Pronouns can also be directly linked to particles. Specifically, they are found attached to the ends of Ḥarf Jarr and Naṣb particles. Singular inanimate objects are referred to by the Third Person pronoun such as [هُ] or [ها], while their plurals are usually referred by the feminine singular [ها].

Table 9: Attached Pronouns [الضَّمائِر الْمُتَّصِلَة]

Plural	Dual	Single	
هُمْ	هُما	هُ	3rd Person masculine
هُنَّ	هُما	ها	3rd Person feminine
كُمْ	كُما	كَ	2nd Person masculine
كُنَّ	كُما	كِ	2nd Person feminine
نا	نا	[ي or نِي][39]	1st Person

➤ Attached Pronoun Structure

i. Third Person pronouns start with [ه].

ii. Dual pronouns end with [ما].

iii. Masculine 2nd and 3rd Person plurals end with [مْ].

iv. Feminine 2nd and 3rd Person plurals end with [نَّ].

v. Second Person masculine and feminine start with [كـ].

vi. First Person singular is either [ي] or [نِي].

[39] [نِي] is only attached to verbs, and is called نون الْوِقاية.

Table 10: Conjugation of Attached Nouns in Three I'rābs[40] [كِتاب]								
كِتابٍ (Jarr)			كِتابًا (Naṣb)			كِتابٌ (Raf')		
كِتابِهِم	كِتابِهِما	كِتابِهِ	كِتابَهُم	كِتابَهُما	كِتابَهُ	كِتابُهُم	كِتابُهُما	كِتابُهُ
كِتابِهِنَّ	كِتابِهِما	كِتابِها	كِتابَهُنَّ	كِتابَهُما	كِتابَها	كِتابُهُنَّ	كِتابُهُما	كِتابُها
كِتابِكُم	كِتابِكُما	كِتابِكَ	كِتابَكُم	كِتابَكُما	كِتابَكَ	كِتابُكُم	كِتابُكُما	كِتابُكَ
كِتابِكُنَّ	كِتابِكُما	كِتابِكِ	كِتابَكُنَّ	كِتابَكُما	كِتابَكِ	كِتابُكُنَّ	كِتابُكُما	كِتابُكِ
كِتابِنا	كِتابِنا	كِتابِي	كِتابَنا	كِتابَنا	كِتابِي	كِتابُنا	كِتابُنا	كِتابِي

C. Examples of Pronouns from the Qur'ān

Qur'ānic Āyah	Translation of Selected Pronoun	Type of Pronoun	I'rāb of pronoun
﴿ يَا أَيُّهَا ٱلنَّاسُ ٱعْبُدُواْ رَبَّكُمُ ٱلَّذِي خَلَقَكُمْ وَٱلَّذِينَ مِن قَبْلِكُمْ لَعَلَّكُمْ تَتَّقُونَ ﴾ "O mankind, worship your Lord, who created you and those before you, that you may become righteous" (2:21)	رَبَّكُم [your Lord]	Attached to Noun	Jarr
	خَلَقَكُمْ [He created you]	Attached to Verb	Naṣb
	قَبْلِكُمْ [before you]	Attached to Ḥarf Jarr	Jarr
	لَعَلَّكُمْ [so that you]	Attached to Ḥarf Naṣb	Naṣb
﴿ وَقُلْنَا يَا آدَمُ ٱسْكُنْ أَنتَ وَزَوْجُكَ ٱلْجَنَّةَ وَكُلاَ مِنْهَا رَغَداً حَيْثُ شِئْتُمَا وَلاَ تَقْرَبَا هَـٰذِهِ ٱلشَّجَرَةَ فَتَكُونَا مِنَ ٱلْظَّالِمِينَ ﴾ "And We said, "O Ādam, dwell, you and your wife, in Paradise and eat therefrom in [ease and] abundance from wherever you will. But do not approach this tree, lest you be among the wrongdoers." (2:35)	أَنتَ [you]	Detached Pronoun	Raf'
	زَوْجُكَ [your wife]	Attached to noun	Jarr
	مِنْهَا [from it]	Attached to Ḥarf Jarr	Jarr

40 Please note that the conjugated structure of [كِتاب] with an Attached Pronoun (or for that matter any noun) can be altered due to phonetics [الصَّرف]. For example, [كِتابِهُ] is changed to [كِتابِهِ] because it is awkward in pronouncing [هُ] directly after a Kasrah. Similarly, there is only one possible pattern in [كِتابِي] due to the [ي]. These changes in vowel do not cause any change in the meaning of the word or its I'rāb. It is simply an issue of phonetics and morphology. More variances like this will be seen in later lessons. The modification of the Attached Pronoun vowel can have variance in some cases. For example, in Sūrah Fatḥ (48:10) ﴿...وَمَنْ أَوْفَىٰ بِمَا عَاهَدَ عَلَيْهُ ٱللَّهَ فَسَيُؤْتِيهِ أَجْرًا عَظِيمًا﴾, the shaded word [عَلَيْهُ] is expected to be [عَلَيْهِ]. Here the Ḍammah functions rhetorically in exalting the oath/promise [عَاهَدَ].

II. Pointing Nouns [أسْماءُ الْإِشارَة]

These nouns as expected possess all four characteristics present in nouns such as gender, number, definiteness, and I'rāb. Like pronouns, Pointing Nouns are always Definite and Inflexible. In contrast, however, they can take all three I'rāb depending on their context in a respective sentence. Masculine Pointing Nouns usually start with the letter [ه] while the feminine nouns usually start with the letter [ت]. There are two types of Pointing Nouns, "Near" [اَلْقَرِيب] and "Far" [اَلْبَعِيد]. The "Far" Pointing Noun is used to refer to something far literally or figuratively. The "Near" Pointing Noun, on the other hand is used for something closer, or near.

A. Pointing Nouns - [أسْماءُ الْإِشارَة]

1. **"This/These"** - denotes nearness

Table 11: Pointing Nouns - Near [أسْماءُ الْإِشارَةِ الْقَرِيب]			
Plural	**Dual**	**Single**	
هٰؤُلاءِ *These*	هٰذَانِ / هٰذَيْنِ *These (two)*	هٰذَا *this*	3rd Person masculine
هٰؤُلاءِ *These*	هٰتَيْنِ / هٰتانِ *These (two)*	هٰذِهِ *this*	3rd Person feminine

﴿ هٰذَانِ خَصْمَانِ ٱخْتَصَمُوا فِي رَبِّهِمْ... ﴾

"These two antagonists dispute with each other about their Lord..." (22:19)

2. **" That/Those "** - denotes being far away

Table 12: Pointing Nouns: Far [أسْماءُ الْإِشارَةِ الْبَعِيد]			
Plural	**Dual**	**Single**	
أُوْلَٰئِكَ *Those (all)*	ذانِكَ / ذَيْنِكَ *Those (two)*[41]	ذٰلِكَ *That*	3rd Person masculine
أُوْلَٰئِكَ *Those (all)*	تانِكَ / تَيْنِكَ *Those (two)*	تِلْكَ *That*	3rd Person feminine

[41] The "Far" Pointing Nouns for dual are rarely used.

- Instead of [ذَٰلِكَ], you can also use [ذَٰلِكُمْ] or [ذَٰلِكُمَا], which have similar meaning and, are <u>singular</u>.

  i. ﴿... ذَٰلِكُمُ ٱللَّهُ رَبُّكُمْ ...﴾

  "...That is Allah, your Lord..." (10:3).

  ii. ﴿ أُوْلَٰٓئِكَ ٱلَّذِينَ ٱشْتَرَوُاْ ٱلضَّلَٰلَةَ بِٱلْهُدَىٰ... ﴾

  "Those are the ones who have sold guidance for error ...."(2:16).

B. Additional Pointing Nouns

Table 13: Additional Pointing Nouns	
كَذَٰلِكَ	like this
هَٰكَذَا	in this way
هَٰهُنَا / هُنَا	Here
هُنَاكَ	There
ثَمَّ	there/over there

﴿ وَإِذَا رَأَيْتَ ثَمَّ رَأَيْتَ نَعِيمًا وَمُلْكًا كَبِيرًا ﴾

"And when you look <u>there</u> [in Paradise], you will see pleasure and great dominion." (76:20)

Lesson 4: Particles (اَلْحُروف) and Broken Plurals (جَمعُ التَّكْسِير)

Particles (حُرُوف/حَرْف)

Particles are the third category of words in Arabic. As mentioned before, particles are words that require being associated to another word to have a meaning in speech. They come directly in front of nouns and verbs. Some particles can impart a new meaning to a noun or verb while others do not. Among the particles are subcategories that function differently in terms of grammar. In this book, we will focus upon the most common and high-yield particles. The particles that cause a change in I'rāb will be discussed in detail such as Ḥarf Jarr (حُرُوف الْجَرّ), Ḥarf Naṣb (حُرُوف النَّصْب), and Ḥarf Jazm (حُرُوف الْجَزْم). Other particles that do not affect I'rāb (حُروفٌ غَيْرُ عامِلَةٍ) will be covered briefly here in Volume 1.

I. Particles of Jarr (حُرُوفُ الْجَرّ)

These particles are prepositions that cause nouns immediately following them to be in the Jarr (جَرّ) state. As particles, they require another word to have a useful meaning. Please note that the Jarr state is specific only to nouns, therefore Ḥarf Jarr do not act on verbs. See Table 14 on the following page for a listing of common Ḥarf Jarr. When a Jarr particle acts on a noun causing the noun to take the Jarr I'rāb, it becomes a unit called "Jarr Construction". This unit has some important grammar functions in sentences, which we will later see.

A. Examples of Jarr Particles

The Ḥarf Jarr shown below (underlined) cause the word after it to be Jarr. In some cases, the Ḥarf Jarr is attached directly to the noun.

1. ﴿وَمِنَ ٱلنَّاسِ مَن يَقُولُ آمَنَّا بِٱللَّهِ وَبِٱلْيَوْمِ ٱلآخِرِ وَمَا هُم بِمُؤْمِنِينَ﴾

   "And from the people are some who say, "We believe in Allah and the Last Day," but they are not believers." (2:8)

2. ﴿وَإِذْ قَالَ رَبُّكَ لِلْمَلَائِكَةِ إِنِّي جَاعِلٌ فِي ٱلْأَرْضِ خَلِيفَةً...﴾

   "And (remember) when your Lord said to the angels: "Verily, I am going to place a representative on earth." (2:30)

B. Ḥarf Jarr [حُرُوفُ الْجَرّ]

Table 14: Ḥarf Jarr [حُرُوفُ الْجَرّ]

إِلى	to/towards	فِي	in
بِ	in/with	كَ	like (similarity)
تَ	by (oath)	لِ	for/to
حَتَّى	until	وَ	by (oath)
عَنْ	from/about	مِن	from
عَلى	upon/on		

C. Ḥarf Jarr Attached to Pronouns (Variant Conjugations)

In the examples below, we see that when Ḥarf Jarr attach to pronouns, in certain cases, they modify one of their vowels. This is similar to nouns as was shown in Table 10 (pg. 46) with the example of [كِتاب]. In some cases, when nouns attach to pronouns, they cause slight modification of the vowels of pronouns. Please refer to footnote #40 for a more detailed discussion.

Jarr Particle	⇨	Pronoun	⇨	Jarr Construction	Incorrect form
لِ		هُ		لَهُ	~~لِهُ~~
إِلى		هُ		إِلَيْهِ	~~إِلَيْهُ~~
فِي	+	هُما		فِيهِما	~~فِيهُما~~
عَلى		هُنَّ		عَلَيْهِنَّ	~~عَلَيْهُنَّ~~
بِ		هُم		بِهِمْ	~~بِهُمْ~~
مِن		هُ		مِنْهُ	~~مِنْهِ~~

D. Ḥarf Jarr-like Nouns and [الظُّروف]

Sometimes nouns can act as Jarr particles. This occurs with nouns that are always found attached to another noun in a "Possession Construction". Thus, these nouns are seldom if ever found alone in Arabic. In this way, those words act like Ḥarf Jarr and cause the word after it to be in the Jarr state. However, despite being like particles, they are still nouns since their ends get affected by a Ḥarf Jarr. Most of these nouns below belong to a category of words known as [اِسْمُ الظَّرْف] or [الظَّرْف]. These words are found in the Naṣb case and point to the relative place [ظَرْفُ المكان] or the relative time [ظَرْفُ الزَّمان] that a certain action occurs in.[42] These nouns are being listed here for completion.

1. Examples of Ḥarf Jarr-like Nouns

بَعْض	some (of)
حَوْلَ	around
قَبْلَ	before
بَعْدَ	after
دُونَ	besides/other than
مِنْ دُونِ / غَيْرَ	other than
لَدُنْ / لَدَى	from/with

42 These nouns also known as [مفعول فِيهِ] can however take the Jarr case if acted upon by a Ḥarf Jarr. Please see examples (i) and (ii) on the next page.

2. Nouns of Place and Time

Table 15: Nouns of Place [ظَرْفُ الْمَكَان] and Nouns of Time [ظَرْفُ الزَّمان]			
Nouns of Place		**Nouns of Place**	
أَمامَ	in front of/before	قَبْلَ	before
بَيْنَ	between	بَعْدَ	after
فَوْقَ	above	اليَوْمَ	today
تَحْتَ	under	أَبَدًا	always
وَراءَ	behind	حِيْنًا	for a period of time
خَلْفَ	after	صَباحًا	morning
مَعَ or عِنْدَ	with	بُكْرَةً/سَحَرًا	early morning

3. Qur'ānic Examples:

i. ﴿ ثُمَّ بَعَثْنَاكُم مِّنْ بَعْدِ مَوْتِكُمْ لَعَلَّكُمْ تَشْكُرُونَ ﴾

"Then We revived you after your death that perhaps you would be grateful." (2:56)

ii. ﴿ تِلْكَ حُدُودُ ٱللَّهِ وَمَن يُطِعِ ٱللَّهَ وَرَسُولَهُ يُدْخِلْهُ جَنَّاتٍ تَجْرِي مِن تَحْتِهَا ٱلْأَنْهَارُ ﴾

"These are the limits of Allah, and whoever obeys Allah and His Messenger will be admitted by Him to gardens under which rivers flow". (4:13)

iii. ﴿... لَا يَسْتَوِي مِنكُم مَّنْ أَنفَقَ مِن قَبْلِ ٱلْفَتْحِ وَقَاتَلَ أُوْلَٰئِكَ أَعْظَمُ دَرَجَةً مِّنَ ٱلَّذِينَ أَنفَقُوا مِن بَعْدُ وَقَاتَلُوا... ﴾

"Not equal among you are those who spent before the conquest [of Makkah] and fought [and those who did so after it]."[43] (57:10)

43 In the above Āyah, we see an occurrence that is found frequently in the Qur'ān: the presence of a Ḍammah on [بَعْدُ] and also often on [قَبْلُ]. This is related to what follows the Noun of Place/Time and if it is connected to it (i.e. Possession construction). If the noun is not connected and does not link with the word after, it carries a single Ḍammah as in [بَعْدُ] above. Here we see that [قَبْلِ] has Kasrah because it forms a Possession construction with [الفتح]. On the other hand [بَعْدُ] does not form a link with [و قاتلوا] thus resulting in a Ḍammah.

E. Particles of Oaths [حُرُوف القَسَم]

Three particles are used in making an oath in Arabic. These are Wāw, Tā, and Bā. The Wāw is the most common particle for making an oath and is differentiated by other types of Wāw by the sign of Jarr on words it is associated with.

Table 16: Particles of Oaths [حُرُوف القَسَم]	
﴿ وَٱلشَّمْسِ وَضُحَاهَا ﴾	"By the sun and its brightness"
﴿ وَٱلْقَمَرِ إِذَا تَلَاهَا ﴾	"And by the moon when it follows it"
﴿ وَٱلنَّهَارِ إِذَا جَلَّاهَا ﴾	"And by the day when it displays it" (91:1-3)
﴿ قَالَ تَٱللَّهِ إِن كِدتَّ لَتُرْدِينِ ۝ وَلَوْلَا نِعْمَةُ رَبِّي لَكُنتُ مِنَ ٱلْمُحْضَرِينَ ﴾ "He will say, "By Allah, you almost ruined me. If not for the favor of my Lord, I would have been of those brought in [to Hell]." (37:56-57)	
﴿ لَآ أُقْسِمُ بِيَوْمِ ٱلْقِيَامَةِ ﴾ "I swear by the Day of Resurrection." (75:1)	

II. Particles of Naṣb [حُرُوف النَّصب]

A. Particles on Naṣb on Nouns [إِنَّ و أَخواتها]

These Ḥarfs cause words following them to go into the Naṣb state. Particles of Naṣb that act on nouns are called [إِنَّ و أَخواتها] or "Inna and its Sisters" in grammar terminology. These particles typically act on a subject in a Nominal sentence. The most common particle is [إِنَّ], which is seen frequently in the Qur'ān and Ḥadīth. Inna imparts emphasis on its associated noun. It is easier to memorize these six Ḥarf Naṣb particles phonetically from right to left [إِنَّ أَنَّ كَأَنَّ لَيتَ لَكِنَّ لَعَلَّ].

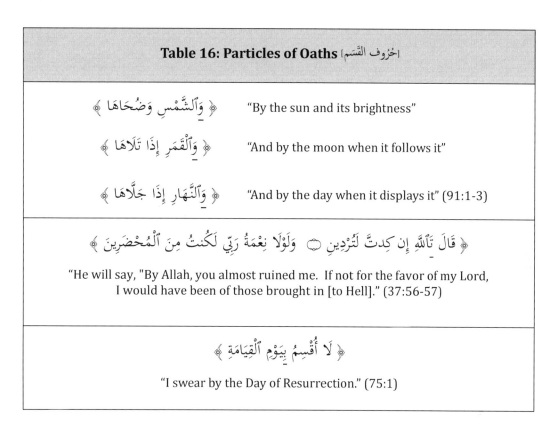

B. Inna and its Sisters

Table 17: Inna and its Sisters إِنَّ وَ أَخَوَاتُهَا	
إِنَّ	surely, verily (used in the beginning)
أَنَّ	surely, verily (used in the middle)
كَأَنَّ	as though (used to draw a parallel)
لَيْتَ	if only, (used to wish for what could have been)
لَكِنَّ	but, on the contrary, actually
لَعَلَّ	perhaps, maybe, so as to

C. Examples from the Qur'ān and Ḥadīth

1. ﴿كُتِبَ عَلَيْكُمُ ٱلصِّيَامُ كَمَا كُتِبَ عَلَى ٱلَّذِينَ مِن قَبْلِكُمْ لَعَلَّكُمْ تَتَّقُونَ﴾
"...Fasting is prescribed for you as it was prescribed for those before you, that you may gain Taqwah (2:183)."

2. ﴿إِنَّ اللهَ لا يَنْظُرُ إِلَى صُوَرِكُم وَ أَمْوَالِكُم وَ لَكِنْ يَنْظُرُ إِلَى قُلُوبِكُمْ وَ أَعْمَالِكُمْ﴾
"Indeed, Allah does not like to look at your forms or your wealth, but He looks at your hearts and your actions.[44]"

3. ﴿أَنْ تَعْبُدَ اللهَ كَأَنَّكَ تَرَاهُ فَإِنْ لَمْ تَكُنْ تَرَاهُ فَإِنَّهُ يَرَاكَ..﴾
"... That you worship Allah as if you see Him, And if you cannot see Him, then Indeed He sees you...".[45]

D. Particles of Naṣb for Verbs [حروف النَّصب]

These particles only work on Present Tense [المضارع] verbs.[46] These are discussed in further detail in Lesson 10. They cause the Ḍammah at the end of single Present Tense verbs to become Fatḥah (like nouns). They cause the Nūn at the end of a dual or plural verb to be cut off.[47] The most common Particles of Naṣb for verbs are listed

44 Ṣaḥīḥ Muslim, The Book of Virtue, Good Manners and Joining of the Ties of Relationship: كِتَاب الْبِرِّ وَالصِّلَةِ وَالْآدَابِ, Ḥadīth # 2564.

45 Ṣaḥīḥ al-Bukhāri, Chapter on Imān: كِتَاب الْإِيمَانِ Ḥadīth #50.

46 The one exception to this is the particle [حَتَّى] that also acts as a Ḥarf Jarr on nouns.

47 The exception is the Nūn of femininity present in feminine plural Present Tense verb conjugation(s), which cannot be truncated.

below. The most common Ḥarf Naṣb are (أَنْ) and (لَنْ). It is easier to memorize these particles in the following rhyming order from right to left: (أَنْ لَنْ لِأَنْ كَيْ إِذًا حَتَّى).

E. Ḥarf Naṣb for Verbs

Table 18: Ḥarf Naṣb for Verbs			
أَنْ	that/to	إِذًا	therefore
لَنْ	will never (future)	حَتَّى	until
لِ	so that	أَلَّا	may not
لِكَيْ /كَيْ	so that	لِأَنْ	for that

F. Examples from the Qur'ān

1. ﴿لَن تُغْنِيَ عَنْهُمْ أَمْوَالُهُمْ وَلَا أَوْلَادُهُم مِّنَ ٱللَّهِ شَيْـًٔا﴾
   "Never will their wealth or their children avail them against Allah at all.." (58:17)

2. ﴿وَإِذْ قَالَ مُوسَىٰ لِقَوْمِهِۦٓ إِنَّ ٱللَّهَ يَأْمُرُكُمْ أَن تَذْبَحُوا۟ بَقَرَةً قَالُوٓا۟ أَتَتَّخِذُنَا هُزُوًا قَالَ أَعُوذُ بِٱللَّهِ أَنْ أَكُونَ مِنَ ٱلْجَٰهِلِينَ﴾
   "And remember when Mūsa said to his people, "Indeed, Allah commands you to slaughter a cow." They said, "Do you take us in ridicule?" He said, "I seek refuge in Allah from being among the ignorant." (2:67)

III. Particles of Jazm (حُرُوف الْجَزْم)

The Jazm case is specific to Present Tense verbs, and characterized by a Sukūn on the end of Jazm verbs (singular form). Present Tense verbs can also go in Raf' and Naṣb states but they never go into the Jarr state. Instead, they can go into the Jazm state. There are several particles that cause Jazm and these outnumber the other Jarr and Naṣb Particles. Please note that Ḥarf Jazm particles are discussed in further detail in Lesson 10, a chapter dedicated to verbs.

A. Common Ḥarf Jazm

لِ	should (encouraging/admonishing)
لاَ	negation (forbidding)
لَمْ	did not (Past Tense)
إِنْ	If (condition)
لَمَّا	not yet/ when

B. Examples from the Qur'ān

1. ﴿ وَلاَ تُطِعْ مَنْ أَغْفَلْنَا قَلْبَهُ عَن ذِكْرِنَا وَاتَّبَعَ هَوَاهُ وَكَانَ أَمْرُهُ فُرُطًا ﴾

"...and do not obey one whose heart We have made heedless of Our remembrance and who follows his desire and whose affair is ever [in] neglect". (18:28)

2. ﴿ لَمْ يَلِدْ وَلَمْ يُولَدْ ۝ وَلَمْ يَكُن لَّهُ كُفُوًا أَحَدٌ ﴾

"He begets not, nor has he been born, nor has there been to Him any equivalent." (112:2-3).

IV. Broken Plural Patterns [جَمْعُ التَّكْسِيرِ]

We briefly discussed Broken Plurals in Lesson 1. We are discussing them in more detail here since students need to be familiar with their grammar and intricacies. Please note that the majority of nouns take Broken Plurals. Typically, there is not set rule for the Broken Plural pattern that any specific noun takes. Some patterns however are more common than others are. Nonetheless, it is understood that the plural should be memorized along with its singular. The actual Broken Plural pattern for a noun can be determined by using an Arabic dictionary like Hans Wehr[48], unless it is known already. There are more patterns than the ones listed in this lesson, but these are the most common. Remember that the I'rāb for Broken Plural is <u>feminine singular</u>, even when the singular noun is masculine[49]. This is essential to remember since Arabic grammar places much emphasis on gender distinction. It is also important to remember the structures of male and female Proper Plurals as was discussed in the first lesson.

---

[48] See Lesson #10 on the section on using Arabic Dictionaries.

[49] Please note that there are occasional variances. Consider the following Āyah (3:6): ﴿ ... هُوَ الَّذِي أَنزَلَ عَلَيْكَ الْكِتَابَ مِنْهُ آيَاتٌ مُّحْكَمَاتٌ هُنَّ أُمُّ الْكِتَابِ وَأُخَرُ مُتَشَابِهَاتٌ ﴾. Here, it is expected that the pronoun referring to آيَات would be اها. However the plural هُنَّ is used for rhetorical function of magnifying the importance of آيَات.

The most common plural patterns for three-letter words are **patterns #1 through #4** shown in the table below. The most common patterns for four-letter words are **plural patterns #7 through #9.** Please note that Plural patterns #7 through #11 are **Partially Flexible** and do not take Tanwīn when they are Indefinite. Addition plural patterns also listed are #12 through 14, which are less common. Memorizing the most common plural patterns on the [فعل] stem allows the student to identify plurals even if one does not know the meaning of the words itself. Identifying and analyzing words from Āyāt of the Qur'ān is the first step in reading comprehension.

Table 19: Broken Plural Patterns

Broken Plural Pattern #	Broken Plural Pattern [فعل] Stem	Singular Noun Example [مُفْرَد]		Plural [جَمْع]
1	أَفْعالٌ	قَلَم	pen	أَقْلَامٌ
2	فُعُولٌ	قَلْب	heart	قُلُوبٌ
3	فِعَالٌ	كَبِير	big	كِبارٌ
4	فُعُلٌ	مَدِينَة	city	مُدُنٌ
5	فُعَلٌ	غُرْفَةٌ	room	غُرَفٌ
6	فُعَّالٌ	كَافِرٌ	disbeliever	كُفَّارٌ
7	مَفاعِلُ	إِصْبَعٌ	finger	أَصابِعُ
8	فُعَلاءُ	شَرِيكٌ	partner	شُرَكَاءُ
9	فَوَاعِلُ	كَوْكَبٌ	star	كَوَاكِب
10	فَوَاعِيلُ	مِحْراب	prayer corner	مَحَارِيب
11	مَفَاعِيلُ	مِفْتَاحٌ	key	مَفَاتِيحُ
12	أَفِعَّلَةٌ	ذَلِيلٌ	humble/low	أَذِلَّةٌ
13	أَفْعِلَةٌ	فُؤَادٌ	heart	أَفْئِدَةٌ
14	فَعَلٌ	عِمَادٌ	pillar	عَمَدٌ

Lesson 5: Word Constructions [الْمُرَكَّبَات]

I. Introduction to Word Constructions

Understanding Word Constructions is required to properly analyze and translate sentences. In this lesson, we will discuss the different types of Word Constructions. A construction [مُرَكَّب] is composed of two or more words that join to form one unit in a respective sentence. These include the following: Describing Constructions, Pointing Constructions, Possession Constructions, and Jarr Constructions. We will also see that adjacent constructions can often be merged together into one larger Construction. Learning the Word Constructions enables the student to analyze sentences. This lesson will also examine Relative Pronouns since they act like Possession Constructions (in describing a Definite noun). These nouns are found frequently in the Qur'ān.

II. The Describing Construction [الْمُرَكَّبُ التَّوْصِيفِيّ]

In Arabic, the word being described [مَوْصُوف] comes first and the adjective follows (as opposed to English). The adjective [صِفَة] used adopts all four characteristics of the noun being described; gender, definiteness, plurality, and I'rāb. The adjective typically directly follows the described word without any word coming in-between. The word and its adjective(s) that follow form a "Describing Construction" know as [الْمُرَكَّبُ التَّوْصِيفِيّ].

In the examples of Describing Constructions on the next page, the noun described is underlined once while the adjective is underlined twice. Remember that if the adjective of a noun is a Broken Plural, it will be grammatically *feminine singular*. This is shown in examples #1 [أَزْوَاجٌ مُّطَهَّرَةٌ] and in #4 [فُرُشٍ مَّرْفُوعَةٍ]. In example #2, we see that a [مَوْصُوف] can have many adjectives describing it sequentially. However, if you look closely we see that there is a word [مِنكُنَّ] in-between the [مَوْصُوف] and [صِفَة]. This can sometimes happen, but in this case, this Jarr Construction acts functionally as a [صِفَة][50]. A similar phenomenon occurs in example #4 with [لَّا مَقْطُوعَةٍ وَلَا مَمْنُوعَةٍ], a term that functions in describing [فَاكِهَةٍ]. In example #5, we see that the adjective [ٱلْمُؤْمِنِينَ] describes the Possession Construction [عِبَادِنَآ]. Here, the [مَوْصُوف] is one unit, even though it is composed of two words. The [مَوْصُوف] is Jarr and plural because of [عِبَادِ], and it Definite because Possession Constructions are Definite.

[50] Sometimes Jarr Constructions, Verbs, and other words can act functionally as a [صِفَة]. Obviously, in these cases, the rules that were presented in the above paragraph are excluded. Please note that this topic is more of an advanced grammar discussion at this point.

➢ Examples of Describing Constructions from the Qur'ān and Ḥadīth

1. ﴿...وَلَهُمْ فِيهَا أَزْوَاجٌ مُّطَهَّرَةٌ وَهُمْ فِيهَا خَالِدُونَ﴾

   "...And they will have therein purified spouses, and they will abide therein eternally." (2:25)

2. ﴿عَسَىٰ رَبُّهُ إِن طَلَّقَكُنَّ أَن يُبْدِلَهُ أَزْوَاجًا خَيْرًا مِّنكُنَّ مُسْلِمَاتٍ مُّؤْمِنَاتٍ قَانِتَاتٍ تَائِبَاتٍ عَابِدَاتٍ سَائِحَاتٍ ثَيِّبَاتٍ وَأَبْكَارًا﴾

   "Perhaps his Lord, if he divorced you [all], would substitute for him wives better than you submitting [to Allah], believing, devoutly obedient, repentant, worshipping, and traveling [ones] previously married and virgins."(66:5)

3. ﴿إِنَّ ٱلَّذِينَ يُحَادُّونَ ٱللَّهَ وَرَسُولَهُۥ كُبِتُوا كَمَا كُبِتَ ٱلَّذِينَ مِن قَبْلِهِمْ وَقَدْ أَنزَلْنَا آيَاتٍ بَيِّنَاتٍ وَلِلْكَافِرِينَ عَذَابٌ مُّهِينٌ﴾

   "Indeed, those who oppose Allah and His Messenger are abased as those before them were abased. And We have certainly sent down verses of clear evidence. And for the disbelievers is a humiliating punishment."(58:5)

4. ﴿وَأَصْحَابُ ٱلْيَمِينِ مَا أَصْحَابُ ٱلْيَمِينِ ۝ فِي سِدْرٍ مَّخْضُودٍ ۝ وَطَلْحٍ مَّنضُودٍ ۝ وَظِلٍّ مَّمْدُودٍ ۝ وَمَاءٍ مَّسْكُوبٍ ۝
   وَفَاكِهَةٍ كَثِيرَةٍ ۝ لَّا مَقْطُوعَةٍ وَلَا مَمْنُوعَةٍ ۝ وَفُرُشٍ مَّرْفُوعَةٍ﴾

   "The companions of the right what are the companions of the right? [They will be] among lote trees with thorns removed, And trees layered, And shade extended, And water poured out, And fruit, abundant, Neither limited [to season] nor forbidden, And [upon] thrones raised high."(56:27-34)

5. ﴿إِنَّهُ مِنْ عِبَادِنَا ٱلْمُؤْمِنِينَ﴾

   "Indeed, he was of Our believing servants." (37:132)

6. ﴿اَلْمُؤْمِنُ الْقَوِيُّ خَيرٌ وَ أَحَبُّ إِلَى اللهِ مِنَ الْمُؤْمِنِ الضَّعِيفِ﴾

   "The strong believer is better and more beloved to Allah than the weak believer" (Muslim)[51]

7. ﴿التَّاجِرُ الصَّدُوقُ الْأَمِينُ مَعَ النَّبِيِّينَ وَ الشُّهَدَاءِ وَ الصَّالِحِينَ﴾

   "The trustworthy, truthful merchant is with the prophets and the martyrs, and the righteous." (Tirmidhi)[52]

---

[51] Ṣaḥīḥ Muslim, Chapter on Predestination: كتاب القدر, Ḥadīth #4822.

[52] Sunan Tirmidhi, Chapter on Transactions: كتاب البيوع Ḥadīth #1126. This Ḥadīth is generally classified as weak by most scholars even though Tirmidhi regarded it as Ḥasan.

III. Pointing Constructions

When a Pointing Noun such as [هٰذَا] or [ذٰلِكَ] is used to refer to a noun, it becomes one unit, which is termed "Pointing Construction". Similar to Describing Constructions, both the Pointing Noun and the noun being pointed to have the same four characteristics (gender, plurality, definiteness, and I'rāb). If the noun associated with a Pointing Noun is **Indefinite** but matches the other remaining three characteristics, then a Nominal Sentence [جُمْلَة اِسْمِيَّة] is formed (not a Pointing Construction). A Pointing Construction on the other hand like the other Constructions is not a complete sentence.

A. Examples of Pointing Constructions

Near Pointing Nouns [القريب] include the following nouns: [هٰذَا/ هٰذِهِ / هٰؤُلاءِ]. Far Pointing nouns [البَعيد] include the following: [ذٰلِكَ / تِلْكَ / أُولٰئِكَ]. Dual Pointing Nouns are seldom used and do not need to be emphasized. Let us look at the following Pointing Construction from the Āyah below.

1. ﴿ وَأُوحِيَ إِلَيَّ هَٰذَا ٱلْقُرْآنُ لِأُنذِرَكُم بِهِۦ وَمَنۢ بَلَغَ ﴾

"...And this Qur'ān was revealed to me that I may warn you thereby and whomever it reaches..." (6:19).

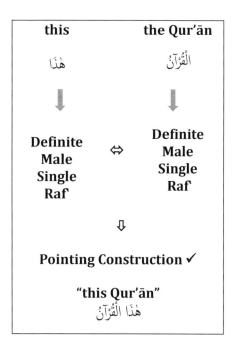

this — هٰذَا ⬇ **Definite / Male / Single / Raf'**

⇔

the Qur'ān — الْقُرْآنُ ⬇ **Definite / Male / Single / Raf'**

⇩

Pointing Construction ✓

"this Qur'ān"
هٰذَا الْقُرْآنُ

2. ﴿...وَهٰذَا كِتَابٌ أَنْزَلْنَاهُ مُبَارَكٌ مُصَدِّقُ ٱلَّذِي بَيْنَ يَدَيْهِ..﴾

"...And this is a Book which We have sent down, blessed, and confirming what was before it..." (6:72)

this		a book
هٰذَا		كِتَابٌ
⇓		⇓
Indefinite	≠	**Definite**
Male	=	**male**
Single	=	**single**
Rafʿ	=	**Rafʿ**

⇩

~~Pointing Construction~~ ×
Nominal Sentence ✓

"This is a book"
هٰذَا الْكِتابُ

B. Examples from the Qur'ān

1. ﴿تِلْكَ ٱلْقُرَىٰ نَقُصُّ عَلَيْكَ مِنْ أَنْبَائِهَا...﴾

"Those cities - We relate to you, [O Muḥammad], some of their news...." (7:101)

2. ﴿...وَكُلَا مِنْهَا رَغَدًا حَيْثُ شِئْتُمَا وَلَا تَقْرَبَا هٰذِهِ ٱلشَّجَرَةَ فَتَكُونَا مِنَ ٱلظَّالِمِينَ﴾

"... and eat therefrom in [ease and] abundance from wherever you will. But do not approach this tree, lest you be among the wrongdoers."(2:35)

3. ﴿وَتِلْكَ ٱلْأَمْثَالُ نَضْرِبُهَا لِلنَّاسِ لَعَلَّهُمْ يَتَفَكَّرُونَ﴾

"...And these examples We present to the people that perhaps they will give thought." (59:21)

IV. Iḍāfah - The Possession Construction [المُرَكَّبُ الإضافِيّ]

The Possession Construction or Iḍāfah [المُرَكَّبُ الإضافِيّ] occurs frequently in Arabic, and need to be mastered before analyzing Arabic sentences. We have briefly touched upon them when we examined nouns attached to pronouns, which essentially are Iḍāfah. An Iḍāfah is composed of two components, a Muḍāf [المُضاف], and a Muḍāf I'laih [مُضافٌ إلَيْه]. The Muḍāf is the thing that **belongs** to the noun that directly follows it. Conversely, the Muḍāf I'laih is the person or thing that possesses the Muḍāf (preceding it). As we saw for the Attached Pronouns, the pronoun linked to the preceding noun "possesses" it. Aside from Jarr Particles, an Iḍāfah is the only other instance that a noun can be Jarr (Muḍāf I'laih).

A. Rules of Iḍāfah/Possession Construction

1. The Muḍāf [المُضاف]

i. The Muḍāf is the object that "**belongs"** to the noun, or is possessed by the noun that directly follows it. In other words, the Muḍāf is possessed.

ii. The Muḍāf **never** takes "Al". This does not mean that is not Definite though. It is Definite when its Muḍāf I'laih is Definite.

iii. The Muḍāf has no Tanwīn, and has no Nūn ending (Nūn is cut off in dual endings and sound plural endings). See the following examples.

his two hands	يَدانِ /يَدَيْنِ	+	هُ	=	~~يَدانِهِ/يَدَيْنِهِ~~	يَدَاهُ/يَدَيْهِ
her two eyes	عَيْنانِ/عَيْنَيْنِ	+	ها	=	~~عَيْنانِها/عَيْنَيْنِها~~	عَيْناها/عَيْنَيْها
Muslims of Makkah	مُسْلِمُونَ	+	مَكَّة	=	~~مُسْلِمُونَ مَكَّة~~	مُسْلِمُوا مَكَّة

iv. The Muḍāf can be in **any** of the three states of I'rāb [Raf', Naṣb, or Jarr]. It determines the I'rāb of the Possession Construction. This is the case even if the I'rāb of its Muḍāf I'laih is different. Please note gender and number **do not** need to match (e.g. her brothers, his sisters).

v. The properties of the Iḍāfah (Gender/plurality/definiteness/I'rāb) are determined by the **Muḍāf.**

2. The Muḍāf I'laih [مُضافٌ إِلَيْه]

i. The Muḍāf I'laih is the person or thing that "**possesses**" the Muḍāf (preceding it).

ii. The Muḍāf I'laih is **always** in the Jarr state.

iii. **No word** comes in-between the Muḍāf and the Muḍāf I'laih in the Iḍāfah.

iv. The Iḍāfah is typically considered Definite (exception is when the Muḍāf I'laih is Indefinite. (e.g. man of **a** village **versus** man of **the** village).

v. The Muḍāf I'laih usually takes "Al". However, there are three cases in which this does not occur. These are the following :

  a. When Muḍāf I'laih is Indefinite,

  b. When there is a "Double Muḍāf I'laih" where the first Muḍāf I'laih acts as a Muḍāf for the second, and

  c. When the Muḍāf I'laih is a word that cannot take "al" such as a pointing noun [هٰذا], proper name [مَكَّة], etc. Please see the following examples below.

  d. [رَجُلُ قَرْيَةٍ] "a man of a village"

  e. [مٰلِكِ يَوْمِ ٱلدِّينِ] "Master of the Day of Judgment"

  f. [فَلْيَعْبُدُوا رَبَّ هَٰذَا ٱلْبَيْتِ] "Let them worship the Lord of this House" (106:3)

3. Determining an Iḍāfah

Muḍāf I'laih	**Muḍāf**
الْعالِمُ	قلمٌ
the scholar	*pen*
⇓	⇓
Definite Jarr	**no Tanwīn**

⇩

Possession Construction ✓

الْعالِمِ قلمُ

"pen of the scholar"

قَلَمُ الْعالِمِ

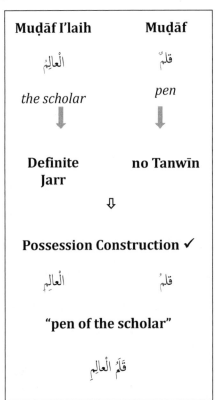

B. Examples from the Qur'ān

1. ﴿...إِنِّي أَخَافُ ٱللَّهَ رَبَّ ٱلْعَالَمِينَ﴾

"...Indeed, I fear Allah, Lord of the worlds."(59:16)

2. ﴿وَإِذْ قَالَ مُوسَىٰ لِقَوْمِهِ يَا قَوْمِ[53] لِمَ تُؤْذُونَنِي وَقَد تَّعْلَمُونَ أَنِّي رَسُولُ ٱللَّهِ إِلَيْكُمْ فَلَمَّا زَاغُوا أَزَاغَ ٱللَّهُ قُلُوبَهُمْ وَٱللَّهُ لَا يَهْدِي ٱلْقَوْمَ ٱلْفَاسِقِينَ﴾

"And remember when Mūsa said to his people, "O my people, why do you harm me while you certainly know that I am the Messenger of Allah to you?" And when they deviated, Allah caused their hearts to deviate. And Allah does not guide the rebellious people." (61:5)

3. ﴿تَبَّتْ يَدَا أَبِي لَهَبٍ وَتَبَّ﴾

"May the hands of Abū Lahab be ruined, and ruined is he". (111:1)

C. Embedded Constructions with Iḍāfah/Possession Constructions

An Iḍāfah can be associated or linked to other constructions such as Jarr Constructions, Describing Constructions, or Pointing Constructions. In these cases, the Iḍāfah is embedded within these constructions (and not the reverse). For example, when an Iḍāfah is associated with a Jarr Construction, the entire unit becomes a Jarr Construction.

D. Describing Iḍāfah Constructions

When an Iḍāfah is described by an adjective, it has to match the I'rāb, number, and gender of the Muḍāf. Definiteness is determined by looking at the Muḍāf I'laih. The adjective (صِفَة) comes **after** the Iḍāfah Construction. Let us look at a couple of examples below to clarify this rule.

Adjective	+	Iḍāfah Described	=	Describing construction
truthful صَادِقَة	+	woman of the land اِمْرَأَةُ الْبَلَدِ	=	truthful woman of the land اِمْرَأَةُ الْبَلَدِ الصَّادِقَةُ
generous كَرِيم	+	two men of a mosque رَجُلَا مَسْجِدٍ	=	Two generous men of a mosque رَجُلَا مَسْجِدٍ كَرِيمَانِ

[53] In the word (قَوْمِ), the (يِ) has been omitted, despite there being no subtraction from its pronunciation. The Kasrah is retained as the sign of the Yā. We see omission of the Yā in several places in the Qur'ān. The phenomenon of (حَذْف) or omission of words sometimes occurs in the Qur'ān for purposes of eloquence and rhetoric.

In the first example, the adjective [الصَّادِقَةُ] describes the Muḍāf [امْرَأَةُ], but is Definite because the Muḍāf I'laih is Definite. In the second example, the adjective describes a dual noun [رَجُلَانِ] whose Nūn is cut off because it is a Muḍāf. The adjective does not have [ال-] because the Muḍāf I'laih is Indefinite.

E. Pointing Nouns and Iḍāfah

We run into a dilemma when pointing to an Iḍāfah with a Pointing Noun. This is because a Pointing Noun directly followed by an Iḍāfah is not a Pointing Construction, but is really a Nominal Sentence. For example, suppose we wanted to point to the Iḍāfah "book of Fāṭimah" by the statement "this book of Fāṭimah". Adding the pointing noun [هذا] to [كِتابُ فاطِمَةَ] would yield [هذاكِتابُ فاطِمَةَ], which would be wrong. The meaning of this statement becomes "This **is** the book of Fāṭimah", not "this book of Fāṭimah". This is similar to when a Pointing Noun is followed by an Indefinite noun (being pointed to) as in [هذا كِتابٌ], or "This is a book". In both these cases, the Construction or word following the Definite Pointing Noun acts as the Predicate. Because of this dilemma, the Pointing Noun can point to an Iḍāfah **when it is placed directly after the Iḍāfah** (at the end). Let us look at the following two examples to illustrate this point.

Iḍāfah being pointed to	+	**Pointing Noun**	=	**Pointing Construction**	≠	**Nominal Sentence**
Messenger of Allah رَسُولُ اللهِ	+	هٰذا	=	this Messenger of Allah رَسُولُ اللهِ هٰذا	≠	This is the Messenger of Allah هذا رَسُولُ اللهِ
your books كُتُبُكَ	+	those[54] تِلْكَ	=	those books of yours كُتُبُكَ تِلْكَ	≠	Those are your books. هٰذا كُتُبُكَ

[54] Here since the feminine singular pointing noun [تِلْكَ] is referring to Broken Plural, the meaning shifts from that to those. This would be similar for [هٰذِهِ] which would be "these" in this case.

F. Qur'ānic Examples of Embedded Iḍāfah Constructions

In the following examples, the entire merged Constructions are highlighted gray, the Jarr Particles are underlined once, the adjectives (صِفَة) are underlined twice, and Pointing Nouns are underlined with dashes. In example (1), there are two Jarr Constructions. Within each, there is an Iḍāfah, namely (إِذْنِ ٱللَّهِ) and (كُلِّ شَيْءٍ). In example (3), we again have two embedded Jarr Constructions as in (1). In example (4), we have an adjective (الحكيم) that describes the Iḍāfah (آيَاتُ ٱلْكِتَابِ). Altogether, it is a Describing Construction with an embedded Iḍāfah. In example (5), we have two Iḍāfahs merged together (رَبِّكَ) and (كِتَابِ رَبِّكَ) within a Jarr Construction. Examples (6) and (7) show Pointing Constructions with embedded Iḍāfah.

1. ﴿ مَا أَصَابَ مِن مُّصِيبَةٍ إِلَّا بِإِذْنِ ٱللَّهِ وَمَن يُؤْمِن بِٱللَّهِ يَهْدِ قَلْبَهُ وَٱللَّهُ بِكُلِّ شَيْءٍ عَلِيمٌ ﴾

"No disaster strikes except by the permission of Allah. And whoever believes in Allah, He will guide his heart. And Allah is of all things Knowledgeable." (64:11).

2. ﴿ مَالِكِ يَوْمِ ٱلدِّينِ ﴾

"Master of the Day of Judgment" (1:4)

3. ﴿ يَا أَيُّهَا ٱلنَّبِيُّ إِذَا طَلَّقْتُمُ ٱلنِّسَاءَ فَطَلِّقُوهُنَّ لِعِدَّتِهِنَّ وَأَحْصُوا ٱلْعِدَّةَ وَٱتَّقُوا ٱللَّهَ رَبَّكُمْ لَا تُخْرِجُوهُنَّ مِن بُيُوتِهِنَّ وَلَا يَخْرُجْنَ إِلَّا أَن يَأْتِينَ بِفَاحِشَةٍ... ﴾

"O Prophet, when you divorce women, divorce them for [the commencement of] their waiting period and keep count of the waiting period, and fear Allah, your Lord. Do not turn them out from their houses, nor should they leave [during that period] unless they are committing a clear immorality..." (65:1)

4. ﴿ الر تِلْكَ آيَاتُ ٱلْكِتَابِ ٱلْحَكِيمِ ﴾

"Alif, Lām, Rā. These are the Āyāt of the Wise Book". (10:1).

5. ﴿ وَٱتْلُ مَا أُوحِيَ إِلَيْكَ مِن كِتَابِ رَبِّكَ... ﴾

"And recite, what has been revealed to you of the Book of your Lord..." (18:27)

6. ﴿ فَذُوقُوا بِمَا نَسِيتُمْ لِقَاءَ يَوْمِكُمْ هَٰذَا إِنَّا نَسِينَاكُمْ وَذُوقُوا عَذَابَ ٱلْخُلْدِ بِمَا كُنتُمْ تَعْمَلُونَ ﴾

"So taste [the punishment] because you forgot the meeting of this Day of yours, indeed, We have forgotten you. And taste the punishment of eternity for what you used to do." (32:14).

7. ﴿ ...فَٱبْعَثُوا أَحَدَكُم بِوَرِقِكُمْ هَٰذِهِ إِلَى ٱلْمَدِينَةِ... ﴾

"...So send one of you with this coin/money of yours to the town.."(18:19).

V. Relative Pronouns [أَسْماءُ الْمَوْصُولَة]

A Relative Pronoun connects the Definite word **before it** to the sentence **after** it. The statement after the Relative Pronoun [صِلَةُ الْمَوْصُول] functions as a description of the Definite word preceding it. In English, it includes the following words: who, whom, whose, and those. Relative Pronouns similar to Pointing Nouns retain all four characteristics of nouns, are Inflexible, and can take all three cases of I'rāb. They are always Definite like the word they describe. Relative Pronouns are used frequently in the Qur'ān.

A. Relative Pronouns [اَلَّذِينَ / اَلَّذِي]

Table 20: Relative Pronouns: [اَلَّذِينَ / اَلَّذِي]			
Plural	**Dual**	**Single**	
اَلَّذِينَ *Those who*	اَلَّذَانِ / اَلَّذَيْنِ *These (two) who*	اَلَّذِي *The one who*	masculine
اَلَّائِي / اَلَّاتِي *Those who*	اَلَّتَانِ / اَلَّتَيْنِ *These (two) who*	اَلَّتِي *The one who*	feminine

B. Additional Relative Pronouns: [مَنْ] & [مَا]

The Relative Pronoun [مَنْ] is used only for people. It is not gender or number specific. Do not confuse this Relative Pronoun with the Interrogative Particle [مَنْ] that has the same structure. The Ḥarf Jarr [مِنْ] also has a very similar appearance. As the Relative Pronouns just listed previously, both [مَنْ] and [مَا] follow the same rules in describing a Definite noun.

The Relative Pronoun [مَا] is used for non-humans. It is also not gender or number specific. Do not confuse this with the Negation Particle [مَا], or the Interrogative particle [مَا]. When a word is used whose morphology is identical to others with a different grammatical function, the true identify of the word can be identified by context.

1. Examples from Qur'ān and Ḥadīth:

i. ﴿ وَمِنَ ٱلنَّاسِ مَنْ يُجَادِلُ فِي ٱللَّهِ بِغَيْرِ عِلْمٍ ﴾

"And among men there are those who disputing about Allah without knowledge." (22:3)

ii. ﴿ ما نَهَيْتُكُمْ عَنْهُ فَٱجْتَنِبُوهُ وَ ما أَمَرْتُكُمْ بِهِ فَأْتُوا مِنْهُ ما ٱسْتَطَعْتُمْ ﴾

"What I have forbidden upon you, avoid; what I have ordered you, do as much of it as you can...."[55]

C. Relative Pronouns in sentences

Please note that a Relative Pronoun essentially functions in describing a Definite noun. The description comes after the Relative Pronoun and is known in grammar as the [صِلَة]. The [صِلَة] serves as the [صِفَة] for the noun before the Relative Pronoun. Often in sentences with Relative Pronouns, we may see a pronoun that appears redundant in meaning. This is the Connector or [عائِد] and connects the Relative Pronoun back to the Definite noun being described. This word is not present in English, and translating it from Arabic may give an awkward meaning if it is not omitted (in translation). Let us look at the following Arabic sentence below to clarify this point.

هٰذا الكِتابُ الَّذِي اشْتَرَيْتُهُ

"This book is the one that I bought."

In this example, the Relative Pronoun is underlined once, while the Connector is underlined twice. Focus your attention on the pronoun [هُ] attached to the verb [اشْتَرَيْتُ] which means "I bought". The pronoun [هُ] is the Connector, and connects back to the Definite noun being described, which is [هذا الكِتاب]. If the sentence is literally translated in English, it would read incorrectly as "This book is the one that I bought **it**". Here, we also see that the words following the Relative Pronoun [الَّذِي] acts as an adjective to describe the Definite noun before it (هذا الكِتاب). The noun is a Pointing Construction and acts like a single unit.

[55] Ṣaḥīḥ al-Bukhāri, Chapter on Holding Fast to the Book and Sunnah; كِتاب الاعْتِصام بِالكِتابِ والسُّنَّة Ḥadīth # 6777. Also in Ṣaḥīḥ Muslim, كِتاب الفَضائِل, Ḥadīth #1337.

D. Examples of [عائد] from the Qur'ān and Ḥadīth

In following two examples below, the [اسم مَوْصول] is underlined once while the [عائِد] is underlined twice.

1. ﴿ ٱلَّذِينَ يَأْكُلُونَ ٱلرِّبَا لَا يَقُومُونَ إِلَّا كَمَا يَقُومُ ٱلَّذِي يَتَخَبَّطُهُ ٱلشَّيْطَانُ مِنَ ٱلْمَسِّ... ﴾
"Those who consume interest cannot stand [on the Day of Resurrection] except as one stands the one that is beaten by Shaytān into insanity..." (2:275)

2. ﴿ ما نَهَيْتُكُمْ عَنْهُ فَٱجْتَنِبُوهُ وَ ما أَمَرْتُكُمْ بِهِ فَأْتُوا مِنْهُ ما ٱسْتَطَعْتُمْ ﴾
"What I have forbidden upon you, avoid; what I have ordered you, do as much of it [what] you can..." (Bukhāri)

In example #1, the [هُ] connects to the verb [يَقُومُ] that translates as "one standing". In example #2, we see that each underlined [هُ] connects back to preceding Relative Pronoun [مَا]. Please note that there may not be an explicit [عائِد] in every sentence with a Relative Pronoun. In cases where the [عائِد] is omitted, it is implied in a grammatical sense.

VI. Jarr Constructions and Sentences as Adjectives

We have just learned that Relative Pronouns act essentially as Describers for Definite nouns. Often, the [صِلَة] is an entire sentence that acts as a [صِفَة] and describes a Definite noun (preceding the Relative Pronoun). But what about an Indefinite noun? Is there another way to describe it other than the conventional Describing Construction methodology? The answer is yes, and in fact, it is an easier concept than that of Relative Pronouns we have studied here. Indefinite words can be described directly by a **sentence** or a **Jarr Construction**, which follows it. The more the student masters sentences and Word Constructions, these alternate Describers will be more easily recognized.

In the following examples below, the Indefinite noun being described is underlined once while the [صِفَة] is underlined twice. In the first example, the Indefinite word [خُبْزًا] is being described by the sentence [تَأْكُلُ ٱلطَّيْرُ مِنْهُ]. Note that the Indefinite word is immediately followed by its [صِفَة], a sentence. In the second example, we have two [صِفَة] of the Indefinite word [قِصَّةٌ]. First, we have the word [عَجِيبَةٌ] that matches all of the attributes of its described noun. Then, we have the Jarr Construction [فِي القُرآنِ], which acts as an adjective to describe the Indefinite word [قِصَّةٌ].

1. ﴿ قَالَ ٱلْآخَرُ إِنِّي أَرَانِي أَحْمِلُ فَوْقَ رَأْسِي خُبْزًا تَأْكُلُ ٱلطَّيْرُ مِنْهُ ﴾
"The other said, Verily I see myself carrying on my head bread, birds are eating from it." (12:36)

2. [يُوسُفُ لَهُ قِصَّةٌ عَجِيبَةٌ فِي القُرآنِ]
"Yūsuf has a wondrous story in the Qur'ān."

VII. The Five Special Nouns [الأَسْماءُ الْخَمْسَةُ]

The Five Special Nouns [أَبٌ / أَخٌ / فَمٌ / ذُو / ذَاتٌ] occur frequently in Arabic and have a variant conjugation when they occur as Muḍāf. A discussion on these Five Special Nouns is being included here since their conjugation requires understanding of Iḍāfah. These words behave like normal words in terms of inflection when **not** in an Iḍāfah Construction. For example, the word [أب] in I'rāb of Raf', Naṣb, and Jarr is respectively [أَبٌ], [أَبًا], and [أَبٍ].

Table 21: The Five Special Nouns [الأَسْماءُ الْخَمْسَةُ]			
Plural	**Dual**	**Single**	
آباءُ	أَبَوانِ / أَبَوَيْنِ	أَبٌ	father
إِخْوانٌ	أَخَوانِ / أَخَوَيْنِ	أَخٌ	brother
أَفْواهٌ	فَمانِ / فَمَيْنِ	فَمٌ	mouth
أُولُو	ذَوانِ / ذَوَيْنِ	ذُو	owner of/possessor (masculine)
أُولاتٌ	ذَواتانِ / ذَوتَيْنِ	ذَاتٌ	owner of/possessor (feminine)

The thing that differentiates the Special Nouns from other nouns is the situation when they are Muḍāf. When this occurs, then their ending takes one of three vowels based on their I'rāb. The Raf' case is denoted by a Wāw ending, the Naṣb case by the Alif ending, and the Jarr case by the Yā. Other than that, the grammar does not change. Please note that the words [ذات] or [أُولات] do not fit into this paradigm since they have a Tā Marbūṭah, and whose conjugation has been discussed previously.

A. Five Special Nouns as Muḍāf

Table 22: Conjugation of Five Special Nouns as Muḍāf			
Jarr[56]	**Naṣb**	**Raf'**	**Five Special Nouns in single form**
أَبِي	أَبَا	أَبُو	أَبٌ
أَخِي	أَخَا	أَخُو	أَخٌ
فِي	فَا	فُو	فَمٌ
ذِي	ذَا	ذُو	ذُو[57]
أُوْلِي	أُوْلِي	أُوْلُو	أُوْلُو
ذَاتِ	ذَاتَ	ذَاتُ	ذَاتٌ
أُوْلاتِ	أُوْلاتِ	أُوْلاتُ	أُوْلاتٌ

B. Examples from the Qur'ān

1. ﴿...يَا أَبَانَا مُنِعَ مِنَّا ٱلْكَيْلُ فَأَرْسِلْ مَعَنَا أَخَانَا نَكْتَلْ...﴾

   "...O our father, measure has been denied to us, so send with us our brother [that] we will be given measure... (12:63)

2. ﴿وَلَمَّا جَهَّزَهُمْ بِجَهَازِهِمْ قَالَ ٱئْتُونِي بِأَخٍ لَكُمْ مِنْ أَبِيكُمْ...﴾

   "And when he had furnished them with their supplies, he said, "Bring me a brother of yours from your father..." (12:59)

3. ﴿أَنْ كَانَ ذَا مَالٍ وَبَنِينَ﴾

   "Because he is a possessor of wealth and children," (68:14)

4. ﴿...وَٱللَّهُ يَخْتَصُّ بِرَحْمَتِهِ مَنْ يَشَاءُ وَٱللَّهُ ذُو ٱلْفَضْلِ ٱلْعَظِيمِ﴾

   "..But Allah selects for His mercy that He wills, and Allah is the possessor of great bounty."(2:105)

56 Please note that from these Five Special Nouns, (أخي) and (أبي) in the Jarr state as Muḍāf have the same appearance as when they are attached to the pronoun of first person (ي). You can differentiate them from their Iḍāfah forms by their context in the sentence. This is however not the case for فَم which retains the Meem when attached to the (ي) pronoun.

57 Please note that (ذُو) is always found in the form of a Muḍāf, but does not attach to pronouns. See examples #3 and #4.

Lesson 6: The Nominal Sentence [الْجُمْلَةُ الْاِسْمِيَّةُ]

I. The Basic Nominal Sentence [الْجُمْلَةُ الْاِسْمِيَّةُ]

Arabic sentences are of two types, Nominal and Verbal. The type of sentence is identified simply by examining the word at the beginning of the sentence. If the word is a noun, then the sentence is a "Non-Verbal" nominal sentence or a [الْجُمْلَةُ الْاِسْمِيَّةُ]. If the sentence begins with a verb, then you have a Verbal Sentence or [الْجُمْلَةُ الْفِعْلِيَّةُ]. Each sentence type has its own rules. Since we have thoroughly discussed the grammar of words and word constructions, familiarization with the Nominal sentence should not take too long.

Nominal sentences have two components: a Subject [مُبْتَدَأ] and a Predicate [خَبَر]. The Predicate serves to give information about the Subject. Unlike English, Arabic has no specific word for "is". In Arabic, there is a hidden or implied "is" between the Subject and Predicate. A simple way to differentiate the Subject and Predicate from the noun and adjective is by looking at the definiteness of the two. Since the Predicate gives information about the Subject, both have to match in gender, number and in the Raf' case[58]. The key difference is that Predicate is typically Indefinite. Another concept that is important to keep in mind is that both Subject and Predicate can be entire Word Constructions.

➢ **<u>Please note the following rules for a Nominal Sentence:</u>**

1. It consists of two components, a Subject [مُبْتَدَأ] and a Predicate [خَبَر].
2. There is an implied unwritten **"is"** between the Subject and Predicate.
3. The Subject comes **before** the implied "is" and is generally <u>Definite.</u> *If the sentence starts with a noun (Ism), that noun is the Subject.* Please note that both Nominal Sentences and Verbal Sentences can begin with a particle. The particle is overlooked as its "first" word when screening a sentence for a Nominal Sentence.
4. The Predicate comes after the implied "is" and is generally <u>Indefinite</u>.
5. Both the Subject and Predicate are **Raf'** independently.
6. The Nominal sentence can have other details after the Predicate that give additional information.

[58] Please note however that the Subject and the Predicate are independently Raf', for they do not follow the I'rāb if one of them changes, for example by a Naṣb particle like Inna.

➢ **Let us look at the diagram below, which shows how a basic Nominal sentence is formed.**

The house is big.

كَبِيرٌ　　اَلْبَيْتُ

Predicate　　**Subject**

big　　the house

خَبَر　　مُبتَدَأ

⬇　　⬇

Indefinite　　**Definite**

Raf'　　**Raf'**

⇩

Nominal Sentence ✓

اَلْبَيْتُ كَبِيرٌ

Other examples:

This is a book. [هٰذَا كِتَابٌ]

Those are Muslims. [أُوْلَٰئِكَ مُسْلِمُونَ]

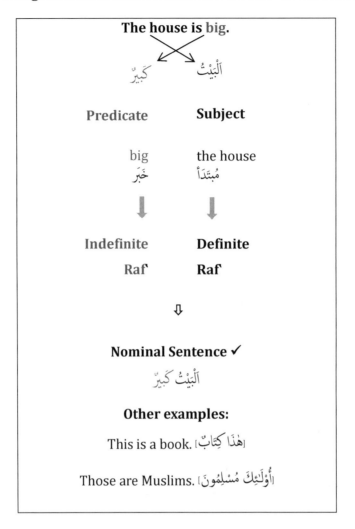

II. Subject and Predicate [اَلْمُبْتَدَأ] and [اَلْخَبَر]

A. Subject [اَلْمُبْتَدَأ]

1. It is generally **Definite** and **Raf'**. It can be Naṣb however, when [إِنَّ] begins a sentence[59].
2. It is present at the start of a "sentence". Please note that a typical Āyah of the Qur'ān is often composed of many sentences, and thus can have many embedded Nominal and Verbal Sentences within.
3. The Subject can be an entire Word Construction (Possession, Pointing, or Describing Constructions) and thus be composed of two or more nouns.

[59] Inna and its sisters [إِنَّ وَ أَخَوَاتُهَا] are present in Nominal Sentences, but are grammatically classified differently than Nominal sentences. In this 2-Volume Series, this is not essential to know, however one may come across this in other grammar textbooks. These Naṣb particles act on a Nominal sentence and cause it to gain a verb-like meaning depending of on the particle used. That is why, when the particle [إِنَّ] acts on a sentence, the subject becomes Naṣb and is termed [اِسْمُ إِنَّ], while the Predicate is termed [خَبَرُ إِنَّ].

B. The Predicate (اَلْخَبَر)

1. The Predicate generally comes after the Subject.
2. It is Raf'.
3. The Predicate agrees in gender, plurality, and I'rāb since it gives information about its Subject, but not in definiteness.
4. It is typically **Indefinite**, but please note that exceptions do exist. Cases where the Predicate is Definite are discussed here later.
5. The Predicate can be an entire Word Construction (Possession, Pointing, or Describing Constructions) and thus can be composed of two or more nouns.
6. There are four types of Predicate. The simplest one is termed (مُفْرَد) or "single word", which we looked at in the previous examples.

C. Examples from the Qur'ān and Ḥadīth

Subject is underlined once, Predicate is underlined twice. Additional words not underlined can be considered extra detail at this point.

1. ﴿ وَهُوَ[60] عَلِيمٌ بِذَاتِ ٱلصُّدُورِ ﴾

   "...and He is knowing of what is in within the breasts..." (57:6)

2. ﴿ وَ الصَّلاةُ نورٌ ، وَالصَّدَقَةُ بُرْهانٌ ، وَ الصَّبْرُ ضِياءٌ ، وَ الْقُرْآنُ حُجَّةٌ لَكَ أَوْ عَلَيْكَ... ﴾

   "...And the prayer is a light, and charity is a proof, and patience is a shine, and the Qur'ān is an evidence for or against you..." (Muslim)[61]

3. ﴿ وَٱللَّهُ بَصِيرٌ بِمَا تَعْمَلُونَ ﴾

   "...and Allah is seeing of what you do."(49:18)

4. ﴿ اَلدُّنْيا سِجْنُ الْمُؤْمِنِ وَ جَنَّةُ الْكافِرِ ﴾

   "The world is a prison for the believer and a paradise for the disbeliever". (Muslim)[62]

5. ﴿ آيَةُ الْمُنَافِقِ ثَلاثٌ... ﴾

   "The signs of the hypocrite are three...." (Bukhāri)[63]

60 Please note that in all these examples, there is a (وَ) present before the Subject (مُبْتَدَأ). This is because these examples were taken from in between the respective Qur'ānic Āyah or Ḥadīth. A Wāw often serves as a particle, which connects two adjacent sentences. There are many different types of Wāws in Arabic grammar, but the Wāw mainly functions as a connector, without affecting I'rāb.

61 Ṣaḥīḥ Muslim: Chapter on Book of Purification,كتاب الطَّهارة, Ḥadīth # 223.

62 Ṣaḥīḥ Muslim, Chapter on Piety and Softening of the Hearts: كتاب الزُّهدِ وَالرَّقائِق, Ḥadīth # 2956.

63 Ṣaḥīḥ al-Bukhāri, Chapter on Imān: كتاب الإيمان, Ḥadīth #33.

6. ﴿إِنَّمَا ٱلْمُؤْمِنُونَ ٱلَّذِينَ آمَنُوا بِٱللَّهِ وَرَسُولِهِ ثُمَّ لَمْ يَرْتَابُوا وَجَاهَدُوا بِأَمْوَالِهِمْ وَأَنفُسِهِمْ فِي سَبِيلِ ٱللَّهِ..﴾

"The believers are only those who have believed in Allah and His Messenger and then doubt not but strive with their properties and their lives in the cause of Allah...." (49:15)

III. The Four Types of Predicates [أَخْبار]

A. Predicate as a Single word or Word Construction: [مُفْرَد]

There are four types of Predicates. The [مُفْرَد] type is the major type of Predicate that we will be studying. Sometimes the Predicate is a single word as in prior examples # 1, 2, 3, and 5 just examined. Sometimes, it is a Word Construction such an Iḍāfah/Possession Construction as in example #4. Please note that sometimes the Subject can itself be a Word Construction as shown in Example #5. Whatever the case, it is essential to identify Word Constructions when analyzing the sentence. Incorrect identification can inherently lead to erroneous and confused translations. Sometimes the Predicate can be a Relative Pronoun that is encompassed within an entire sentence. In example #6, the Predicate is the Relative Pronoun [ٱلَّذِينَ]. Since all Relative Pronouns are connected with a [صِلَة], the entire sentence (dotted) after it becomes part of the Predicate. These types of sentences incorporating Relative Pronouns are frequently seen in the Qur'ān and Ḥadīth. Also, please note that addition details can follow the Predicate such as a Jarr constructions (example #1 and 3), conjunctions (example #4), other words, etc. At this point, it is a bit premature to discuss these details that are explained in more detail in the Second Volume.

B. Predicate as a Ḥarf Jarr Construction [جارٌ وَالْمَجْرور]

These include nouns like [الظُّروف] that act like Jarr particles[64] (see Table 15). The implied "is" is placed between the Jarr Construction and the Subject. Since the Jarr Construction is the Predicate, it is considered Raf' functionally even though its appearance is not. In the following examples, the basic Nominal Sentence is underlined, which contains the Predicate that is highlighted in gray. Additional words after the underlined basic Nominal sentence are "extra detail" that add additional information to the basic sentence unit.

1. ﴿أُوْلَٰئِكَ عَلَىٰ هُدًى مِّن رَّبِّهِمْ...﴾

"They are on guidance from their Lord..." (2:5)

64 In Arabic Grammar terminology, this category of [خبَر] is termed [شبه جملة], and includes Jarr Constructions and those words associated with [الظُّروف].

2. ﴿...إِنَّ يَدَ اللهِ عَلَى الْجَمَاعَةِ﴾

"The hand of Allah is on the group".[65]

3. ﴿إِنَّ ٱلْمُنَافِقِينَ فِي ٱلدَّرْكِ ٱلْأَسْفَلِ مِنَ ٱلنَّارِ وَلَن تَجِدَ لَهُمْ نَصِيرًا﴾

"Indeed, the hypocrites will be in the lowest depths of the Fire and never will you find for them a helper". (4:145)

C. Nominal sentence [الجُملَةُ الاِسْمِيَّة]

Sometimes the Predicate can come in the form of a sentence, such as Nominal sentence. This embedded sentence directly follows the Subject that initiates a sentence and acts as the Predicate. This is often done for purposes of placing emphasis on the Subject itself. This is because there is often a redundancy in bringing forth an extra Subject. Furthermore, it is not proper to translate an implied "is" between the Subject and Predicate. Let us look at the following diagram.

1. Nominal Sentence as Predicate

الرَّجُلُ هُوَ صادِقٌ

Predicate	Subject
هُوَ صادِقٌ	الرَّجُلُ
Predicate خَبَر	**Subject** مُبتَدَأ
⇩	⇩
الجُملَةُ الاِسْمِيَّة	**Definite Rafʿ**

⇩

Nominal Sentence ✓

الرَّجُلُ هُوَ صادِقٌ

The man, he is truthful.

~~(The man is he is truthful.)~~

65 Sunan Tirmidhi: Chapter on Tribulation from كتاب الفِتَن Ḥadīth #2166. Ṣaḥīḥ as per Sheikh Albānī.

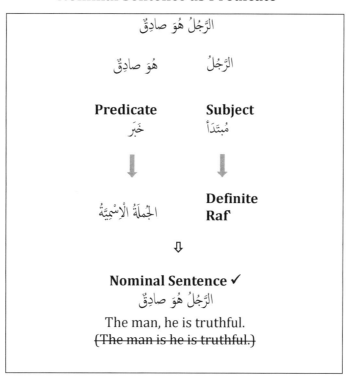

2. Single Word as Predicate [مُفْرَد]

الرَّجُلُ صادِقٌ

Predicate	Subject
صادِقٌ	الرَّجُلُ
Predicate	**Subject**
خَبَر	مُبتَدَأ
⇓	⇓
[مُفْرَد]	**Definite Raf'**

⇩

Nominal Sentence ✓

الرَّجُلُ صادِقٌ

The man is truthful.

D. Verbal Sentence [الْجُمْلَةُ الفِعْلِيَّة]

Similar to the previous discussion, the Predicate can also be a Verbal Sentence. Again, the embedded sentence follows the Subject that initiates a Nominal Sentence and acts as the Predicate. Similar to a Nominal Sentence Predicate, it is inappropriate to place an implied "is" in-between the Subject and the Verbal Sentence. One rhetorical purpose for this is that extra emphasis is placed on the Subject being discussed. The Subject is really mentioned twice. Please recall that a Verbal Sentence is always initiated by a verb. Let us look at the following examples where the Verbal Sentence is underlined.

1. [اَلْمُؤْمِنُونَ جاهِدُوا فِي سَبِيلِ اللهِ]

   "The Believers, they struggle in the way of Allah."

2. ﴿ ...وَ ٱللَّهُ يَعْلَمُ مَا فِي ٱلسَّمَاوَاتِ وَمَا فِي ٱلْأَرْضِ... ﴾

   "...and Allah (He) knows whatever is in the heavens and whatever is on the earth..." (49:16)

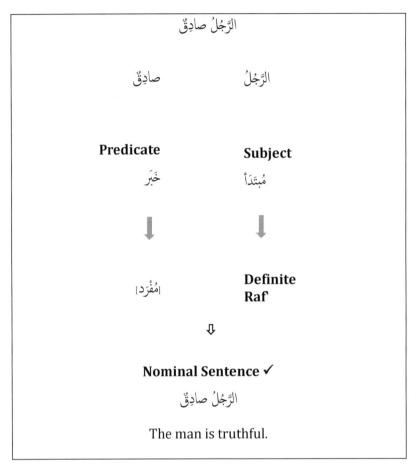

IV. Important Miscellaneous Particles in Sentences

Numerous particles occur frequently in Arabic sentences that the student should be familiar with. We have already discussed those that affect I'rāb such as Ḥarf Naṣb, Jarr, and Jazm. In this section, we will briefly discuss the important particles that have no effect on I'rāb, or [حُروفٌ غَيْرُ عامِلَةٍ].

A. Categories of Miscellaneous Particles [حُروفٌ غَيْرُ عامِلَةٍ]

1. Particles of Negation [حُرُوف النَّفْي]

These particles presented here cause negation without affecting I'rāb. Thus, the other particles of negation that cause a change in I'rāb do not fit into this category. These are particles such as [لَنْ] , [لَمْ], and the Forbidding [لا]. The Particles of Exception [حُرُوف الاسْتِثْناء] such as [إِلَّا] are also not categorized here since they cause a change in I'rāb.

Table 23: Particles of Negation [حُرُوف النَّفْي] *Examples shown on pgs. 81-82*		
لا	no	Example #1
ما	no	Examples #2 and 3
إِنْ	no[66]	Example #8
كَلَّا	Never!/by no means![67]	Example #9

2. Particles of Interrogation [حُرُوفُ الاِسْتِفْهام].

Please see Section V of this lesson.

3. Connecting Particles [حُرُوف الْعَطْف]

Connecting Particles connect two words or phrases together in a sentence. Similar to English conjunctions, these particles allow for less redundancy in the language. These particles transfer I'rāb of the first word onto the following word that the particle connects to. Please see Qur'ānic examples #7 in the next section which shows how [عَطْف] works. In these examples, the underlined nouns are connected by a [حَرْفُ الْعَطْف] that retains the same I'rāb.

---

[66] There are different grammatical functions of [إِنْ], the most common being that of a conditional particle. It serves as a negation particle only when followed by the exception particle [إِلَّا] later in the sentence. See Example #8 on pg. 82.

[67] This particle stands out from the other particles, as it is a solitary particle, which used as an exclamation. It can also be used in rebuttal of a statement. For example in 104:3-4, ﴿ يَحْسَبُ أَنَّ مَالَهُ أَخْلَدَهُ ۝ كَلَّا ۖ لَيُنبَذَنَّ فِي الْحُطَمَةِ ﴾, the particle [كَلَّا] is used to negate the statement. "He thinks that his wealth will make him immortal. No! He will surely be thrown into the Crusher."

Table 24: Connecting Particles [حُرُوف الْعَطْف] *Examples shown on pgs. 81-82*		
وَ	"and"	Examples #5 and 7
فَ	"and/then" (immediately following)	Example #2
ثُمَّ	"then" (after a period of time)	Examples #6, 7, and 9
أَوْ	"or" (alternation or doubt)	Example #10
أَمْ	"or"/rather (used in questions)	Example #11
بَلْ	but/rather	Example #10
لَكِنْ	but[68]	Example #1

4. Particles of Emphasis [حُرُوف التَّوْكِيد]

These particles function in causing emphasis. Please note that the particle [لَ] can attach to the beginning of a particle, noun, or a verb. The most common particle that is used for emphasis is the Naṣb particle Inna which has been discussed.

Table 25: Particles of Emphasis [حُرُوف التَّوْكِيد] *Examples shown on pg. 82*		
لَ	Indeed	Examples #3, 6 and 8
قَدْ	Indeed/certainly[69]	------
إِنَّمَا	only[70]	Example #7

68 This particle is very similar in meaning and form to [لَكِنَّ], which is also a Naṣb Particle.

69 Even though this particle has been grouped under [حُرُوف التَّوْكِيد], it is more accurately termed [حَرْف التَّحْقِيق], being a particle of certainty.

70 This particle unlike the particle [إِنَّ] does not cause Naṣb even though it appears to be similar.

5. Particles of Condition (حُرُوف الشَّرْط)

Conditional Particles function in initiating a Conditional Statement (if/then statement). This consists of two parts: the Condition (شَرْط) and the Response (جَوابُ الْشَّرْط). These particles can act on both nouns and verbs. If they act on a Present Tense verb, then they cause Jazm. Otherwise, they have no effect on I'rāb. The Response Particle Fā (فَ) is used to indicate a Response Statement. The Fā is typically not used when Present Tense verbs are used in both the condition and the response.

Table 26: Particles of Condition (حُرُوف الشَّرْط) *Examples shown on pgs. 82*		
لَوْ	If	Example #9
إِنْ	If	Example #5 and 10
مَنْ	who	-----
ما	what	-----
لَوْلا	had it not been/ were it not for	Example #6
أَمَّا	as for	Example #4
فَ	"then" Response Particle[71]	Example #4, 5, and 10

B. Examples from the Qur'ān

Particles are underlined.

1. ﴿أَلَآ إِنَّهُمْ هُمُ ٱلْمُفْسِدُونَ وَلَٰكِن لَّا يَشْعُرُونَ﴾

"Unquestionably, it is they who are the corrupters, but they perceive [it] not."(2:12)

2. ﴿أُولَٰٓئِكَ ٱلَّذِينَ ٱشْتَرَوُا۟ ٱلضَّلَٰلَةَ بِٱلْهُدَىٰ فَمَا رَبِحَت تِّجَٰرَتُهُمْ وَمَا كَانُوا۟ مُهْتَدِينَ﴾

"Those are the ones who have purchased error [in exchange] for guidance, so their transaction has brought no profit, nor were they guided."(2:16)

[71] This Fā is actually a "Response Particle" and frequently precedes the Response Statement of a Conditional Statement.

3. ﴿...وَمَا كَانَ ٱللَّهُ لِيُضِيعَ إِيمَانَكُمْ إِنَّ ٱللَّهَ بِٱلنَّاسِ لَرَءُوفٌ رَّحِيمٌ﴾

"...and never would Allah have caused you to lose your faith. Indeed Allah is, to the people, Kind and Merciful."(2:143)

4. ﴿...فَأَمَّا ٱلَّذِينَ ءَامَنُوا۟ فَيَعْلَمُونَ أَنَّهُ ٱلْحَقُّ مِن رَّبِّهِمْ وَأَمَّا ٱلَّذِينَ كَفَرُوا۟ فَيَقُولُونَ مَاذَآ أَرَادَ ٱللَّهُ بِهَٰذَا مَثَلًا...﴾

"...and (as for) those who have believed, they know that it is the truth from their Lord. But as for those who disbelieve, they say, "What did Allah intend by this as an example?..."(2:26)

5. ﴿فَإِن لَّمْ تَفْعَلُوا۟ وَلَن تَفْعَلُوا۟ فَٱتَّقُوا۟ ٱلنَّارَ ٱلَّتِى وَقُودُهَا ٱلنَّاسُ وَٱلْحِجَارَةُ أُعِدَّتْ لِلْكَافِرِينَ﴾

"But if you do not and you will never be able to then fear the Fire, whose fuel is men and stones, prepared for the disbelievers."(2:24)

6. ﴿ثُمَّ تَوَلَّيْتُم مِّنۢ بَعْدِ ذَٰلِكَ فَلَوْلَا فَضْلُ ٱللَّهِ عَلَيْكُمْ وَرَحْمَتُهُۥ لَكُنتُم مِّنَ ٱلْخَاسِرِينَ﴾

"Then you turned away after that. And if not for the favor of Allah upon you and His mercy, you would have been among the losers."(2:64)

7. ﴿إِنَّمَا ٱلْمُؤْمِنُونَ ٱلَّذِينَ ءَامَنُوا بِٱللَّهِ وَرَسُولِهِۦ ثُمَّ لَمْ يَرْتَابُوا وَجَاهَدُوا بِأَمْوَالِهِمْ وَأَنفُسِهِمْ فِى سَبِيلِ ٱللَّهِ أُو۟لَٰٓئِكَ هُمُ ٱلصَّادِقُونَ﴾

"The believers are only the ones who have believed in Allah and His Messenger and then do not doubt but strive with their properties and their lives in the cause of Allah. It is those who are the truthful."(49:15)

8. ﴿لَقَالَ ٱلَّذِينَ كَفَرُوا إِنْ هَٰذَا إِلَّا سِحْرٌ مُّبِينٌ...﴾

"...the disbelievers would say, "This is not but obvious magic..." (6:7)

9. ﴿كَلَّا سَوْفَ تَعْلَمُونَ ۝ ثُمَّ كَلَّا سَوْفَ تَعْلَمُونَ ۝ كَلَّا لَوْ تَعْلَمُونَ عِلْمَ ٱلْيَقِينِ ۝﴾

"Nay! You are going to know. Then nay! You are going to know. Nay! If you only knew with knowledge of certainty" (102:2-5)

10. ﴿..قُلْ فَمَن يَمْلِكُ لَكُم مِّنَ ٱللَّهِ شَيْـًٔا إِنْ أَرَادَ بِكُمْ ضَرًّا أَوْ أَرَادَ بِكُمْ نَفْعًا بَلْ كَانَ ٱللَّهُ بِمَا تَعْمَلُونَ خَبِيرًا﴾

"...Say, "Then who could prevent Allah at all if He intended for you harm or intended for you benefit? Rather, ever is Allah, with what you do, Acquainted."(48:11)

11. ﴿أَمْ خُلِقُوا مِنْ غَيْرِ شَيْءٍ أَمْ هُمُ الْخَالِقُونَ﴾

"Or were they created by nothing, or were they the creators [of themselves]?" (52:35)

V. Interrogative Sentences [اَلْاِسْتِفْهام]

Interrogative Particles, when placed at the beginning of a respective sentence cause it to become a question. They do not have any effect on I'rāb, and can act on both Nominal and Verbal Sentences alike. For example, the particle [أ] or [هَلْ] directly converts any sentence into a question form. Please note that some Interrogative Particles like [ما] and [مَنْ] can have other grammatical roles even though they may be present at the beginning of a sentence. For example, [ما] can act in negation, as a Relative Pronoun, or as an Interrogative. The particle [مَنْ] can act as a Relative Pronoun, Conditional Particle, or an an Interrogative.

Table 27: Interrogative Particles [حُروفُ الْاِسْتِفْهام]

Interrogative Particle	أ / هَلْ	or / do	أَمْ
When	مَتَى / أَيَّانَ	Who	مَنْ
What	ما / ماذا	Where	أَيْنَ
Why	لِماذا / لِمَا	Which (this is **Muḍāf)**	أَيٌّ
How	كَيْفَ	How many	كَمْ
from where/how	أَنَّى	About what	عَمَّ

➢ Examples from the Qur'ān

1. ﴿قُلْ يَا أَهْلَ الْكِتَابِ لِمَ تَكْفُرُونَ بِآيَاتِ اللَّهِ....﴾
“Say, "O People of the Book, why do you disbelieve in the Āyāt of Allah..?” (3:98)

2. ﴿وَمَا لَكُمْ لَا تُؤْمِنُونَ بِاللَّهِ...﴾
“And why do you not believe in Allah...” (57:8)

3. ﴿ هَلْ أَتَاكَ حَدِيثُ مُوسَىٰ ﴾
“Has there reached you the story of Mūsa?”(79:15)

4. ﴿قَالُوا أَإِنَّكَ لَأَنتَ يُوسُفُ...﴾
“They said, "Are you indeed Yūsuf?.."(12:90)

5. ﴿أَمْ حَسِبْتُمْ أَنْ تَدْخُلُوا ٱلْجَنَّةَ وَلَمَّا يَعْلَمِ ٱللَّهُ ٱلَّذِينَ جَاهَدُوا مِنْكُمْ....﴾

"Or do you think that you will enter Paradise while Allah has not yet made evident those of you who fight in His cause"... (3:142)

6. ﴿كَيْفَ تَكْفُرُونَ بِٱللَّهِ وَكُنتُمْ أَمْوَاتاً فَأَحْيَاكُمْ...﴾

"How can you disbelieve in Allah when you were lifeless and He brought you to life..?"(2:28)

7. ﴿....فَمَنْ أَظْلَمُ مِمَّنِ ٱفْتَرَى عَلَى ٱللَّهِ كَذِبًا﴾

"...And who is more unjust than one who invents about Allah a lie?""(18:15)

8. ﴿...قَالَ قَائِلٌ مِّنْهُمْ كَمْ لَبِثْتُمْ..﴾

"...a speaker said from among them, How long have you remained?..." (18:19)

9. ﴿قَالَتْ أَنَّى يَكُونُ لِي غُلَامٌ وَلَمْ يَمْسَسْنِي بَشَرٌ وَلَمْ أَكُ بَغِيًّا﴾

"She said, "How can I have a boy while no man has touched me and I have not been unchaste?"(19:20)

10. ﴿عَمَّ يَتَسَاءَلُونَ﴾

"Concerning what are they disputing?"(78:1)

11. ﴿ٱلَّذِي خَلَقَ ٱلْمَوْتَ وَٱلْحَيَاةَ لِيَبْلُوَكُمْ أَيُّكُمْ أَحْسَنُ عَمَلًا..﴾

"The One who created death and life to test you which of you is best in deeds..." (67:2)

Lesson 7: Types of Nominal Sentences [أَنْوَاعُ الجُمَل]

I. Nominal Sentences and its Variances

In Lesson 6, the rules for the standard Nominal Sentence were studied. Being familiar with their principles will allow us to also examine and study "atypical" or variant types of Nominal Sentences. Their study is important since Arabic including the Qur'ān is filled with variances. For example, we have studied that in the typical Nominal Sentence, the Predicate is Indefinite. However, there a few important situations in which the Predicate is in fact Definite.

➤ **Examples of typical Nominal Sentences where the Predicate (underlined) is Indefinite**

1. ﴿ وَهَٰذَا كِتَابٌ أَنزَلْنَاهُ مُبَارَكٌ مُّصَدِّقُ ٱلَّذِي بَيْنَ يَدَيْهِ ﴾
   "And this is a Book which We have sent down, blessed and confirming what was before it" (6:92)

2. ﴿..إِنَّمَا أَنَا بَشَرٌ مِّثْلُكُمْ..﴾
   "..I am only a man like you..." (41:6)

3. ﴿ وَقَاتِلُوا فِي سَبِيلِ ٱللَّهِ وَٱعْلَمُوا أَنَّ ٱللَّهَ سَمِيعٌ عَلِيمٌ ﴾
   "And fight in the cause of Allah and know that Allah is Hearing and Knowing."(2:244)

4. [هُوَ رَجُلُ عِلْمٍ]
   "He is a man of knowledge".

5. [رَجُلُ الْبَلَدِ حَسَنٌ]
   "The man of the city is good".

II. Cases when the Predicate is Definite

There are situations when the Predicate is Definite in a Nominal Sentence. When this occurs, we can run into a dilemma. Since there are two consecutive nouns that possess that same four inherent characteristics including definiteness, it may be difficult to differentiate the sentence from a Describing Construction. Here, context will be the important factor that differentiates between these two possibilities.

Situation #1: A pronoun is placed between the Subject and Predicate

In order to avoid making this a Describing Construction, We can place another word in between these two words, remove any ambiguity, and make it a Nominal Sentence. The word that is placed in-between is **the pronoun** of the Subject. Remember, the pronoun **needs to match** in number and gender of the Subject. This pronoun essentially is the implied "is" of a Nominal Sentence, and is translated as such. In the following examples, this pronoun is underlined, and is between the Subject and Predicate.

1. ﴿ فَمَنْ تَوَلَّىٰ بَعْدَ ذَٰلِكَ فَأُولَٰئِكَ هُمُ ٱلْفَاسِقُونَ ﴾
"And whoever turned away after that - they were the defiantly disobedient."(3:82)

2. ﴿ ...إِنَّكَ أَنْتَ ٱلسَّمِيعُ الْعَلِيمُ ﴾
"Indeed, You are the All-Hearing." (2:127)

3. ﴿ ...لَا تَبْدِيلَ لِكَلِمَاتِ ٱللَّهِ ذَٰلِكَ هُوَ ٱلْفَوْزُ ٱلْعَظِيمُ ﴾
"..No change is there in the words of Allah. That is what the great attainment is."(10:64)

Situation #2: Nothing is placed between the Subject and Predicate

In some circumstances, both the Subject and the Predicate are Definite, without any pronoun as in the previous situation. In this instance, there is an implied "is" between **two continuous Definite nouns**. This is more of an exception to the above stated rules even though these types of sentences are found in the Qur'ān. This meaning is determined by the context of the words. We often see this in many simple sentences, and this is understood. For example, He is Aḥmad, She is Fāṭimah, This is Baghdād, etc. Please note that in these cases which start with a pronoun or pointing noun, there is no other way that these can be stated other than by having a Definite Predicate, if it is proper name. However, in other cases when the Predicate contains the Definite article, then context should be used to identify it as a sentence. Please see the following examples where the Predicate has been underlined.

1. ﴿...أَنَا يُوسُفُ...﴾
"..I am Yūsuf..." (12:90).

2. ﴿ ...فَسَيَكْفِيكَهُمُ ٱللَّهُ وَهُوَ ٱلسَّمِيعُ ٱلْعَلِيمُ ﴾
"...and Allah will be sufficient for you against them. And He is the Hearing, the Knowing."(2:137)

3. ﴿ ذَٰلِكَ ٱلْكِتَابُ لَا رَيْبَ فِيهِ هُدًى لِّلْمُتَّقِينَ ﴾
"This is the Book about which there is no doubt, a guidance for those conscious of Allah" (2:2)

4. ﴿مَنْ يُصْرَفْ عَنْهُ يَوْمَئِذٍ فَقَدْ رَحِمَهُ وَذَٰلِكَ ٱلْفَوْزُ ٱلْمُبِينُ﴾
"He from whom it is averted that Day, He has granted him mercy. And that is the clear attainment."(6:16)

III. Review of Nominal Sentences with Embedded Constructions

In the following Nominal Sentences, the Predicate is underlined. Please note that the Subject precedes the Predicate. In these examples, the Subject and/or Predicate take the form of a Word Construction.

1. ﴿اَلْكِبْرُ بَطَرُ الْحَقِّ وَ غَمْطُ النَّاسِ﴾ "Arrogance is rejecting the truth and looking down on people". (Muslim)[72]
2. ﴿طَلَبُ الْعِلْمِ فَرِيضَةٌ عَلى كُلِّ مُسْلِمٍ﴾ "Seeking knowledge is obligatory on every Muslim"(Abū Dawūd).[73]
3. ﴿ما أنا بِقارِئٍ﴾ "I am not a reciter".[74]
4. [اَلْإِسْلامُ دِينُ قَوْمِ مِصْرَ] "Islam is the religion of the people of Egypt".
5. [وَقْتُ الصَّلاةِ قَرِيبٌ] "The time for prayer is near".
6. [بِنْتُكِ طِفْلَةٌ جَمِيلَةٌ] "Your daughter is a pretty infant."
7. [اَلْمَساجِدُ الْقَدِيمَةُ مَحْبُوبَةٌ لَنا] "The old mosques are beloved to us."
8. [هَلْ بَيْتُ زَيْدٍ الْكَبِيرٌ أَوْ الصَّغِيرٌ] "Is the house of Zaid big or small?
9. [اَلْمُؤْمِنُونَ على الصِّراطِ الْمُسْتَقِيمِ] "The believers are on the straight path".
10. [اَلْكافِرُونَ هُمْ الْخاسِرُونَ] "The disbelievers, they are the losers."
11. [اَلْمُعَلِّمُ عَلَّمَ فِي الْجامِعَةِ الْمَدِينَةِ] "The teacher, he taught in Madīnah University".

[72] Ṣaḥīḥ Muslim: Book of Imān, كِتاب الايمان باب تَحْرِيمِ الْكِبْرِ وَبَيَانِهِ, Ḥadīth #91.

[73] Sunan Abu Dawūd, [ونقله ايضا عن المزي وقد صححه الشيخ الالباني في صحيح الجامع], Ḥadīth #224. Classified as Authenthic by Albāni and Suyūṭi.

[74] Ṣaḥīḥ Bukhāri, Hadith #4597, from كتاب تفسير القرآن.

1. Additional Practice with Word Constructions and Sentences

The following exercises are designed to review principles that were covered for Nominal Sentences and Word Constructions.

a) Exercise 1: Translate the following phrases or sentences and identify specific Word Constructions that are present.

1. هٰذَا الرَّجُلُ
2. هٰذَا رَجُلٌ
3. رَجُلُ الْبَلَدِ
4. هٰذَا رَجُلُ الْبَلَدِ
5. هٰذَا رَجُلُ بَلَدٍ
6. رَجُلُ الْبَلَدِ هٰذَا
7. رَسُولُ اللّٰهِ هٰذَا

Answers for Exercise 1:

1. **this man**: Describing Construction & Pointing Construction.
2. **This is a man.** Nominal Sentence.
3. **the man of the city.** Possession Construction.
4. **This is the man of the city**: Nominal Sentence with a Possession Construction.
5. This is **a** man of **a** city. Nominal Sentence with a Possession Construction.
6. **this man of the city:** Possession Construction with a Pointing Construction.
7. **this Messenger of Allah**. Possession Construction with a Pointing Construction.

b) Exercise 2: *Let us go further with this and take it to the next level.*

8. رَجُلُ الْبَلَدِ الْحَسَنُ
9. رَجُلُ الْبَلَدِ حَسَنٌ
10. إِنَّكَ أَنْتَ الْغَفُورُ
11. أَنْتِ فاطِمَةُ

Answers for Exercise 2:

8. **the good man of the city.** Describing Construction with Possession Construction.
9. **The man of the city is good.** Possession Construction with a Nominal Sentence.
10. **Indeed, You are All Forgiving.** Nominal Sentence.
11. **You are Fāṭimah.** Nominal Sentence (both Subject and Predicate are Definite).

IV. Methodology for Analyzing Nominal Sentences[75]

Correctly analyzing and translating a Nominal Sentence requires that one be very familiar with I'rāb and Word Constructions. A Nominal Sentence is identified by looking at the first word of the sentence. If the first word is a particle, then the next word is examined to see if it is a noun. From this, we should go systematically in analysis of the sentence. Let us examine this methodology.

1. The first step before analyzing the sentence in question, each word should be analyzed thoroughly and be categorized (noun, particle, or verb). If the word is a noun, then its gender, plurality, definiteness, flexibility, and I'rāb should be identified. If the word is a particle, then it should also be appropriately categorized.
2. The second step should be to identify Word Constructions (Possession, Pointing, Describing, and Jarr Constructions) and merge words together. Relative Pronouns also should be looked at carefully since they are associated with embedded sentences. Then, merge any Word Constructions together, and or words joined by connecting particles [حروف العطف]. Merging allows one to simplify analysis of a sentence into grammar units so that the Subject and Predicate can be easily identified.
3. Finally, the third step is to identify the Subject and the Predicate of all embedded sentences, and then translate the sentence. Please look at the algorithm on the next page detailing the methodology to analyze Nominal Sentences.

[75] This methodology is not a novel one, and has been used in some traditional institutions where Arabic is not a first language. For example this methodology was taught to me by my teachers at the online Sunnipath Academy (now Qibla for the Islāmic Sciences). If one uses this methodology well, mistranslations and errors will be decreased.

Methodology of Analyzing a Nominal Sentence:

كُلُّ بَنِي آدَمَ خَطَّاءٌ وَ خَيْرُ الْخَطَّائِينَ التَّوَّابُونَ [Tirmidhi][76]

	التَّوَّابُونَ	الْخَطَّائِينَ	خَيْرُ	وَ	خَطَّاءٌ	آدَمَ	بَنِي	كُلُّ
Step #1 **Word Analysis**	Ism male proper-plural Definite Flexible Raf'	Ism male proper-plural Definite Flexible Jarr	Ism male single Indef. Flexible Raf'	Connect -ing particle	Ism male single Indefinite Flexible Raf'	Ism male single Definite Partially Flexible Jarr	Ism male plural Indefinite Flexible Jarr	Ism male plural Indefinite Flexible Raf'
Step #2 **Word Construction**	التَّوَّابُونَ	Possession Construction خَيْرِ الْخَطَّائِينَ			خَطَّاءٌ	Possession Construction بَنِي آدَمَ		كُلُّ
						Possession Construction كُلُّ بَنِي آدَمَ		
Merging words		Possession Construction خَيْرِ الْخَطَّائِينَ				Possession Construction كُلُّ بَنِي آدَمَ		
Step #4 **Identify Subject & Predicate and then Translate**	التَّوَّابُونَ Predicate "Those who repent repeatedly"	خَيْرِ الْخَطَّائِينَ Subject "the best of those who commit sin"		وَ Connects both sentences "and"	خَطَّاءٌ Predicate "those who commit sins"	كُلُّ بَنِي آدَمَ = Subject "All of the Children of Ādam"		

"All the Children of Ādam commit sins,
and the best of those who commit sins are those who seek repentance."

[76] Sunan Ibn Mājah, كتاب الزهد, Ḥadīth # 4251. Classified as Ḥasan by Sheikh Albāni.

Lesson 8: Introduction to Verbs [أَفْعَال]

I. Introduction to Verb Classification

We have at this point Alḥamdulillah reached the halfway point of this book. We will now start discussion on verbs, which will encompass the entire second half of this book. Since Arabic roots are based on verbs, even the discussions of nouns, in many ways, are linked to verbs and their derivatives.

A. Verbs are divided into two types based on <u>Root</u> letters.

    1. Three-letter roots [اَلْفِعْلُ الثُّلَاثِي]: these constitute the majority from verbs. These three-letter verbs will be our primary focus.

    2. Four-letter Root [اَلْفِعْلُ الرُّبَاعِي]: these are not common and are discussed in Volume 2.

B. Verbs have two different types of conjugations.

    1. Past Tense [اَلْفِعْلُ الْمَاضِي]

    2. Present/Future tense [اَلْفِعْلُ الْمُضَارِع]

C. Each Verb has an associated Verbal Noun [مَصْدَر].

D. The Verb and its associated three-letter root. Many nouns are derived from this Verbal Noun related to the verb in meaning in some way.

E. The three-letter root verb [اَلْفِعْلُ الثُّلَاثِي الْمُجَرَّد] will be referred to as <u>Verb Family I</u> in this book to avoid confusion with technical Arabic terminology. This is the origin of most Arabic words. Each Verb in Family I (based on a specific three-letter root) can generate from it, other families of verbs by adding to its three-letter root.

    1. These verbs with extra letters added to its three-letter root is termed [اَلْفِعْلُ الثُّلَاثِي الْمَزِيد فِيهِ].

    2. These verb families are termed according to Orientalist classification by Roman Numerals II through X. This classification scheme is very simple and is easier for learning Introductory Arabic, and thus used in this series.

F. Verbs can be regular or irregular. This occurs when any of the root letters of a verb are weak which are also termed [حروف الْعِلَّة]. The weak letters are the following letters: [ا / ي / و / أ] with the additional inclusion if any of the letter that has a Shadda [ـّ] (or consecutive doubled letters of a three-letter root). At this early stage, we do not recommend studying the Irregular verbs in detail since they can be confusing.

Once the rules for regular verbs (including higher verb families) are mastered, then the student should study the grammar of the Irregular verbs.

G. Verbs can be attached to the following pronouns at their ends.

1. [هُنَّ / ها / هُما / هُم / هُ]
2. [كُنَّ / كُما / كِ / كَ]
3. [انا / ني] (Please note that [ني] instead of [اي] is attached to verbs.)
4. All the above act as <u>Direct Objects</u> [مَفْعُول بِهِ] for the respective verb they are attached to.

II. The Past Tense Verb [اَلْفِعْلُ الْماضي]

A. Family I Past tense Verbs

Verb Family I, from which most of words of the Arabic language are derived, is composed of <u>three</u> basic root letters. Specifically, the Past Tense of Verb Family I is a ***male Third Person single conjugation***. All other conjugations contain more than three letters. Even though other verb conjugations carry more than three letters, every conjugation contains the original three root letters.

1. Using the [فعل] stem[77] nomenclature.

Let us take an example of a common verb: [نَصَرَ], which means to help.

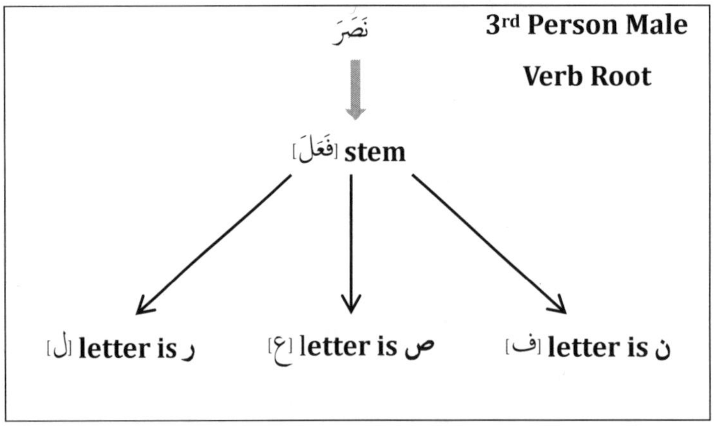

2. The Root Verb [فَعَلَ] and its derivatives.

   i. It typically has Fatḥah on the beginning and end letter.

[77] In Arabic grammar, the [فعل] stem is routinely utilized to derive various conjugations or patterns of both verbs and nouns. Recall, it was used to characterize the various Broken Plural patterns that were discussed earlier.

ii. The middle [ع] letter vowel <u>varies</u> and is **key** in verb conjugation to the Present Tense form. For example, the verbs [كَرُمَ/سَمِعَ/ضَرَبَ] are all Verb Family I with the same conjugation.

iii. Each verb has its own Verbal Noun [مَصْدَر]. Similar to Broken Plurals, they are found in several different patterns. Each verb has its own distinct Verbal Noun.

iv. A root verb is the source of numerous words and Verb Families that are connected in by similar meanings. For example, from the verb [عَلِمَ] (to learn), the following verbs are derived:

عَلَّمَ	أَعْلَمَ	تَعَلَّمَ	إِسْتَعْلَمَ
To teach (knowledge)	To notify	To learn (knowledge)	To ask for information

- The verb [عَلِمَ] also gives rise to other "action" nouns directly and indirectly related to its meaning shown below.

عِلْم	knowledge	عَلَم	mark/token
تَعْلِيم	learning	إِسْتِعْلَمَات	information
عالِم	knowledgeable	عُلُوم	sciences
مُعَلِّم	teacher	مُعَلَّم	student
إِسْتِعْلام	inquiry	مَعْلُوم	known

B. <u>Verb Conjugation of Past Tense Family I Verbs</u>

In review, the basic verb unit is in the *Third Person Masculine Single Past Tense form*. In it, we see that both the first stem [ف] and the third stem [ل] letters carry the Fatḥah vowel. The middle [ع] stem letter however can carry a Fatḥah, Ḍammah, or Kasrah. In Table 28, the verb conjugation has been detailed for Family I Verbs in the Past Tense based on the [فعل] stem. Please note that each conjugated form reflects a specific pronoun. That pronoun is the Doer of the action if the Doer is not mentioned explicitly.

Perhaps the easier way to memorize the Past Tense Conjugation Table is to go from right to left starting from the single masculine Third Person (root) line and then proceeding downwards. You will notice that in the conjugations, the first three root letters remain the same; additional letters are added on at their ends. This contrasts with Present Tense verbs where letters are added on at both the beginning and at the end of the 3-root letters.

Table 28: Verb Conjugation of Past Tense Family I Verbs			
Plural	**Dual**	**Singular**	
فَعَلُوْا [هُمْ]	فَعَلاَ [هُمَا]	فَعَلَ [هُوَ] ***root verb***	3rd Person masculine
فَعَلْنَ [هُنَّ]	فَعَلَتَا [هُمَا]	فَعَلَتْ [هِيَ]	3rd Person feminine
فَعَلْتُمْ [أَنْتُمْ]	فَعَلْتُمَا [أَنْتُمَا]	فَعَلْتَ [أَنْتَ]	2nd Person masculine
فَعَلْتُنَّ [أَنْتُنَّ]	فَعَلْتُمَا [أَنْتُمَا]	فَعَلْتِ [أَنْتِ]	2nd Person feminine
فَعَلْنَا [نَحْنُ]	فَعَلْنَا [نَحْنُ]	فَعَلْتُ [أَنَا]	1st Person (masculine/feminine)

C. <u>Example of Past Tense Conjugation:</u> [فَتَحَ] "to open"

Plural	**Dual**	**Singular**	
فَتَحُوْا They (all) opened	فَتَحَا They (two) opened	فَتَحَ He opened	3rd Person masculine
فَتَحْنَ They (feminine) opened	فَتَحَتَا They (two) opened	فَتَحَتْ She opened	3rd Person feminine
فَتَحْتُمْ You (all) opened	فَتَحْتُمَا You (two) opened	فَتَحْتَ You (masculine) opened	2nd Person masculine
فَتَحْتُنَّ You (all feminine) opened	فَتَحْتُمَا You two opened	فَتَحْتِ You (feminine)opened	2nd Person feminine
فَتَحْنَا we opened	فَتَحْنَا we opened	فَتَحْتُ I opened	1st Person (masculine/ feminine)

D. Examples of Past Tense Verbs in the Qur'ān

After thoroughly reviewing the Past Tense conjugation tables, you should be able to identify most Past Tense verbs. Please note that any pronoun attached to a verb at its end is its Direct Object. Do not confuse the Direct Object with the extra letters that cannot be separated from a particular conjugation. In the following examples, pay attention to the underlined Past Tense verbs.

1. ﴿ٱلْحَمْدُ لِلَّهِ ٱلَّذِي خَلَقَ ٱلسَّمَاوَاتِ وَٱلْأَرْضَ وَجَعَلَ ٱلظُّلُمَاتِ وَٱلنُّورَ...﴾
   "All praise is [due] to Allah, who created the heavens and the earth and made the darkness and the light..." (6:1)

2. ﴿قَالَ مَا مَنَعَكَ أَلَّا تَسْجُدَ إِذْ أَمَرْتُكَ قَالَ أَنَا خَيْرٌ مِنْهُ خَلَقْتَنِي مِنْ نَارٍ وَخَلَقْتَهُ مِنْ طِينٍ﴾
   "[Allah] said, "What prevented you from prostrating when I commanded you?" [Shayṭān] said, "I am better than him. You created me from fire and created him from clay."(7:12)

3. ﴿وَٱلَّذِينَ إِذَا فَعَلُوا فَاحِشَةً أَوْ ظَلَمُوا أَنْفُسَهُمْ ذَكَرُوا ٱللَّهَ...﴾
   "And those who, when they commit an immorality or wrong themselves remember Allah..." (3:135)

4. ﴿وَإِذْ أَخَذْنَا مِيثَاقَكُمْ وَرَفَعْنَا فَوْقَكُمُ ٱلطُّورَ...﴾
   "And [recall] when We took your covenant, and We raised over you the mount." (2:63)

5. ﴿تِلْكَ أُمَّةٌ قَدْ خَلَتْ لَهَا مَا كَسَبَتْ وَلَكُمْ مَا كَسَبْتُمْ...﴾
   "That was a nation which has passed on. It will have what it earned, and you will have what you have earned..." (2:134)

III. The Present Tense Verb [اَلْفِعْلُ الْمُضَارِعُ]

Present Tense verb conjugates have extra letters attached to the front **and** the end of their root letters. Recall that Past Tense verbs add extra letters only to the ends of their 3-letter roots. Present Tense verbs start with one of the following letters: [ن / ت / أ / ي]. Please note that although most Present Tense verbs begin with the letter [ي][78], very few verbs actually have the [ي] letter root as their first [ف] stem letter.

There, if a word starts with the letter [ي], you can assume it a verb because very few nouns start with [ي]. The following nouns begin with the letter [ي]: [يَسير / يُسْر / يَقِين / يَتيم / يَمِين / يوم]. Another distinct characteristic of Present Tense verbs is that they take an I'rāb. This is unlike the Past or Command Tenses that do not take I'rāb. Like nouns, the

[78] In the Qur'ān, only three verbs start with the Yā letter, [يَسَّرَ], [يَئِسَ], and [يُوقِنُ].

"default" I'rāb for Present Tense verbs is Raf'. A Present Tense Verb goes into Naṣb or Jazm when a Ḥarf acts on it (i.e. a Ḥarf Naṣb or Ḥarf Jazm). The Jarr case does not exist for verbs just as the Jazm does not exist for nouns.

Please note that Present Tense verbs can sometimes actually refer to the Future Tense. This differentiation depends on context. To specify the Future Tense without ambiguity, the particles [سَ] or [سَوْفَ] is placed directly before the respective Present Tense verb. These particles are discussed at the end of Lesson 10.

A. Verb Conjugation of [اَلْفِعْلُ الْمُضارِع]

It is essential to memorize the Past and Present verb conjugation Tables completely before moving forward. Learning the two verb conjugation tables (28 and 29) in this lesson should allow you to conjugate most Family I Verbs fully in all forms in the Past or Present Tense. Perhaps the easiest way to memorize the Present Tense Conjugation Table (#29) is going from top to bottom and moving left.

Knowing the Past and Present Tense Tables furthermore allows the student to theoretically conjugate verbs of all 3-letter roots in addition to their Verb Families (I through X). Please note that conjugation of Irregular Verbs also utilizes these two tables with some modification(s) due to vowel letters. The conjugation of Irregular Verbs is discussed in depth in "Volume 2". To be proficient in verb conjugation, it is essential that the student study and memorize the assigned high-yield verbs from the "80% of Qur'ānic Vocabulary" collection.

B. Verb Conjugation of [الفعل المضارع]

Table 29: Verb Conjugation of Present Tense Family I Verbs [الفعل المضارع]			
Plural	**Dual**	**Single**	
يَفْعَلُونَ [هُمْ]	يَفْعَلانِ [هُما]	يَفْعَلُ [هُوَ] ***root verb***	3rd Person masculine
يَفْعَلْنَ [هُنَّ]	تَفْعَلانِ [هُما]	تَفْعَلُ [هِيَ]	3rd Person feminine
تَفْعَلُونَ [أَنْتُمْ]	تَفْعَلانِ [أَنْتُما]	تَفْعَلُ [أَنْتَ]	2nd Person masculine
تَفْعَلْنَ [أَنْتُنَّ]	تَفْعَلانِ [أَنْتُما]	تَفْعَلِينَ [أَنْتِ]	2nd Person feminine
نَفْعَلُ [نَحْنُ]	نَفْعَلُ [نَحْنُ]	أَفْعَلُ [أَنَا]	1st Person (masculine/ feminine)

C. Example of Present Tense Conjugation: [فَتَحَ] "to open"

Plural	Dual	Single	
يَفْتَحُونَ [هُمْ]	يَفْتَحانِ [هُما]	يَفْتَحُ [هُوَ] ***root verb***	3rd Person masculine
يَفْتَحْنَ [هُنَّ]	تَفْتَحانِ [هُما]	تَفْتَحُ [هِيَ]	3rd Person feminine
تَفْتَحُونَ [أَنْتُمْ]	تَفْتَحانِ [أَنْتُما]	تَفْتَحُ [أَنْتَ]	2nd Person masculine
تَفْتَحْنَ [أَنْتُنَّ]	تَفْتَحانِ [أَنْتُما]	تَفْتَحِينَ [أَنْتِ]	2nd Person feminine
نَفْتَحُ [نَحْنُ]	نَفْتَحُ [نَحْنُ]	أَفْتَحُ [أَنَا]	1st Person (masculine/feminine)

D. Relationship between Past and Present Tense verbs

When studying any particular verb, it is essential to memorize the Root form (Past Tense 3rd Person male singular form) and its Present Tense counterpart. By memorizing these two conjugations, the student should be able to conjugate all forms detailed (on Tables 28 and 29). There is one caveat however. That is the issue of the middle [ع] vowel, which often changes when switching between Past and Present Tense for any specific verb. Let us look at the following diagram.

Converting Past Tense Verbs to Present Tense		
اَلْفِعْلُ الْمَاضِي	→	اَلْفِعْلُ الْمُضارِعُ
	↱	يَفْعُلُ
فَعَلَ	→	يَفْعَلُ
	↳	يَفْعِلُ
فَعِلَ	→	يَفْعَلُ
فَعُلَ	→	يَفْعُلُ

1. **For Past Tense verbs with a Fatḥah on the middle [ع] letter,** the middle letter can take a <u>Fatḥah, Kasrah, or Ḍammah</u> in the Present Tense. Thus, in these cases the [ع] letter vowel on the Present Tense verb needs to be memorized since there is no set pattern. Each of the following verbs below with a [ع] Fatḥah vowel is found in only one of three possible Present Tense patterns. The one correct form for these three verbs is highlighted below.

نَصَرَ			ضَرَبَ			فَتَحَ		
⇙	⇓	⇘	⇙	⇓	⇘	⇙	⇓	⇘
~~يَنْصَرُ~~	يَنْصُرُ	~~يَنْصِرُ~~	~~يَضْرَبُ~~	يَضْرِبُ	~~يَضْرُبُ~~	~~يَفْتُحُ~~	يَفْتَحُ	~~يَفْتِحُ~~
✗	✓	✗	✗	✓	✗	✗	✓	✗

2. One trick to aid in memorizing Past Tense verbs is knowing the following principle: In Past Tense verbs where the [ع] letter takes a <u>Fatḥah</u> **and** where <u>one of its last two letters is a **letter of the throat**</u>, then the middle letter takes a <u>Fatḥah</u> in the Present Tense. The letters of the throat are the following: [ه / ء / خ / ح / غ / ع]. Look at the examples below.

   (i) [قَرَأَ] ⇒ [يَقْرَأُ]

   (ii) [جَعَلَ] ⇒ [يَجْعَلُ]

3. For Past Tense verbs with a <u>Ḍammah on the [ع] letter</u>, the [ع] letter <u>always</u> takes a Ḍammah in the Present Tense. Please note that this **does not work** in the opposite direction as most random Present Tense verbs with a [ع] Ḍammah actually have a [ع] Fatḥah in the Past Tense. The examples below illustrate this principle of the Past Tense [ع] Ḍammah.

   (i) [كَرُمَ] ⇒ [يَكْرُمُ]

   (ii) [بَصُرَ] ⇒ [يَبْصُرُ]

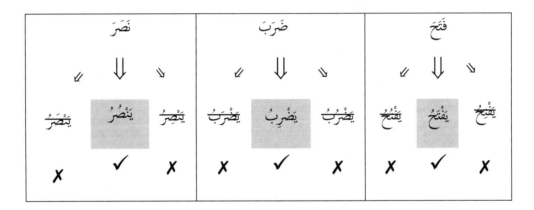

4. For Past Tense verbs with a Kasrah on the [ع] letter, the [ع] takes a Fatḥah in the Present Tense with rare exception[79]. Please again note that this principle often does not work in the opposite direction. For example, if you take any random Present Tense verb whose [ع] letter has a Fatḥah, its Past Tense [ع] letter is usually a Fatḥah. Please see the examples below.

(i) سَمِعَ ⇒ يَسْمَعُ

(ii) عَلِمَ ⇒ يَعْلَمُ

E. Examples of Present Tense Verbs from the Qur'ān

1. ﴿لَئِنْ أُخْرِجُوا لَا يَخْرُجُونَ مَعَهُمْ وَلَئِن قُوتِلُوا لَا يَنْصُرُونَهُمْ...﴾

"If they are expelled, they will not leave with them, and if they are fought, they will not aid them..." (59:12)

2. ﴿وَكَأَيِّنْ مِنْ دَابَّةٍ لَا تَحْمِلُ رِزْقَهَا ٱللَّهُ يَرْزُقُهَا وَإِيَّاكُمْ...﴾

"And how many a creature carries not its provision. Allah provides for it and for you ..." (29:60)

3. ﴿قُلْ يَا أَهْلَ ٱلْكِتَابِ لِمَ تَكْفُرُونَ بِآيَاتِ ٱللَّهِ وَٱللَّهُ شَهِيدٌ عَلَى مَا تَعْمَلُونَ﴾

"O people of the book, why do you disbelieve in the verses of Allah while Allah is Witness over what you do?"(3:98)

4. ﴿لَا أَعْبُدُ مَا تَعْبُدُونَ﴾

"I do not worship what you worship."(109:2)

5. ﴿قَالُواْ يَا شُعَيْبُ أَصَلَاتُكَ تَأْمُرُكَ أَن نَّتْرُكَ مَا يَعْبُدُ آبَاؤُنَا أَوْ أَن نَّفْعَلَ فِي أَمْوَالِنَا مَا نَشَاءُ...﴾

"They said, "O Shu'ayb, does your prayer command you that we should leave what our fathers worship or not do with our wealth what we please?..."(11:87)[80]

[79] It is allowed that Verbs with a Kasrah on the [ع] in Past Tense yields a Kasrah in the Present Tense but this is rare. In fact, this principle is often mentioned in Grammar books. An example of this verb is [حَسِبَ]. But, even in the Qur'ān, the verb [حَسِبَ] takes a Fatḥah as an [ع] vowel, since it can take either Kasrah or Fatḥah vowel. Please refer to the last row of Table 30 on pg. 100 for an example of their conjugation.

[80] Please note that for the verbs [نَتْرُكَ] and [نَفْعَلَ] have a Fatḥah at the end instead of the Ḍammah. This is because these two verbs are in the Naṣb state due to the Ḥarf [أَنْ].

Table 30 - Conjugation of All Family I Forms[81] [اَلْفِعْلُ الثُّلاثِي الْمُجَرَّد]							
إِسْم الْمَفْعول Passive Noun	إِسْم الفاعِل Doer Noun	مَصْدَر Verbal Noun	الفِعل الأَمْر Command	الْمُضارِع Present	الماضي Past	[ع] Vowel Variations in Past/Present	
مَفْعُوْلٌ مَكْتُوْبٌ	فَاعِلٌ كَاتِبٌ	فِعَالَةٌ كِتَابَةٌ	أُفْعُلْ أُكْتُبْ	يَفْعُلُ يَكْتُبُ	فَعَلَ كَتَبَ	Past ـَ	Present ـُ
مَفْعُوْلٌ مَجْلُوْسٌ	فَاعِلٌ جَالِسٌ	فُلُوسٌ جُلُوْسٌ	اِفْعِلْ اِجْلِسْ	يَفْعِلُ يَجْلِسُ	فَعَلَ جَلَسَ	Past ـَ	Present ـِ
مَفْعُوْلٌ مَذْهُوْبٌ	فَاعِلٌ ذَاهِبٌ	فَعَالٌ ذَهَابٌ	اِفْعَلْ اِذْهَبْ	يَفْعَلُ يَذْهَبُ	فَعَلَ ذَهَبَ	Past ـَ	Present ـَ
مَفْعُوْلٌ مَكْبُوْرٌ	فَاعِلٌ كَابِرٌ	فُعْلٌ كُبْرٌ	أُفْعُلْ أُكْبُرْ	يَفْعُلُ يَكْبُرُ	فَعُلَ كَبُرَ	Past ـُ	Present ـُ
مَفْعُوْلٌ مَشْرُوْبٌ	فَاعِلٌ شَارِبٌ	فعْلٌ شرْبٌ	اِفْعَلْ اِشْرَبْ	يَفْعَلُ يَشْرَبُ	فَعِلَ شَرِبَ	Past ـِ	Present ـَ
مَفْعُوْلٌ مَيْئُوْسٌ	فَاعِلٌ يَائِسٌ	فَعْلٌ يَأْسٌ	اِفْعِلْ اِيْئِسْ	يَفْعِلُ يَيْئِسُ	فَعِلَ يَئِسَ	Past[82] ـِ	Present ـِ

[81] In the above noted table, please focus on the first three columns on the right for now. The other columns to the left are further discussed in later lessons of the book. The columns on the left show the conjugation of the Doer, the Passive Noun, and the Verbal Noun. These are all intrinsically related to its Type I Verb by meaning. These are discussed later in Lesson 11.

[82] This [ع] vowel variation is not common and thus not discussed earlier. Vast majority of Past Tense verbs with a [ع] Kasrah yield a Present Tense verb with a [ع] Fatḥah.

Lesson 9: The Verbal Sentence [اَلْجُمْلَةُ الْفِعْلِيَّةُ]

I. Introduction to Verbal Sentences

A Verbal Sentence [جُمْلَة فعليّة] is a sentence that starts with a verb. This is in contrast to a Nominal Sentence that starts with a noun. In Arabic, verbs can come in one of three tenses, two of which have been studied. They come in the Past Tense, Present Tense, or the Command Tense (Lesson 10). In a Verbal Sentence, the verb is typically followed directly by the Doer [فاعِل], and then a Direct Object [مَفْعولٌ بِهِ] if applicable. In a Verbal Sentence, the Doer is always Rafʿ while the Direct Object is always Naṣb. Furthermore, please remember that any pronoun attached to the end of a verb is its Direct Object. In this case, the specified Doer will follow the Direct Object (as opposed to the Direct Object coming after the Doer).

Please note that neither the Doer nor the Direct Object needs to be mentioned to form a grammatically correct Verbal Sentence. In general, deviation from the default sequence of the Verb, Doer, and Direct Object in a Verbal Sentence is possible, but occurs usually for specific rhetorical benefits. Again, it is important to focus on the most common "mainstream" grammar principles before looking at variances and exceptions. Let us look at the following grammatically correct Verbal Sentences to get some familiarity.

1.	كَتَبَ	He wrote.
2.	كَتَبَ زَيْدٌ	Zaid wrote.
3.	كَتَبَ زَيْدٌ كِتابًا	Zaid wrote a book.
4.	كَتَبَ زَيْدٌ الْكِتابَ	Zaid wrote the book.
5.	كَتَبَهُ زَيْدٌ	Zaid wrote it.
6.	كَتَبَهُ	He wrote it.
7.	كَتَبَ كِتاباً وَ رِسالَةً	He wrote a book and a letter.
8.	ما كَتَبَهُ	He did not write it
9.	هَلْ كَتَبَ الْكِتابَ	Did he write the book?
10.	كَتَبَ زَيْدٌ الْكِتابَ الصَّغيرَ الْيَوْمَ	Zaid wrote the small book today.
11.	كَتَبَ زَيْدٌ الْكِتابَ الصَّغيرَ فِي بَيْتِهِ الْيَوْمَ	Zaid wrote the small book in his home today.
12.	يَكْتُبُهُ	He is writing it.
13.	يَكْتُبُهُ غَدًا إِنْ شاءَ اللهُ	He will write it tomorrow Inshā Allah.

All of the previous sentences are correct Verbal Sentences, but differ in the details that they contain. The most important detail that should be identified first in any Verbal Sentence after analyzing the verb is the Doer. This is because all actions require a Doer, whether explicit or implicit. In sentence #1 on the previous page, we see a Verbal Sentence with no Doer specified, nor a Direct Object. In this case, the Doer is (هُوَ) and is implied (not explicitly mentioned like in sentence #2).

After identifying the Doer, the Direct Object should be sought. The Direct Object is not mentioned at all in sentences #1 or #2, but is mentioned in later sentences, either as a pronoun or as a specified noun. In examples #8 and #9, we see that using particles in front of verbs are allowed in Verbal Sentences. In examples #10, #11, and #13, there is extra detail provided regarding the time when an action is occurring. This extra detail comes **after** mention of respective Doer and Direct Object.

II. Verbal Sentence with Explicit Subject (Third Person)

Verbal Sentences with verbs using the **Third Person conjugation** follow certain specific rules that the student needs to be familiar with. The following rules occur when the Doer of a Verb in the third Person conjugation **is explicitly mentioned**.

1. In a (جملة فعليّة), the verb always appears in the **singular form** when the Doer (فاعل) is explicitly mentioned, whether is single, dual or plural.
2. The **gender of** the verb matches that of the Doer.

Let us look at the examples below to exemplify these principles. The verb with its corresponding Doer is underlined.

i. ﴿وَقَالَ ٱلَّذِينَ لَا يَعْلَمُونَ لَوْلَا يُكَلِّمُنَا ٱللَّهُ أَوْ تَأْتِينَآ ءَايَةٌ كَذَٰلِكَ قَالَ ٱلَّذِينَ مِن قَبْلِهِم مِّثْلَ قَوْلِهِمْ﴾

"Those who do not know say, "Why does Allah not speak to us or there come to us a sign?" Thus spoke those before them like their words."(2:118)

ii. ﴿قَالَ رَجُلَانِ مِنَ ٱلَّذِينَ يَخَافُونَ أَنْعَمَ ٱللَّهُ عَلَيْهِمَا ٱدْخُلُوا۟ عَلَيْهِمُ ٱلْبَابَ فَإِذَا دَخَلْتُمُوهُ فَإِنَّكُمْ غَٰلِبُونَ وَعَلَى ٱللَّهِ فَتَوَكَّلُوٓا۟ إِن كُنتُم مُّؤْمِنِينَ﴾

"Said two men from those who feared upon whom Allah had bestowed favor, "Enter upon them through the gate, for when you have entered it, you will be predominant. And upon Allah rely, if you should be believers." " (5:23)

iii. ﴿وَإِذَا قِيلَ لَهُمُ ٱتَّبِعُوا۟ مَآ أَنزَلَ ٱللَّهُ قَالُوا۟ بَلْ نَتَّبِعُ مَآ أَلْفَيْنَا عَلَيْهِ ءَابَآءَنَآ أَوَلَوْ كَانَ ءَابَآؤُهُمْ لَا يَعْقِلُونَ شَيْـًٔا وَلَا يَهْتَدُونَ﴾

And when it is said to them, "Follow what Allah has revealed," they say, "Rather, we will follow that which we found our fathers doing." Even though their fathers understood nothing, nor were they guided?"(2:170)

iv. ﴿ إِذْ يَقُولُ الْمُنَافِقُونَ وَالَّذِينَ فِي قُلُوبِهِم مَّرَضٌ غَرَّ هَٰؤُلَاءِ دِينُهُمْ وَمَن يَتَوَكَّلْ عَلَى اللَّهِ فَإِنَّ اللَّهَ عَزِيزٌ حَكِيمٌ ﴾

"[Remember] when the hypocrites and those in whose hearts was disease said, "Their religion has deluded those [Muslims]." But whoever relies upon Allah then indeed, Allah is Exalted in Might and Wise."(8:49)

3. **Contrast the above with these following examples of Verbal Sentences which have no explicit [فاعِل] mentioned. You will note that the conjugated verb necessarily matches the corresponding pronoun.**

(i) ﴿ ضَرَبَ اللَّهُ مَثَلًا لِّلَّذِينَ كَفَرُوا امْرَأَتَ نُوحٍ وَامْرَأَتَ لُوطٍ كَانَتَا تَحْتَ عَبْدَيْنِ مِنْ عِبَادِنَا صَالِحَيْنِ فَخَانَتَاهُمَا فَلَمْ يُغْنِيَا عَنْهُمَا مِنَ اللَّهِ شَيْئًا وَقِيلَ ادْخُلَا النَّارَ مَعَ الدَّاخِلِينَ ﴾

"Allah presents an example of those who disbelieved: the wife of Nūḥ and the wife of Lūṭ. They were under two of Our righteous servants but betrayed them, so those prophets did not avail them from Allah at all, and it was said, "Enter the Fire with those who enter.""(66:10)

In example (i) above, please note that the implied [فاعِل] for the verb [كَانَتَا] underlined represents [هُما]. Specifically [هُما] refers to "wife of Nūḥ ﷺ and the wife of Lūṭ ﷺ" from what is underlined twice before the Verbal Sentence that begins with [كَانَتَا]. Later on, the same conjugation is used in the next Verbal Sentence initiated by [خانَتَا]. This again implicitly refers to "wife of Nūḥ ﷺ and the wife of Lūṭ ﷺ". The overall context of the Āyah makes it clear the actual identity of the [هُما] pronoun.

(ii) ﴿ وَإِذَا قِيلَ لَهُمُ اتَّبِعُوا مَا أَنزَلَ اللَّهُ قَالُوا بَلْ نَتَّبِعُ مَا أَلْفَيْنَا عَلَيْهِ آبَاءَنَا أَوَلَوْ كَانَ آبَاؤُهُمْ لَا يَعْقِلُونَ شَيْئًا وَلَا يَهْتَدُونَ ﴾

"And when it is said to them, "Follow what Allah has revealed," they say, "Rather, we will follow that which we found our fathers doing." Even though their fathers understood nothing, nor were they guided?"(2:170)

In example (ii), the Āyah actually starts by a Conditional Statement, where the Condition is marked by the particle [إذا], and the Response is marked by the verb [قَالُوا]. The verb [قَالُوا] is on the conjugation of [هُمْ]. The identity of [هُمْ] here can be extracted from words before the Verbal Sentence [قَالُوا], specifically from "And when it is said to **them**...". Later on in the Āyah, we see the Present Tense verbs [لاَ يَعْقِلُونَ] and [لاَ يَهْتَدُونَ], both on the conjugation [هُمْ]. However, in this case, the [هُمْ] that they are referring to is not the same as for [قَالُوا]. For these two verbs, the [هُمْ] is actually extracted from the following "Even though **their fathers**.....". To keep track of the identity of the various implied Doers, it is essential to pay attention to the overall sentence.

III. Identifying the Doer and Direct Object in Verbal Sentences

In the typical Verbal Sentence, the verb is followed directly by the Doer when mentioned explicitly, and then a Direct Object [مَفعولٌ بِهِ] if applicable. The Doer is always Rafʿ while the Direct Object is always Naṣb. As we go through more Verbal Sentences, we need to improve proficiency in identifying the Doer and Direct Object. Let us take more examples of Verbal Sentences from the Qur'ān. The Doer is underlined once while the Direct Object is underlined twice. The verb is highlighted gray. Please remember that there is often more than one Verbal Sentence embedded in an Āyah. Each verb essentially represents an individual Verbal Sentence.

- **Examples from the Qur'ān** [جُملَة فعليّة]

1. ﴿ فَهَزَمُوهُم بِإِذْنِ اللهِ وَقَتَلَ دَاوُودُ جَالُوتَ.. ﴾
"So they defeated them by permission of Allah, and Dawūd killed Jālūṭ" (2:251).

2. ﴿...كُلَّمَا دَخَلَتْ أُمَّةٌ لَعَنَتْ أُخْتَهَا...﴾
"...Every time a nation enters, it will curse its sister..." (7:38)

3. ﴿ قَالُوا أَأَنتَ فَعَلْتَ هَذَا بِآلِهَتِنَا يَا إِبْرَاهِيمُ ﴾
"They said: "Are you the one who has done this to our gods, O Ibrāhīm?"(21:62)

4. ﴿ قَالَ مَا مَنَعَكَ أَلاَّ تَسْجُدَ إِذْ أَمَرْتُكَ قَالَ أَنَا خَيْرٌ مِّنْهُ خَلَقْتَنِي مِن نَّارٍ وَخَلَقْتَهُ مِن طِينٍ ﴾
"[Allah] said, "What prevented you from prostrating when I commanded you?" [Shayṭān] said, "I am better than him. You created me from fire and created him from clay."(7:12)

5. ﴿ وَكَأَيِّن مِن دَابَّةٍ لَا تَحْمِلُ رِزْقَهَا ٱللَّهُ يَرْزُقُهَا وَإِيَّاكُمْ.. ﴾
"And how many a creature carries not its provision. Allah provides for it and for you..." (29:60)

IV. Transitive and Intransitive Verbs [اَلْفِعْلُ الْمُتَعَدِّي] & [اَلْفِعْلُ اللاَّزِم]

One important division of verbs is based on Transitivity, or the ability of a verb to transfer the action onto another thing, or entity. We have discussed the Direct Object, or [مَفْعُول بِهِ]. Only verbs which are Transitive [اَلْفِعْلُ الْمُتَعَدِّي], can take a Direct Object. Common examples of Transitive Verbs are the following: He hit, They wrote, She is drinking water.

On the other hand, those verbs that cannot transfer its action onto another thing or entity are termed, Intransitive, or [اَلْفِعْلُ اللاَّزِم]. Examples are the following: We went to a place, He sat on the chair, She is happy. These types of verbs **do not** take a Direct Object. Even though Intransitive Verbs cannot take a Direct Object, they can be associated with another noun. This occurs through a **Ḥarf Jarr.** For example, in the sentence "He sat on a chair", the action of sitting is associated with a chair by the particle "on". It would be improper to say, "He sat chair". The correct sentence is [جَلَسَ عَلَى الْكُرْسِي]. Here, the Ḥarf Jarr [عَلَى] is used to link sitting with a chair. In this sentence, the Jarr Construction [عَلَى الْكُرْسِي] is termed [شِبْهُ الْجُمْلَة]. Here, we will term this the **Indirect Object** for the sake of simplicity. Please note the following examples where the Indirect Object is underlined.

➢ Examples of Intransitive verbs and their Indirect Objects

1. ﴿وَإِذَا جَآؤُوكُمْ قَالُوٓا۟ آمَنَّا وَقَد دَّخَلُوا۟ بِٱلْكُفْرِ وَهُمْ قَدْ خَرَجُوا۟ بِهِ...﴾
   "And when they come to you, they say, "We believe." But they have entered with disbelief, and they have certainly left with it."(5:61)

2. ﴿..رَّضِيَ ٱللَّهُ عَنْهُمْ وَرَضُوا۟ عَنْهُ ذَٰلِكَ ٱلْفَوْزُ ٱلْعَظِيمُ﴾
   "..Allah being pleased with them, and they with Him. That is the great attainment."(5:119)

3. ﴿قُولُوٓا۟ آمَنَّا بِٱللَّهِ وَمَآ أُنزِلَ إِلَيْنَا وَمَآ أُنزِلَ إِلَىٰٓ إِبْرَاهِيمَ..﴾
   "Say, "We have believed in Allah and what has been revealed to us and what has been revealed to Ibrāhīm..." (2:136)

Intransitive Verbs require association with Ḥarf Jarr whenever associated with nouns in a sentence. And this association forms an Indirect Object that functions like a [مَفْعُولٌ بِهِ]. Nevertheless, it is important to note that some Transitive Verbs can sometimes also be associated with a Ḥarf Jarr. For example, the verb [غَفَرَ], which means to forgive is associated with a Ḥarf [لِ] even though the verb is transitive. This verb is not used without the Ḥarf Jarr when a direct object is mentioned. Please also note that Ḥarf Jarr present within a Verbal Sentence need not be connected to the verb, and may be present as detail within the sentence.

From these principles relating to Intransitive Verbs, we see that Ḥarf Jarr are associated to derive a certain verbal meaning. Sometimes, the literal meaning of the particle itself is dropped or not used, and the verbal meaning is incorporated. For example, the verb [آمَنَ] means to believe, but it is inherently associated with the Ḥarf [بِ]. The sentence [آمَنَ بِاللهِ] means "He believed in Allah", not "He believed with Allah". Some Verbs can be associated with different Ḥarf Jarr particles to derive a different verbal meaning. Table 31 shows verbs that are associated with different Ḥarf Jarr. The exact meaning of the verb can be determined from a classical dictionary such as the Hans Wehr Arabic Dictionary.

Table 31: Verbs with an Associated Ḥarf Jarr					
ذَهَبَ	to go	ضَرَبَ	to strike	جاءَ بِ	to bring
ذَهَبَ بِ	to take away	ضَرَبَ في	to travel through/in	تابَ إلى	to repent
ذَهَبَ إلى	to go toward	ضَرَبَ مَثَلاً	to give an example	تابَ على	to accept repentance
ذَهَبَ عَنْ	to go away	ضَرَبَ على	to impose upon	قَضَى	to decree/fulfill
أَتَى	to come	ضَرَبَ لِ	to mention/ give example	قَضَى بَيْنَ	to judge between
أَتَى بِ	to bring	جاءَ	to come	قَضَى عَلَى	to kill

➢ Examples from the Qur'ān

1. ﴿...وَلَوْ شَاءَ ٱللَّهُ لَذَهَبَ بِسَمْعِهِمْ وَأَبْصَارِهِمْ إِنَّ ٱللَّهَ عَلَى كُلِّ شَيْءٍ قَدِيرٌ﴾

   "...and if Allah had willed, He could have taken away their hearing and their sight. Indeed, Allah is over all things competent."(2:20)

2. ﴿وَذَا ٱلنُّونِ إِذ ذَّهَبَ مُغَاضِبًا...﴾

   "And [mention] the man of the fish, when he went off in anger..." (21:87)

3. ﴿إِذْ يُغَشِّيكُمُ ٱلنُّعَاسَ أَمَنَةً مِّنْهُ وَيُنَزِّلُ عَلَيْكُم مِّنَ ٱلسَّمَاءِ مَاءً لِّيُطَهِّرَكُم بِهِ وَيُذْهِبَ عَنكُمْ رِجْزَ ٱلشَّيْطَانِ...﴾

   "[Remember] when He overwhelmed you with drowsiness [giving] security from Him and sent down upon you from the sky, rain by which to purify you and remove from you[83] the evil of Shayṭān" (8:11)

83 Please note that the verb conjugation (يُذْهِبَ) represents the Passive verb form, which has not been studied yet. Passive verbs are discussed in Lesson 11.

V. Exceptions to Rules of Verb Conjugation: Broken Plurals

In Verbal Sentences, when the Doer is a male, the male conjugation is used, and in cases of a female Doer, the female conjugation is used. In certain cases, however, the opposite is true, specifically when the Doer is a Broken Plural. There are a few cases in the Qur'ān when this phenomenon occurs. It is not essential at this point to dwell on this principle of exception too much, as this is being mentioned here for completion.[84] If the Subject is a Broken Plural, the preceding verb can come in the form of the singular of the opposite gender. Therefore, even though Broken Plurals are grammatically feminine singular, they sometimes can take the opposite gender for rhetorical reasons. In example 2 below, we notice that the female Doer [نِسْوَةٌ] takes the masculine verb form [قَالَ] rather than the expected feminine form [قَالَتْ]. The other examples below likewise typify this exception of verb conjugation of Broken Plural Doers in Verbal Sentences. In these examples, the Doer in Broken Plural is underlined in bold, while the verb is underlined in stripes.

➢ Examples from the Qur'ān

1. ﴿قَالَتِ ٱلْأَعْرَابُ آمَنَّا قُل لَّمْ تُؤْمِنُوا وَلَٰكِن قُولُوا أَسْلَمْنَا...﴾
"The Bedouins say, "We have believed." Say, you have not [yet] believed; but say, 'we have submitted...'' (49:14)

2. ﴿وَقَالَ نِسْوَةٌ فِي ٱلْمَدِينَةِ ٱمْرَأَةُ ٱلْعَزِيزِ تُرَاوِدُ فَتَاهَا عَن نَّفْسِهِ...﴾
"And women in the city said, "The wife of al-'Azīz is seeking to seduce her slave boy..." (12:30)

3. ﴿...إِذَا جَاءَكُمُ ٱلْمُؤْمِنَاتُ مُهَاجِرَاتٍ فَٱمْتَحِنُوهُنَّ ٱللَّهُ أَعْلَمُ بِإِيمَانِهِنَّ...﴾
"...when the believing women come to you as emigrants, examine them..." (60:10)

4. ﴿قَالَتْ لَهُمْ رُسُلُهُمْ إِن نَّحْنُ إِلَّا بَشَرٌ مِّثْلُكُمْ وَلَٰكِنَّ ٱللَّهَ يَمُنُّ عَلَىٰ مَن يَشَاءُ مِنْ عِبَادِهِ...﴾
"Their messengers said to them, "We are only men like you, but Allah confers favor upon whom He wills of His servants..." (14:11)

[84] This grammatical phenomenon is seen in the Qur'ān and has rhetorical benefits. Here, the masculine verb denotes the Doers as few in number, while the feminine verb denotes many Doers.

Lesson 10: The Command Tense [اَلْفِعْلُ الأَمْرُ], I'rāb of Verbs, Verbal Particles, and Verbs in the Future Tense

I. The Verb of Command [اَلْفِعْلُ الأَمْرُ]

The Command Tense is the third tense that verbs are found in. Verbs of Command have an important place with respect to Islamic Law since most commands in the Qur'ān and Ḥadīth reflect a religious obligation[85]. Furthermore, the Command Tense is also important with respect to supplication, or "Du'ā". Any supplication directed towards Allahﷻ is in the command form. Verbs of Command have their own unique conjugation, which will be discussed here. Since we have studied the Past and Present Tenses, the Command Tense can now be appropriately studied.

A. Important points on Verbs of Command

Verbs in the Command Tense do not take an I'rāb, and are [مَبْنِي]. These verbs occur only in the Second Person. The conjugation rules are also unique for these verbs. The Command Tense can be identified on most verbs by the Alif that they start with. Few verbs begin with an Alif that are not in the Command Tense[86]. Please recall that any verb in the Command Tense directed toward Allahﷻ is really a request or a Du'ā. Any "command" directed to another person of the same hierarchy is a suggestion or recommendation. A "command" to someone of a lower hierarchy is a true command. Examples of verbs in Command Tense are found in the Vocabulary Section adapted from "80% of Qur'ānic Vocabulary" on the middle third column.

It is noteworthy to mention that the Command Tense is specific only to the Second Person. However, verbs can also go into the "Command" tense functionally when in the First or Third Person. This occurs when the Ḥarf Jazm Lām [لِ] acts on a Present Tense verbs in the First or Third Person. Thus, these verbs in First and Third Person are not [مَبْنِي] and differ from the Command Tense of Second Person.

---

[85] A command in the Qur'ān coming from Allahﷻ is *generally* a religious obligation. However, there are cases in which a "command" can sometimes be something recommended, or simply something that is permissible. For example in 62:9-10 Allahﷻ says the following: ﴿يَا أَيُّهَا الَّذِينَ آمَنُوا إِذَا نُودِيَ لِلصَّلَاةِ مِن يَوْمِ الْجُمُعَةِ فَاسْعَوْا إِلَىٰ ذِكْرِ اللَّهِ وَذَرُوا الْبَيْعَ ۚ ذَٰلِكُمْ خَيْرٌ لَّكُمْ إِن كُنتُمْ تَعْلَمُونَ ۝ فَإِذَا قُضِيَتِ الصَّلَاةُ فَانتَشِرُوا فِي الْأَرْضِ وَابْتَغُوا مِن فَضْلِ اللَّهِ وَاذْكُرُوا اللَّهَ كَثِيرًا لَّعَلَّكُمْ تُفْلِحُونَ﴾. "O you who have believed, when [the adhan] is called for the prayer on the day of Friday, then proceed to the remembrance of Allah and leave trade. That is better for you, if you only knew. And when the prayer has been concluded, disperse within the land and seek from the bounty of Allah, and remember Allah often that you may succeed." In these two Āyahs, the commands have been shaded and underlined. The first two commands are a religious *obligation* as the Friday prayer is the most important of the obligatory prayers. The 3rd and 4th commands reflect things which are *permissible*. In the context of the Āyahs, this meaning fits since these two permissible things were made impermissible with the call of the Friday prayer. The last command is a *recommendation* made. Altogether, commands in the Qur'ān and Ḥadīth reflect a religious obligation, but in certain contexts and juristic principles, they may not reflect a true religious obligation.

[86] Verb families VII, VIII, IX, and X all begin with an Alif. They do not carry a Sukūn at their end unlike Verbs of Command.

B. Rules for Conjugating Command Tense from Present Tense [اَلْفِعْلُ الْمُضارِع]

1. Change the verb into Present Tense [مُضارِع] form specifically Third Person single masculine [يَفْعَلُ].
2. Replace the [يَ] with an Alif [ا]. The Alif can only take either a Kasrah or Ḍammah, but not Fatḥah.
3. The vowel on the middle stem [ع] letter on **Present Tense** [مُضارِع] is key.
    i. If verb has Ḍammah on the [ع] letter, the Command Tense beginning Alif and its [ع] letter both take the **Ḍammah** vowel.
    ii. If the verb has Fatḥah on the [ع] letter, the Command Tense beginning Alif takes a **Kasrah** and the [ع] letter takes a **Fatḥah**.
    iii. If the verb has a Kasrah on the [ع] letter, the beginning Command Tense Alif and the [ع] letter both take the **Kasrah** vowel.
4. A Sukūn is placed on the last letter to obtain the singular masculine form.
5. Conjugate as needed to the appropriate verb in terms of gender and plurality.
6. The different conjugation schemes for Command Tense are shown below and on the next page.

C. Conjugation of Command Verbs

Table 32: Converting Verbs to the Command Tense [اَلْفِعْلُ الْأَمر]

اَلْفِعْلُ الْمَاضي →	اَلْفِعْلُ الْمُضارِع	Replace [يَ] → with [إ] or [أ]	Make last letter Sākin (Sukūn) →	اَلْفِعْلُ الْأَمر
	يَفْعِلُ	إ	اِفْعِلُ	اِفْعِلْ
فَعَلَ	يَفْعَلُ	إ	اِفْعَلُ	اِفْعَلْ
	يَفْعُلُ	أُ	اُفْعُلُ	اُفْعُلْ
فَعِلَ	يَفْعَلُ	إ	اِفْعَلُ	اِفْعَلْ
فَعُلَ	يَفْعُلُ	أُ	اُفْعُلُ	اُفْعُلْ

Table 33: Conjugation of Command Verbs [اِفْعَلْ] and [اِفْعِلْ]				
	plural	dual	single	Verb examples past / present
masculine	اِعْمَلُوا	اِعْمَلا	اِعْمَلْ	يَعْمَلُ/عَمِلَ
feminine	اِعْمَلْنَ	اِعْمَلا	اِعْمَلِي	
masculine	اِضْرِبُوا	اِضْرِبا	اِضْرِبْ	يَضْرِبُ/ضَرَبَ
feminine	اِضْرِبْنَ	اِضْرِبا	اِضْرِبِي	
Conjugation of Command Verb -[اُفْعُلْ]				
	plural	dual	single	Verb examples past / present
masculine	أُنْصُرُوا	أُنْصُرا	أُنْصُرْ	يَنْصُرُ/نَصَرَ
feminine	أُنْصُرْنَ	أُنْصُرا	أُنْصُرِي	

II. I'rāb of Verbs: Some Important Principles

Like nouns, all Present Tense Verbs [اَلْفِعْلُ الْمُضارِع] go into one of three I'rāb. Past Tense verbs [اَلْفِعْلُ الْماضِي] and the Verbs of Command [اَلْفِعْلُ الْأَمْر] **do not** go into any I'rāb and are [مَبْنِى]. Similar to nouns, the default case for any Present Tense is the Raf' state. One important difference concerning I'rāb that has been mentioned is that Present Tense never goes into Jarr state (instead, it goes into Jazm [جَزْم]). For any Present Tense Verb in the Naṣb or Jazm case, **there is a Ḥarf acting on it**. The important principles regarding Naṣb and Jazm conjugations are mentioned in this section.

A. **Raf'** [رَفْع] - This is the default state of Present Tense verbs.

B. **Naṣb** [نَصْب]

1. There is a Fatḥah in place of the Ḍammah at the end of singular verbs. For example, the verbs [يَنْصُرُ] and [يَضْرِبُ] are transformed in Naṣb to [يَنْصُرَ] and [يَضْرِبَ] respectively.

2. The Nūn of duality, male plurals, and the singular feminine Second Person are cut off. However, the exception is the Feminine Plural Nūn, which stays fixed. For example, the verbs [يَنْصُرانِ] and [يَضْرِبُونَ] are transformed in to Naṣb to [يَنْصُرا] and [يَضْرِبُوا] respectively. The verb [يَنْصُرْنَ] in Naṣb remains [يَنْصُرْنَ], since the Feminine Plural Nūn stays fixed.

3. Ḥarf Naṣb that act on verbs are the following: [أَنْ لَنْ لِأَنْ لِ كَيْ إِذًا حَتَّى].

C. Jazm [جَزْم]

1. In the Jazm state, a Sukūn is placed at the end of singular verbs (instead of the Ḍammah) as in the following: [يَفْعَلْ و تَفْعَلْ و نَفْعَلْ].

2. Similar to the Naṣb state, the Nūn of duality, male plurals, and the singular feminine Second Person are cut off. The exception is the Feminine Nūn of plurality, which as previously stated is never cut off. For example, the verbs [يَنْصُرانِ] and [يَضْرِبُونَ] are transformed into Jazm becoming [يَنْصُرا] and [يَضْرِبُوا] respectively. The verb [يَنْصُرْنَ] in Jazm remains [يَنْصُرْنَ], since the Feminine Plural Nūn stays fixed. These changes in I'rāb are identical to those of the Naṣb state for non-singular verbs (except First Person).

3. The Particles of Jazm are **many, the most important of which are the following:**

أَيْنَ / لَمْ / لَمَّا / أَلَمْ / أَلَمَّا / لِ / لَا / إِنْ / مَا / مَنْ / مَتَى / وَ

Table 34 – Verb Conjugation in Naṣb and Jazm								
Raf'			**Naṣb**			**Jazm**		
يَفْعَلُونَ	يَفْعَلانِ	يَفْعَلُ	يَفْعَلُوا	يَفْعَلا	يَفْعَلَ	يَفْعَلُوا	يَفْعَلا	يَفْعَلْ
يَفْعَلْنَ	تَفْعَلانِ	تَفْعَلُ	يَفْعَلْنَ	تَفْعَلا	تَفْعَلَ	يَفْعَلْنَ	تَفْعَلا	تَفْعَلْ
تَفْعَلُونَ	تَفْعَلانِ	تَفْعَلُ	تَفْعَلُوا	تَفْعَلا	تَفْعَلَ	تَفْعَلُوا	تَفْعَلا	تَفْعَلْ
تَفْعَلْنَ	تَفْعَلانِ	تَفْعَلِينَ	تَفْعَلْنَ	تَفْعَلا	تَفْعَلِي	تَفْعَلْنَ	تَفْعَلا	تَفْعَلِي
نَفْعَلُ	نَفْعَلُ	أَفْعَلُ	نَفْعَلَ	نَفْعَلَ	أَفْعَلَ	نَفْعَلْ	نَفْعَلْ	أَفْعَلْ

III. Verbal Particles – Ḥarf Naṣb and Ḥarf Jazm

Table 35: Ḥarf Naṣb on Verbs		
حُروف النَّصْب	Meaning	**Examples from the Qur'ān**
أَنْ	**that/to**	﴿وَإِذْ قَالَ مُوسَى لِقَوْمِهِ إِنَّ ٱللَّهَ يَأْمُرُكُمْ أَنْ تَذْبَحُواْ بَقَرَةً...﴾ "And when Mūsa said to his people: Surely Allah commands you that you should sacrifice a cow..."(2:67)
لَنْ	**will never**	﴿لَن تَنفَعَكُمْ أَرْحَامُكُمْ وَلَا أَوْلَادُكُمْ يَوْمَ ٱلْقِيَامَةِ..﴾ "Never will your relatives or your children benefit you; the Day of Resurrection..."(60:3)
لِ	**so that**	﴿ٱلَّذِي خَلَقَ ٱلْمَوْتَ وَٱلْحَيَاةَ لِيَبْلُوَكُمْ أَيُّكُمْ أَحْسَنُ عَمَلاً...﴾ "[He] who created death and life to test you, which of you is best in deeds". (67:2)
كَيْ / لِكَيْ	**so that**	﴿وَأَشْرِكْهُ فِي أَمْرِي ۝ كَيْ نُسَبِّحَكَ كَثِيرًا﴾ "And let him share my task, That we may exalt You much". (20:32-33)
حَتَّى	**until**	﴿..وَلَا يَزَالُونَ يُقَاتِلُونَكُمْ حَتَّىٰ يَرُدُّوكُمْ عَن دِينِكُمْ إِنِ ٱسْتَطَاعُواْ..﴾ "And they will continue to fight you until they turn you back from your religion if they are able."(2:217)

A. Ḥarf Jazm and Conditional Particles

In Arabic, there are specific particles that are used in Conditional Sentences. Common particles that signal a Conditional Statement are [مَنْ], [ما], and [أَنْ]. These particles specifically cause Jazm on a Present Tense verb when it represents the condition and/or the response. Please refer to Table 35, which gives some examples of Jazm particles in Conditional Statements.

It should be noted that even though the Jazm particles like [مَنْ], [ما], and [أَنْ] act on Present Tense verbs to mark a conditional statement, they are also commonly used with Past Tense verbs in conditional statements. In cases when the Response Particle is not a Present Tense verb, the particle [فَ] is typically used to mark the response of [جَوابُ الشَّرْط]. The Response Statement can be a Past Tense verb, noun phrase, Verb of Command, etc.

B. Ḥarf Jazm on Verbs

Table 36: Ḥarf Jazm on Verbs		
حروف الجَزْم	**Meaning**	**Examples from the Qur'ān**
لَمْ	**past negation**	﴿...وَمَن لَّمْ يَحْكُم بِمَا أَنزَلَ ٱللَّهُ فَأُوْلَٰئِكَ هُمُ ٱلْكَٰفِرُونَ﴾ "..and whoever does not judge by what Allah has revealed, then it is those who are the disbelievers."(5:44)
لَمَّا	**not yet**	﴿..وَلَمَّا يَدْخُلِ ٱلْإِيمَٰنُ فِى قُلُوبِكُمْ..﴾ "... for faith has not yet entered your hearts..."(49:14)
أَلَمْ	**Interrogative of [لَمْ]**	﴿أَلَمْ تَعْلَمْ أَنَّ ٱللَّهَ لَهُۥ مُلْكُ ٱلسَّمَٰوَٰتِ وَٱلْأَرْضِ...﴾ "Do you not know that to Allah belongs the dominion of the heavens and the earth?..."(5:40)
لِ	**Lām of Command**	﴿لِيُنفِقْ ذُو سَعَةٍ مِّن سَعَتِهِۦ...﴾ "Let a man of wealth spend from his wealth..." (65:7)
لا	**Lām of Forbidding**	﴿... فَإِذَا خِفْتِ عَلَيْهِ فَأَلْقِيهِ فِى ٱلْيَمِّ وَلَا تَخَافِى وَلَا تَحْزَنِىٓ...﴾ "...but when you fear for him, cast him into the river and do not fear and do not grieve..."(28:7)
إِنْ	**if (condition)**	﴿إِن يَنصُرْكُمُ ٱللَّهُ فَلَا غَالِبَ لَكُمْ...﴾ "If Allah should aid you, no one can overcome you..."(3:160)
مَا	**What/That (condition)**	﴿...وَمَا تُقَدِّمُوا۟ لِأَنفُسِكُم مِّنْ خَيْرٍ تَجِدُوهُ عِندَ ٱللَّهِ إِنَّ ٱللَّهَ بِمَا تَعْمَلُونَ بَصِيرٌ﴾ "...and whatever good you put forward for yourselves - you will find it with Allah. Indeed, Allah of what you do, is Seeing."(2:110)
مَنْ	**Who (condition)**	﴿مَنْ يُرِدْ اللهُ بِهِ خَيْرًا يُفَقِّهْهُ فِي الدِّينِ﴾ "Whoever Allah wants for him good, He will give him understanding in the Religion."[87]
أَيْنَ	**Where (condition)**	﴿أَيْنَمَا تَكُونُوا۟ يُدْرِككُّمُ ٱلْمَوْتُ وَلَوْ كُنتُمْ فِى بُرُوجٍ مُّشَيَّدَةٍ...﴾ "Wherever you may be, death will overtake you, even if you should be within towers of lofty construction..."(4:78)

[87] Ṣaḥīḥ al-Bukhāri, Chapter on Knowledge: كِتَاب الْعِلْم, subheading before Ḥadīth #68. In this Ḥadīth, the [مَنْ] affects two verbs, the verb, which is part of the condition [الشَّرْط], and the verb that follows the condition [جَوَاب الشَّرْط]. The sign of Jazm is shown on both verbs by the Sukūn at the end.

C. Command Tense for Third/First Person – The Lām of Command/Du'ā

The Lām of Command/Du'ā [لِ][88] is a Ḥarf Jazm that acts only on verbs in the First Person and Third Person. It behaves similar in function to the Command Tense. It has the meaning of "should" or "must". An example is shown in Table 36 (fourth row) on the preceding page. This is identical to what occurs at the **ending** in a Second Person verb in the Command State except the following:

1. There is a Lām before the verb.
2. Second Person Command Tense does not have I'rāb like Past Tense verbs, as this was covered before.

In the Qur'ān, the Lām of Command is usually preceded by a [وَ] or a [فَ], and this causes the Lām to take a Sukūn. Let us look at the following example from Sūrah Kahf.

﴿... فَمَنْ كَانَ يَرْجُو لِقَاءَ رَبِّهِ فَلْيَعْمَلْ عَمَلًا صَالِحًا وَلَا يُشْرِكْ بِعِبَادَةِ رَبِّهِ أَحَدًا﴾

"...so whoever hopes for the meeting with His Lord, then let him work righteous deeds and associate none as a partner in the worship of His Lord". (18:110)

D. The Lām of Emphasis [لَامُ تَوْكِيد]

One particle that is found frequently in the Qur'ān is the Lām of Emphasis [لَ]. It is important to distinguish this from the Ḥarf Jazm Lām of Command from other types of Lām particles. The **Lām of Emphasis** [لَامُ التَّوْكِيد] **does not** cause a change in I'rāb and is not a Ḥarf Jazm. It functions to cause a more emphatic meaning similar to the Ḥarf Naṣb particle Inna. This Lām can act on verbs, particles, and nouns.

The Lām of Emphasis is grammatically categorized into various types of different particles. At this stage, it is important not to get lost in the technicalities of this Lām, and focus on its general meaning and use. In general, the Lām of Emphasis has three basic grammatical functions:

(1) Emphasis [تَوْكِيد]
(2) Response to an oath [جَواب القَسَم]
(3) Response to a condition statement with particle [لَوْ] or [لَوْلَا]

88 Please note that there are different types of Lām in Arabic Grammar; these also include Lām of emphasis (Tawkīd), Lām as a Ḥarf Jarr, Lām as a Ḥarf Naṣb on verbs (known as Lām Ta'līl).

➢ **Qur'ānic examples of the Lām of Emphasis on verbs, nouns, and particles.**

1. ﴿ وَ إِنَّا لَنَعْلَمُ أَنَّ مِنكُم مُّكَذِّبِينَ ﴾

   "And We certainly know that among you are those that are denies". (69:49)

2. ﴿ إِنَّ ٱلْإِنسَانَ لَفِي خُسْرٍ ﴾

   "Indeed, mankind is in loss". (103:2)

3. ﴿ قَالُوٓا۟ أَءِنَّكَ لَأَنتَ يُوسُفُ... ﴾

   "They said, "Are you indeed Yūsuf?..." (12:90)

4. ﴿...لَّمَسْجِدٌ أُسِّسَ عَلَى ٱلتَّقْوَىٰ مِنْ أَوَّلِ يَوْمٍ أَحَقُّ أَن تَقُومَ فِيهِ ۚ فِيهِ رِجَالٌ يُحِبُّونَ أَن يَتَطَهَّرُوا۟ ۚ وَٱللَّهُ يُحِبُّ ٱلْمُطَّهِّرِينَ ﴾

   "....A mosque founded on righteousness from the first day is more worthy for you to stand in. Within it is men who love to purify themselves; and Allah loves those who purify themselves." (9:108)

5. ﴿ أَفَلَا يَتَدَبَّرُونَ ٱلْقُرْءَانَ ۚ وَلَوْ كَانَ مِنْ عِندِ غَيْرِ ٱللَّهِ لَوَجَدُوا۟ فِيهِ ٱخْتِلَٰفًا كَثِيرًا ﴾

   "Then do they not reflect upon the Qur'an? If it had been from [any] other than Allah, they would have found within it much contradiction." (4:82)

6. ﴿ وَلَوْلَا نِعْمَةُ رَبِّي لَكُنتُ مِنَ ٱلْمُحْضَرِينَ ﴾

   "If not for the favor of my Lord, I would have been of those brought in [to Hell]." "If not for the favor of my Lord, I would have been of those brought in [to Hell]." (37:57)

7. ﴿....لَئِن لَّمْ تَنتَهُوا۟ لَنَرْجُمَنَّكُمْ وَلَيَمَسَّنَّكُم مِّنَّا عَذَابٌ أَلِيمٌ ﴾

   "...If you do not desist, we will surely stone you, and there will surely touch you, from us, a painful punishment."(36:18)

8. ﴿ كَلَّا لَوْ تَعْلَمُونَ عِلْمَ ٱلْيَقِينِ ۝ لَتَرَوُنَّ ٱلْجَحِيمَ ۝ ثُمَّ لَتَرَوُنَّهَا عَيْنَ ٱلْيَقِينِ ۝ ثُمَّ لَتُسْـَٔلُنَّ يَوْمَئِذٍ عَنِ ٱلنَّعِيمِ ﴾

   "No! If you only knew with knowledge of certainty. You will surely see the Hellfire. Then, you will surely see it with the eye of certainty. Then you will surely be asked that Day about pleasure". (102:5-8)

In examples (i), (ii), and (iii), the Lām (لَ) comes in the sentence after the particle Inna (إِنَّ), and causes emphasis to be placed on its associated word. This Lām is also known as the "Sliding Lām", or (لَامُ المُزَحْلَقَة وَ التَّوْكِيد)[89]. The Sliding Lām

---

[89] This particle of emphasis is usually referred to as (لَامُ المُزَحْلَقَة وَ التَّوْكِيد), or the "sliding Lām". It acts on the (خَبَر إِنَّ) of the particle Inna, and thus is seen after (إِنَّ).

can also act on nouns, verbs, or even other particles for emphasis. Please look at examples (i), (ii), and (iii) where the Sliding Lām (Lām of Emphasis) is underlined.

Another scenario in which the Lām of Emphasis is found is with the Conditional Particles[90] [لَوْ] and [لَوْلَا]. Here, the Lām of Emphasis, in addition to denoting emphasis acts as a Response Particle similar to the Response Particle [فَ] found in Conditional Statements described in Section IIIB. In examples, (v) and (vi), the Lām of Emphasis (underlined) marks the places of the response statement.

Another scenario in which the Lām of Emphasis occurs is on Present Tense Verbs alongside with the Nūn Shadda [نَّ] of Emphasis. Here, the Present Tense Verb [يَفْعَلُ] is converted to [لَيَفْعَلَنَّ], with the Lām attached to the beginning of the verb and the Nūn attached to its end. This Lām occurs usually in response to an oath or a conditional statement. In example (vii), this is response to a conditional statement signified by particle [لَئِنْ]. In example (viii), the oath is signified by the particle [كَلَّا]. In both these examples, the Lām of Emphasis and Nūn Shadda of Emphasis are underlined.

E. <u>Lā of Forbidding</u> [لا ٱلنَّاهِيَة]

This Ḥarf Jazm functions similar to the Verb of Command but in forbidding an action. It typically denotes religious prohibitions in the Qur'ān and Ḥadīth. Unlike the Command Tense, it can act on the Third Person and the First Person, although this is not common. It is mainly found acting on the Second Person. This Lā needs to be distinguished from the Lā of Negation, which does not cause any change in I'rāb, and can act on verbs and nouns.

1. ﴿ يَا أَيُّهَا ٱلَّذِينَ آمَنُوا لَا <u>تَأْكُلُوا</u> أَمْوَالَكُمْ بَيْنَكُمْ بِٱلْبَاطِلِ... ﴾

   "O you who have believed, do not consume one another's wealth unjustly..." (4:29)

2. ﴿ لَا <u>يَتَّخِذِ</u> ٱلْمُؤْمِنُونَ ٱلْكَافِرِينَ أَوْلِيَاءَ مِن دُونِ ٱلْمُؤْمِنِينَ... ﴾

   "Let not believers take disbelievers as allies rather than believers..." (3:28)

[90] The particles [لَوْ] and [لَوْلَا] are conditional particles which have not been discussed. These particles are not Harf Jazm and do not cause any change in I'rāb. Nonetheless, they are found in the Qur'ān in several places.

F. Lā of Negation [لاءُ ٱلنَّفي]

This Lā is **not** a Ḥarf Jazm, and functions in general negation for verbs and nouns. It is included here to contrast the other types of Lā's being discussed.

1. ﴿ وَٱتَّقُوا۟ يَوْماً لَّا تَجْزِي نَفْسٌ عَن نَّفْسٍ شَيْئاً وَلَا يُقْبَلُ مِنْهَا شَفَاعَةٌ وَلَا يُؤْخَذُ مِنْهَا عَدْلٌ وَلَا هُمْ يُنصَرُونَ ﴾

   "And fear a Day when no soul will suffice for another soul at all, nor will intercession be accepted from it, nor will compensation be taken from it, nor will they be aided."(2:48)

2. ﴿ إِنَّ ٱلَّذِينَ قَالُوا۟ رَبُّنَا ٱللَّهُ ثُمَّ ٱسْتَقَامُوا۟ فَلَا خَوْفٌ عَلَيْهِمْ وَلَا هُمْ يَحْزَنُونَ ﴾

   "Indeed, those who have said, "Our Lord is Allah ," and then remained on a right course - there will be no fear concerning them, nor will they grieve."(46:13)

IV. Future Tense [الاسْتِقْبال]

The normal Present Tense state can be used for "future" tense as was discussed previously. The "future tense" meaning is derived based on context. A more definitive way to express the future tense is by adding the following particles directly in front of the Present Tense verb. There are two particles, which are used to specify the future tense: [سَ] and [سَوْفَ]. One of these particles is placed directly in front of a Present Tense verb without any effect on its I'rāb. The [سَ] specifies the near future while [سَوْفَ] specifies the distant future.

يَذْهَبُ He goes.	→	سَيَذْهَبُ He will go.
أَعْلَمُ I learn.	→	سَأَعْلَمُ I will learn.
يَحْفَظُ الْقُرْآنَ He is memorizing the Qur'ān.	→	سَوْفَ يَحْفَظُ الْقُرْآنَ إِنْ شاءَ اللهُ He will memorize the Qur'ān Inshā-Allah.

➢ **Examples from the Qur'ān**

1. ﴿ كَلَّا سَوْفَ تَعْلَمُونَ ۝ ثُمَّ كَلَّا سَوْفَ تَعْلَمُونَ ﴾

   "By no means, you all will know, again by no means, you all will know". (102:3-4)

2. ﴿ وَٱلَّذِينَ آمَنُوا۟ وَعَمِلُوا۟ ٱلصَّالِحَاتِ سَنُدْخِلُهُمْ جَنَّاتٍ تَجْرِي مِن تَحْتِهَا ٱلْأَنْهَارُ خَالِدِينَ فِيهَا أَبَدًا ﴾

   "But those who believe and do righteous deeds - We will admit them to gardens beneath which rivers flow, wherein they abide forever. For them therein are purified spouses, and We will admit them to deepening shade."(4:57)

Lesson 11: The Passive Verb [اَلْفِعْلُ الْمَجْهول], the Doer Noun [اِسْمُ الفاعِل], the Passive Noun [اِسْمُ المَفْعُول], the Verbal Noun [اَلْمَصْدَر], and using an Arabic Dictionary

I. The Passive Verb Tense [اَلْفِعْلُ الْمَجْهول]

So far, we have studied the active tense of Past and Present Tense verbs. We will now examine the Passive Tense [الفِعل المَجْهُول]. Please note that the basic conjugation patterns that have been studied for the Past and Present Tenses do not change. All what changes are vowels on certain letters such as the [ف] and/or [ع] stem letters. Verbs that are Transitive can go into the Passive Tense. For example, the Passive Tense of the verb "they helped" will be "they were helped". The Passive for "We are striking" is "We are being struck", and so on. Please note that certain verbs cannot take the Passive Tense. And this is typically the case for Intransitive Verbs. For example, for the verb "to sit", you cannot say "it is being sit", or "it was sat".

The hallmark of a Verbal Sentence with a Passive Verb is that it lacks a Doer [فاعِل]. Instead of a Doer, the Passive Verb has what is termed a Deputy Doer or [نائِبُ الفاعِل]. The verb is acting upon this entity. The Deputy Doer is always present, whether implied or explicitly mentioned in a Verbal Sentence with a Passive Verb. The Deputy Doer always takes the case of Rafʿ. <u>The conjugation of the Deputy Doer has to match that of the verb. This is similar to the Doer in terms of gender and plurality.</u>

A. Passive Past Tense [فُعِلَ]

It is easier to remember the phonetic sound "oo ee" that Passive Past Tense verbs start with. The first two vowels are fixed as a Ḍammah on the [ف] and a Kasrah on the [ع]. The remaining morphology is unchanged. So, the verb forms [فَعَلَ/فَعُلَ/فَعِلَ] all get converted into [فُعِلَ].

Table 37: Passive Past Tense [اَلْفِعْلُ الْماضي الْمَجْهُول]		
قَتَلَ He killed.	→	قُتِلَ He was killed.
عَلِمَ He knew.	→	عُلِمَ He was known.
نَصَرَ He helped.	→	نُصِرَ He was helped.

Other conjugations:

قَتَلَتْ She killed.	→	قُتِلَتْ She was killed.
عَلِمُوا They knew.	→	عُلِمُوا They were known.
نَصَرْتِ You helped.	→	نُصِرْتِ You were helped.

B. Passive Present Tense [يُفْعَلُ]

The Present Passive Tense begins with the "oo – aa" sound (with a slight pause due to a Sukūn in the middle). The first letter [ن/أ/ت/ي] **preceding** the [ف] stem letter carries a Ḍammah instead of a Fatḥah in the Active Tense while the [ف] letter itself takes a Sukūn. The [ع] letter carries a Fatḥah in the Passive. So, the verb forms [يَفْعَلُ/يَفْعِلُ/يَفْعُلُ] all gets transformed into [يُفْعَلُ] in the Passive form. Please recall that like the Active Present Tense, the Passive Present Tense is subject to I'rāb changes as needed.

Table 38: Passive Present Tense [اَلْفِعْلُ الْمُضَارِعِ الْمَجْهولِ]		
يَقْتُلُ He is killing.	→	يُقْتَلُ He is being killed.
يَعْرِفُ He will know.	→	يُعْرَفُ He will be known.
يَنْصُرُ He helps.	→	يُنْصَرُ He is being helped.

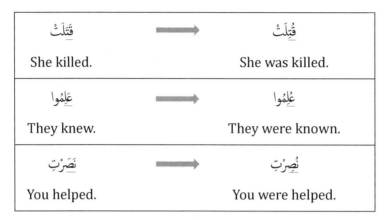

Other conjugations:

تَقْتُلُ She is killing.	→	تُقْتَلُ She is being killed.
يَعْرِفُونَ They will know.	→	يُعْرَفُونَ They will be known.
تَنْصُرِينَ You are helping.	→	تُنْصَرِينَ You are being helped.

C. Examples of Passive Verbs in the Qur'ān

1. ﴿ يُرِيدُ ٱللَّهُ أَن يُخَفِّفَ عَنكُمْ وَخُلِقَ ٱلْإِنسَانُ ضَعِيفًا ﴾
"And Allah wants to lighten for you [your difficulties]; and mankind was created weak."(4:28)

2. ﴿ وَإِذَا ٱلْمَوْءُۥدَةُ سُئِلَتْ ۝ بِأَيِّ ذَنبٍ قُتِلَتْ ۝ وَإِذَا ٱلصُّحُفُ نُشِرَتْ ۝ وَإِذَا ٱلسَّمَاءُ كُشِطَتْ ﴾
"And when the girl buried alive is asked, for what sin she was killed, And when the pages are made public, And when the sky is stripped away..." (81:8-11)

3. ﴿ وَلَا تَقُولُوا لِمَنْ يُقْتَلُ فِي سَبِيلِ اللهِ أَمْوَاتٌ بَلْ أَحْيَاءٌ وَلَكِن لَّا تَشْعُرُونَ ﴾
"And do not say about those who are killed in the way of Allah, "They are dead." Rather, they are alive, but you perceive not."(2:154)

II. The Doer Noun Pattern [اِسْمُ الفاعِل]

In Arabic, there are several important categories of nouns that are directly derived from verbs [اِسْمٌ مُشْتَقٌّ]. One of these nouns is termed a Doer Noun or [اِسْمُ الفاعِل]. This is different from the Doer [فاعِل] that we have studied thus far which serves a specific function in a Verbal sentence. In every Verbal Sentence (with an active Verb), there has to be a Doer, whether implicit or explicit. Not to be confused with the Doer, the Doer Noun inherently carries the **meaning** of doing a certain action. The Doer Noun or has a specific morphology on the stem of [فاعِلٌ]. Thus, any word on this pattern should be assumed to be a Doer Noun, and function as doing the action of the verb (of its root letters). The Doer Noun can take any I'rāb, and in some circumstances acts as the Doer in a Verbal Sentence. However, as was previously stated, it cannot be equated with the Doer, which can only take Raf', and is present only within the context of a Verbal Sentence. The Doer Nouns take the Sound Plural Pattern that was discussed in Lesson 1. Depending on the specific Doer Noun, these nouns sometimes can also take a Broken Plural.

Table 39: The Doer Noun Pattern [إسمُ الفاعِل]		
Verb		**Doer Noun**
عَبَدَ to worship	→	عَابِدٌ a worshiper
نَصَرَ to help	→	نَاصِرٌ a helper
عَلِمَ to know	→	عَالِمٌ one with knowledge
Other Conjugations		
عَابِدٌ a worshiper	→	عَابِدَةٌ a female worshiper
عَابِدٌ a worshiper	→	عابِدُون / عِبادٌ worshipers
كافِرٌ a disbeliever	→	كافِرُونَ/كُفَّارٌ disbelievers

➢ Examples from the Qur'ān:

﴿ إِنَّ ٱلْمُسْلِمِينَ وَٱلْمُسْلِمَاتِ وَٱلْمُؤْمِنِينَ وَٱلْمُؤْمِنَاتِ وَٱلْقَانِتِينَ وَٱلْقَانِتَاتِ وَٱلصَّادِقِينَ وَٱلصَّادِقَاتِ وَٱلصَّابِرِينَ وَٱلصَّابِرَاتِ وَٱلْخَاشِعِينَ وَٱلْخَاشِعَاتِ وَٱلْمُتَصَدِّقِينَ وَٱلْمُتَصَدِّقَاتِ وَٱلصَّائِمِينَ وَٱلصَّائِمَاتِ وَٱلْحَافِظِينَ فُرُوجَهُمْ وَٱلْحَافِظَاتِ وَٱلذَّاكِرِينَ ٱللَّهَ كَثِيرًا وَٱلذَّاكِرَاتِ أَعَدَّ ٱللَّهُ لَهُم مَّغْفِرَةً وَأَجْرًا عَظِيمًا ﴾

"Indeed, the Muslim men and Muslim women, the believing men and believing women, the obedient men and obedient women, the truthful men and truthful women, the patient men and patient women, the humble men and humble women, the charitable men and charitable women, the fasting men and fasting women, the men who guard their private parts and the women who do so, and the men who remember Allah often and the women who do so - for them Allah has prepared forgiveness and a great reward."(33:35)[91]

[91] In this Āyah, there are [اسم الفاعل] that were not highlighted such as [مُؤمِن] ، [مُسْلِم], and [مُتَصَدِّق] that are of Verb Families II and higher. These Verb Families that are discussed in the next two lessons have a different morphology.

III. The Passive Noun Pattern [اِسْمُ المَفْعُول]

Passive Nouns, or [اِسْمُ المَفْعُول] similar to Doer Nouns are also derived from verbs. They specify something that is a recipient of an action. Similar to the Doer Noun, these nouns also take the Sound Plural Pattern. They have a specific morphology based on the [مَفْعُول] stem and typically begin with the letter [م].

Table 40: The Passive Noun Pattern [اِسْمُ المَفْعُول]		
Verb		**Passive Noun**
عَبَدَ to worship	→	مَعْبُودٌ one who is worshiped
نَصَرَ to help	→	مَنْصُورٌ one who is helped
عَلِمَ to know	→	مَعْلُومٌ one who is known
قَتَلَ to kill	→	مَقْتُولٌ/ قَتِيلٌ[92] one that is killed

Other conjugations:

مَنْصُورٌ one who is helped	→	مَنْصُورَةٌ a female who is helped
مَنْصُورٌ	→	مَنْصُورُونَ/مَنْصُورِينَ persons who are helped

➢ Examples from the Qur'ān:

1. ﴿ فَجَعَلَهُمْ كَعَصْفٍ مَّأْكُولٍ ﴾
   "And He made them like eaten straw."(105:5)

2. ﴿ أُولَٰئِكَ لَهُمْ رِزْقٌ مَعْلُومٌ ﴾
   "Those will have a provision determined."(37:41)

[92] Please note the [فعيل] pattern is less common pattern that some [اِسْمُ المَفْعُول] take. Please note that a similar pattern on this stem can be found in superlative words such as the following: [عليم]/[سميع]/[الثقيل], etc.

IV. The Verbal Noun [اَلْمَصْدَر]

The Verbal Noun, or Maṣdar essentially functions as a verb in the infinitive sense, not being confined to a specific time or tense (past, present, or future). Examples of Verbal Nouns in English include words such as knowledge, murder, disbelief, and help. Unlike the previously mentioned Derived Nouns[93], Maṣdars come in several different morphological patterns on the [فعل] stem numbering approximately thirty. Similar to Broken Plurals, a Verbal Noun of any given verb (Family I) can take one of many different morphological patterns. Please note that the Verbal Nouns of the high-yield verbs from "80% of Qur'ānic Vocabulary" are listed on the last column on the left (pgs. 170-175). Among the many Maṣdar patterns that are present, there are a few more common than the rest, which are detailed below in Table 41. Memorizing the Maṣdars for common verbs is strongly recommended, and will facilitate learning the language Inshā Allah. The most common Verbal Noun pattern is of the [فَعْلٌ] pattern like [قَتْلٌ] or [صَبْرٌ]. Other common patterns are on [فُعْلٌ] and [فِعْلٌ] as in [كُفْرٌ] and [عِلْمٌ].

Table 41: Common Verbal Noun Pattern

[فعل] Stem	اَلْمَصْدَر	فِعْل
فَعْلٌ	فَتْحٌ	فَتَحَ
فُعْلٌ	شُكْرٌ	شَكَرَ
فُعُولٌ	قُعُودٌ	قَعَدَ
فِعْلٌ	صِدْقٌ	صَدَقَ
فَعَلٌ	عَمَلٌ	عَمِلَ

➤ Examples from the Qur'ān

1. ﴿ٱلَّذِينَ يَذْكُرُونَ ٱللَّهَ قِيَامًا وَقُعُودًا وَعَلَىٰ جُنُوبِهِمْ وَيَتَفَكَّرُونَ فِي خَلْقِ ٱلسَّمَاوَاتِ وَٱلْأَرْضِ..﴾

"Those who remember Allah while standing or sitting or [lying] on their sides and give thought to the creation of the heavens and the earth..." (3:191)

2. ﴿...فَلَمَّا جَاءَهُم بِٱلْبَيِّنَاتِ قَالُوا هَٰذَا سِحْرٌ مُّبِينٌ﴾

"..But when he came to them with clear evidences, they said, "This is obvious magic"". (61:6)

93 Unlike the Doer Noun [اِسْمُ الفَاعِل] or Passive Noun [اِسْمُ الْمَفْعُول], the Verbal Noun is not considered a Derived Noun [اِسْمٌ مُشْتَقّ]. This is so even though it has a binding relationship with its root verb.

V. Using Arabic Dictionaries[94]

Using an Arabic Dictionary is an essential component in Arabic learning since Arabic has a very deep and rich vocabulary. Furthermore, as you already should have noted, most Arabic words are related and/or derived from a certain root verb or Maṣdar. It helps greatly in acquainting oneself with the root words of a word that is being learned or memorized. Most dictionaries of Classical Arabic are arranged by the Arabic root. Most dictionaries related to conversational Arabic however are often arranged alphabetically. Using a Classical Arabic Dictionary allows the student to connect one word (of a certain root) to several other words having similar meanings and relationships. Furthermore, the vocabulary that is learned is more effectively applied and organized. The past few years has seen the appearance of numerous resources online for Arabic students, both in English and Arabic, and has included online dictionaries. Despite the ease of the internet and search engines, using a dictionary in the traditional way (by the book) is still the more effective method for memorizing vocabulary.

A. Hans Wehr and other Classical Arabic Dictionaries

It is our opinion that the best dictionary for the Arabic student is the Hans Wehr Dictionary[95]. Its organization by root verbs, accurate and easy language, and compact size make it more useful than other dictionaries in its class. Please note that the most detailed Arabic dictionary in English is the eight-volume Lane's Lexicon. It is more detailed and comprehensive, but it is huge, and thus of less utility to the novice student. For those who do wish to obtain a more in-depth meaning than Hans Wehr, Lane's Lexicon is the dictionary to use. Fortunately, it is now available free with an index for root verbs for easy navigation.[96] For in-depth Qur'ānic study, it is best to use a classical "Arabic-Arabic dictionary" such as [لِسانُ العَرَب][97], which is available online[98] or a grammar based Tafsīr. Nonetheless, the Hans Wehr Dictionary does offer meanings that are for the most part in keeping with classical definitions. It is available in a pdf version that can be found online. A new online search engine, Arabic Almanac[99] has now made it very easy to access the knowledge contained within Hans Wehr and Lane's Lexicon, among other sources. It was just a few years ago that both these resources were available only textbook form.

---

[94] The dictionaries in this book that are discussed are best for Qur'ānic Arabic which has a different scope than conversational Arabic

[95] *Arabic-English Dictionary: The Hans Wehr Dictionary*, by Hans Wehr, Edited by J. Milton Cowan, 4th edition, 1994. ISBN 0879500034

[96] Lane's Lexicon, An Arabic-English Lexicon, Volumes 1-8, by Edward W. Lane available for free online at http://www.tyndalearchive.com/tabs/lane/ since the older eight-volume edition is out of copyright.

[97] The dictionary [لِسانُ العَرَب] by Ibn Manzūr (711 A.H.) is among the best-known and most comprehensive dictionaries of the Arabic language encompassing 20 volumes.

[98] The website [الباحِث العربي] at www.baheth.info/ contains this and other Classical Arabic-Arabic dictionaries.

[99] The Arabic Almanac is available for free download from the website http://ejtaal.net/m/aa/ is a search engine which enables the Arabic student to access the knowledge contained within Lane's Lexicon, Hans Wehr, and other dictionaries in English and other languages. By simply inputting a Verb root in either Arabic or English, the student has simultaneous access to these three classical dictionaries.

B. <u>Word Search using the Hans Wehr Dictionary</u>

1. Search the word by the Arabic alphabet of its root word. Remember the order of the Arabic alphabet as shown below. Otherwise, the search will be cumbersome and time consuming.

[ا أ ب ت ث ج ح خ د ذ ر ز س ش ص ض ط ظ ع غ ف ق ك ل م ن ه و ي]

2. **<u>Determining the three-letter root word/root verb.</u>** This will require practice in many cases, especially in cases of long words, words derived from Irregular Verbs, or words derived from the higher Verb Families.

3. **Let us practice by looking up the verb** [عَلِمَ]. Page 128 shows a page from Hans Wehr that defines the verb [علم]. We see the following entry in the dictionary.

- علم **('alima) "a" ('ilm) to know.**

Here, the verb is transliterated in its Past Tense **Family I form**. The term "ilm" represents it the Maṣdar of the verb. The "a" represents the Fatḥah vowel present in its Present Tense [مضارع] form. A Kasrah is represented by "i", while a Ḍammah is a "u". This is the same format for all other verbs. Any Arabic word having the root letters [علم] are listed and defined after the verb.

As you look in the entry for [علم ('alima)], you will note various Roman Numerals. These actually represent the various "higher" Verb Families that are derived from a respective three-letter root. You see the following:

- **II** to teach..........**IV** to let know...... **V** to learn, study...... **X** to inquire...

These Roman Numerals represent the Verb Families II through X. Each verb Root has a certain number of higher Verb Families derived that are actually used in the language. There are certain specific Verb Families (from II through X) which actually exist in Arabic from a given verb Root.

The next entry after the verb [علم] is the noun [علم] 'ilm. We see after it the following:

- **(pl. 'ulūm علوم) science**

This represents the plural of the noun [عِلْم].

4. <u>Looking up a Root with a vowel or a "weak letter"</u>

Even though the Irregular Verbs are not discussed much in this First Volume, it is important for the student to be somewhat acquainted with Irregular Verbs. Recall that Irregular verbs have in their root word one of the following letters: [ا / ـّ / / ي / و]. For example, the following verbs are all Irregular and have one vowel Root letter: [يَقُنَ / دَعا / قَال].

Now, let us look up the verb [دَعا]. The root letters are not [دعا], but are [دعو]. Often in the Irregular Verbs, the [ا] or [ي] can represent a different root letter. For example, for the verb [قَال], the root verb letters are actually [قول]. On page 129, we see the entry for [دعو].

- (دعو and دعي) دعا *da'ā ū* (دعاء *du'ā'*) to call;
  ..To summon (ب or ه s.o.[100])…..; to invite, ask to come (إلى…)…..to invoke God against s.o.), call down evil, invoke evil (على upon s.o.)

As you look through this definition for [دعا], you will notice that there are several Ḥarf Jarr that are associated with a specific shade of meaning from the original "to call". Please note the even though this verb is Transitive, it is associated with certain Ḥarf Jarr which causes a change in its ultimate meaning. For example, using the Ḥarf [على] with this verb [دعا] causes the meaning to change to "invoking God against" versus "calling". Recall that the Transitive Verb [غَفَرَ] that was previously discussed also is associated with a Ḥarf Jarr.

C. <u>Word Search Using Lane's Lexicon</u>

Similar to the Hans Wehr Dictionary, Lane's Lexicon is also organized by three-letter roots. This is the most comprehensive Arabic dictionary in English and is the result of more than thirty years of research. The meanings that this dictionary provides are very detailed and thorough. Lane's Lexicon often references its meanings with sentence examples, specifically how the word is used in an Arabic sentence. Please see the entry for [علم] in Lane's Lexicon on page 130. You will see that compared to Hans Wehr, the information provided on the Verb I form [عَلِمَ] is more in-depth and that several examples are given to correctly show its proper meaning and usage. Nonetheless, the Hans Wehr Dictionary is still more suitable for the beginner and more than adequate for the intermediate student.

[100] These abbreviations such as s.o. (someone) are all explained in the first few pages of the Hans Wehr Dictionary.

Page from the Hans Wehr Dictionary

تعليقة *ta'līqa* pl. *-āt*, تعاليق *ta'ālīq*² marginal note, annotation, note, gloss, scholium

تعلق *ta'alluq* attachment, devotion (ب to), affection (ب for); linkage, connection, relationship (ب with)

معلق *mu'alliq* commentator (radio, press)

معلق *mu'allaq* suspended, hanging; in suspense, in abeyance, pending, undecided; hinging (ب on); depending, dependent, conditional (ب or على on), conditioned (ب or على by) | جسر معلق (*jisr*) suspension bridge; حساب معلق suspense account; قاطرات معلقة suspension railways; مسائل معلقة pending questions; رغبته معلقة ب (*rağbatuhū*) his desire is directed toward ...

معلقة *mu'allaqa* pl. *-āt* placard, poster, bill; المعلقات the oldest collection of complete ancient Arabic kasidas

متعلق *muta'alliq* attached, devoted (ب to); connected (ب with), related, pertaining (ب to), concerning (ب s.o. or s.th.) | متعلق بحبه (*bi-ḥubbihī*) affectionately attached to s.o.; من متعلقاته depending on s.o. or s.th., pertaining to s.o.'s authority

علقم *'alqam* pl. علاقم *'alāqim*² colocynth (*bot.*) | ذاق العلقم to taste bitterness, suffer annoyance, vexation, chicanery or torments (من from)

علك *'alaka u i* (*'alk*) to chew, champ (ه s.th., esp. اللجام the bit, of a horse)

علك *'ilk* mastic

علم *'alima a* (*'ilm*) to know (ب or ه, ه s.o., s.th.), have knowledge, be cognizant, be aware (ب or ه of s.th.), be informed (ب or ه about or of s.th.), be familiar, be acquainted (ب or ه with s.th.); to perceive, discern (ب or ه s.th.), find out (ب or ه about s.th., من from), learn, come to know (ب or ه s.th. or about s.th., من from); to distinguish, differentiate (من ه s.th. from) II to teach (ب ه or ه ه s.o. s.th.), instruct, brief (ب ه or ه ه s.o. in s.th.); to train, school, educate (ه s.o.); to designate, mark, earmark, provide with a distinctive mark (على s.th.); to put a mark (على on) IV to let (ه s.o.) know (ب or ه s.th. or about s.th.), tell (ب or ه ه s.o. about), notify, advise, apprise, inform (ب ه or ه ه s.o. of or about s.th.), acquaint (ب ه or ه ه s.o. with) V to learn, study (ه s.th.); to know (ه s.th.) X to inquire (عن ه or ه ه of s.o. about), ask, query (عن ه or ه ه s.o. about), inform o.s. (عن ه or ه ه through s.o. about), gather information (عن ه or ه ه from s.o. about)

علم *'ilm* knowledge, learning, lore; cognizance, acquaintance; information; cognition, intellection, perception, knowledge; (pl. علوم *'ulūm*) science; pl. العلوم the (natural) sciences | علما وعملا *'ilman wa-'amalan* theoretically and practically; ليكن فى علمه (*li-yakun*) be it known to him, may he know, for his information; كان على علم تام ب (*tāmm*) to know s.th. inside out, be thoroughly familiar with s.th.; to have full cognizance of s.th.; علم الجراثيم bacteriology; علم الاجتماع sociology; علم الحساب arithmetic; علم الحياة *'i. al-ḥayāh* biology; علم الاحياء do.; علم الحيوان *'i. al-ḥayawān* zoology; علم الاخلاق ethics; علم الذرات *'i. aḏ-ḏarrāt* nuclear physics; علم التربية *'i. at-tarbiya* pedagogy; علم الصحة *'i. aṣ-ṣiḥḥa* hygiene; علم الاصوات phonetics; علم المعادن *'i. al-ma'ādin* mineralogy; علم اللغة *'i. al-luğa* lexicography; علم النباتات *'i. an-nabātāt* botany; علم النفس *'i. an-nafs* psychology; علم وظائف الاعضاء *'i. w. al-a'ḍā'* physiology; طالب علم *ṭālib 'ilm* student; كلية العلوم *kullīyat al-'u.* the Faculty of Science of the Egyptian University

علمى *'ilmī* scientific; erudite (book); learned (society)

Adapted from page 635 from Third edition of "Hans Wehr: A Dictionary of Modern Written Arabic".

Page from the Hans Wehr Dictionary

(دعو and دعى) دعا *daʿā u* (دعاء *duʿāʾ*) to call (ه s.o.); to summon (ب or ه s.o.), call or send for s.o. (ب or ه); to call up (ه s.o., الى, ل for); to call upon s.o. (ه), appeal to s.o. (ه) for s.th. or to do s.th. (ل, الى), invite, urge (ل, الى ه s.o. to do s.th.); to invite, ask to come (الى ه s.o. to; e.g., to a banquet); to move, induce, prompt (ل, الى ه s.o. to do s.th.), prevail (ل, الى ه on s.o. to do s.th.); to call (ب, ه ه s.o. by a name), name (ب, ه ه s.o. so and so), pass.: دعى *duʿiya* to be called, be named; to invoke (الله God = to pray to); to wish (ل s.o.) well, bless (ل s.o.; properly: to invoke God in favor of s.o.), invoke a blessing (ب) upon s.o. (ل), pray (ب for s.th., ل on behalf of s.o.), implore (ب ل for s.o. s.th.); to curse (على s.o.; properly: to invoke God against s.o.), call down evil, invoke evil (على upon s.o.); to propagate, propagandize (ل s.th.), make propaganda, make publicity (ل for); to demand, require (الى s.th.), call for (الى); to call forth, bring about, cause, provoke, occasion (الى s.th.), give rise (الى to) | دعى للاجتماع (*duʿiya*) to be summoned, be called into session (parliament); دعى الى حمل السلاح *duʿiya ilā ḥamli s-silāḥ* to be called up for military service, be called to the colors; رجل يدعى ... (*yudʿā*) a man called ..., a man by the name of ...; دعا له بطول العمر (*ṭūli l-ʿumr*) he wished him a long life III to challenge (ه s.o.); to pick a quarrel (ه with); to proceed judicially (ه against), prosecute (ه s.o.) VI to challenge each other, call each

Adapted from page 282 from Third edition of "Hans Wehr: A Dictionary of Modern Written Arabic".

Page from Lane's Lexicon

علم

1. عَلِمَهُ, aor. ـَ, inf. n. عِلْمٌ, *He knew it; or he was, or became, acquainted with it;* syn. عَرَفَهُ: (Ṣ, Ḳ:) or *he knew it* (عَرَفَهُ) *truly,* or *certainly:* (B, TA:) by what is said above, and by what is afterwards said in the Ḳ, العِلْمُ and المَعْرِفَةُ and الشُّعُورُ are made to have one meaning; and this is nearly what is said by most of the lexicologists: but most of the critics discriminate every one of these from the others; and العِلْمُ, accord. to them, denotes the highest quality, because it is that which they allow to be an attribute of God; whereas they did not say [that He is] عَارِفٌ, in the most correct language, nor شَاعِرٌ: (TA:) [respecting other differences between العِلْمُ and المَعْرِفَةُ, the former of which is more general in signification than the latter, see the first paragraph of art. عرف: much might be added to what is there stated on that subject, and in explanation of العِلْمُ, from the TA, but not without controversy:] or عَلِمَ signifies تَيَقَّنَ [i.e. *he knew a thing, intuitively,* and *inferentially,* as expl. in the Mṣb in art. يقن]; العِلْمُ being syn. with اليَقِينُ; but it occurs with the meaning of المَعْرِفَةُ, like as المَعْرِفَةُ occurs with the meaning of العِلْمُ, each being made to import the meaning of the other because each is preceded by ignorance [when not attributed to God]: Zuheyr says, [in his Mo'allaḳah,]

• وَأَعْلَمُ عِلْمَ اليَوْمِ وَالأَمْسِ قَبْلَهُ •
• وَلٰكِنَّنِى عَنْ عِلْمِ مَا فِى غَدٍ عَمِ •

خَارِجٌ is a phrase used in the place of عَلِمْتُ [as meaning *I knew,* or, emphatically, *I know, that such a one was,* or *is, going forth*]; adding, [however,] when it is said to thee, اِعْلَمْ أَنَّ زَيْدًا خَارِجٌ [*Know thou that Zeyd is going forth*], thou sayest قَدْ عَلِمْتُ [lit. *I have known,* meaning *I do know*]; but when it is said, تَعَلَّمْ أَنَّ زَيْدًا خَارِجٌ, thou dost not say, قَدْ تَعَلَّمْتُ; (Ṣ:) accord. to IB, these two verbs are not used as syn. except in the imperative forms: (TA:) [or] عَلِمَ الأَمْرَ and ▾ تَعَلَّمَهُ are syn. as signifying أَتْقَنَهُ [app. meaning *he knew,* or *learned, the case,* or *affair, soundly, thoroughly,* or *well:* see art. تقن: but I think it not improbable, though I do not find it in any copy of the Ḳ, that the right reading may be أَيْقَنَهُ, which is syn. with تَيَقَّنَهُ; an explanation of عَلِمَ in the Mṣb, as mentioned above, being تَيَقَّنَ]. (Ḳ, TA.) And ▾ تعالمهُ الجَمِيعُ means عَلِمُوهُ [i.e. *All knew him;* &c.]. (Ṣ, Ḳ.) —— عَلِمْتُ عِلْمَهُ [lit. *I knew his knowledge,* or *what he knew,* app. meaning *I tried, proved,* or *tested, him, and so knew what he knew;* and hence *I knew his case* or *state* or *condition,* or *his qualities;*] is a phrase mentioned by Fr in explanation of رَبَأْتُ فِيهِ. (TA voce رَبَأَ, q. v. See also the explanation of لَأَخْبُرَنَّ خَبَرَكَ, in the first paragraph of art. خبر: and see غَبِنُوا خَبَرَهَا, in art. غبن.) —— عَلِمْتُ is also used in the manner of a verb signifying swearing, or asseveration, so as to have a similar complement; as in the saying,

• وَلَقَدْ عَلِمْتُ لَتَأْتِيَنَّ عَشِيَّةً •

Adapted from pages 423 and 424 from Volume 5 of "Arabic –English Lexicon" (1968) by Edward W. Lane.

D. Other Important Qur'ānic Arabic References in English

It is important for the novice student not to overwhelm themselves with the numerous resources and books available on Arabic learning. It is important to adhere to one primary resource or Arabic curriculum, and take to its finale. It is far more effective to learn the grammar and vocabulary well presented here than to go tangentially into other areas prematurely. Nonetheless, when the need arises or when finishes the curriculum, one should certainly explore other resources for better understanding. We have already discussed some excellent supplementary material in learning Qur'ānic Arabic. Listed below are other excellent resources that can be used.

1. Islamic Online University – Diploma Series Course "Introduction to Qur'ānic Arabic"- **http://www.islamiconlineuniversity.com/opencampus/**. This is a free online three level course with videos and exams is actually based on this textbook series. It is ideal that student study this textbook series in concert with this course or the like.

2. The Quranic Arabic Corpus at **http://corpus.quran.com/.** This is the most comprehensive website on Qur'ānic grammar in English. As one goes forward in Qur'ānic Arabic studies, this website is a great tool for studying Qur'ānic Grammar.

3. HdO Arabic-English Dictionary of Qur'ān Usage[101], Elsaid M. Badawai, Muḥammad Abel Ḥaleem: This dictionary is the most comprehensive Arabic-English dictionary of the Qur'ān, and based on Classical Arabic Dictionaries and Qur'ānic commentaries.

4. Arabic Tutor - Volumes 1 through 4, 'Abdul Sattar Khān: This four volume series is among the best grammar series on Classical Arabic translated in the English Language.

5. From the Treasures of Arabic Morphology, Muḥammad, Ebrāhīm. This is the best book on the topic of Morphology or Ṣarf in the English language.

6. *Bayyinah Institute Tafsīr Podcast* at **http://podcast.bayyinah.com/**. This excellent initiative by Ustādh Noumān 'Ali Khān and Sheikh 'Abdul-Nāṣir Jungda explains the Qur'ānic Āyāt in detail and depth. This Tafsīr series places much focus on the Qur'ān's eloquence, cohesiveness, and its inimitable grammar. There is much that is expounded upon of the Qur'ān from several classical Tafsīrs of the past. There is also excellent commentary with respect to contemporary issues.

[101] Koninklijke Brill NV (2008), Leiden, The Netherlands. ISBN 9789004149489.

Lesson 12: Verb Families II, III, and IV - اَلْفِعْلُ الثُّلاثي الْمَزيدُ فيهِ

Up until this point in our study of verbs, we have been focusing on the verbs based on a 3-letter root [اَلْفِعْلُ الثُّلاثي]. In particular, we have been studying what we have termed Family I Verbs, which have a minimum of three base letters [اَلْفِعْلُ الثلاثي الْمُجَرَّد]. In this lesson, we will look at verbs of higher Verb Families derived from a 3-letter Root, which have more than three base letters. These represent Families II through X.

We have already studied the conjugations in the Past, Present, Future, Command, and Passive Tenses of Family I Verbs. We have also looked at verb-like nouns that stem from all respective verbs such as the Verbal Noun, the Doer Noun, and the Passive Noun. We have also examined particles that affect verbs and the rules that govern Verbal Sentences. All these grammatical points relative to verbs should be mastered before discussing the higher Verb Families. Please note that we will also continue to shy away from discussing the Irregular Verbs of the higher families just like those of Verb Family I. That topic will be left to Volume 2 of this series.

I. Review of Verb Family I Conjugations

Table 42: Review of Verb Family I [الفِعْلُ الثلاثي المُجَرَّدِ]

اَلْفِعْلُ الْماضي	اَلْفِعْلُ الْمُضارِع		اَلْفِعْلُ الأَمْر
فَعَلَ	يَفْعَلُ		اِفْعَلْ / اُفْعُلْ
فَعِلَ	يَفْعَلُ		اِفْعَلْ
فَعُلَ	يَفْعُلُ		اُفْعُلْ
مَجْهول	مَجْهول	نَصْب	يَفْعُلَ
فُعِلَ	يُفْعَلُ	جَزْم	يَفْعُلْ
فَعْلٌ [المصدر]	فاعِلٌ [اسم الفاعل]		مَفْعولٌ [اسم المفعول]

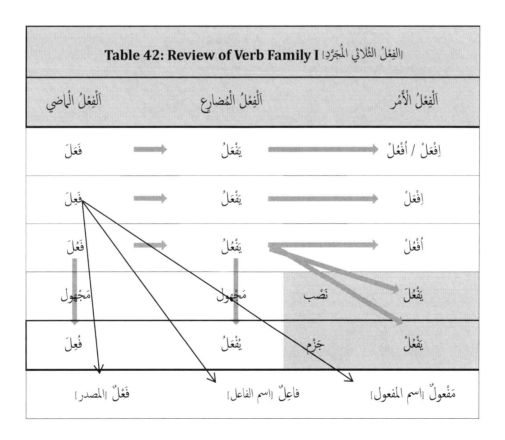

A. Diagram of Verb Families I through X

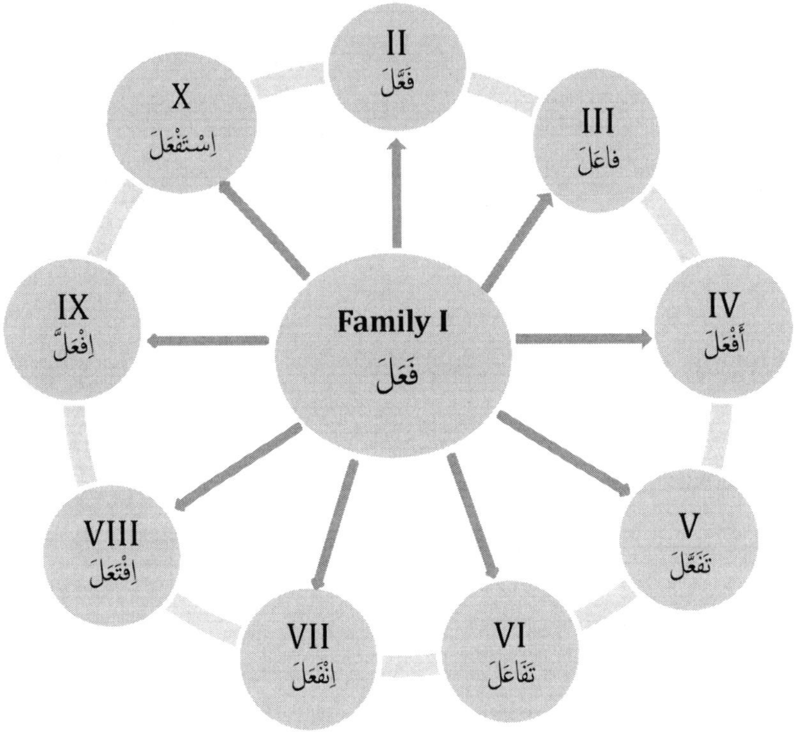

Table 43: Word Count for Verbs in the Qur'ān	
Verb Family	**Number of Words**
I	12,347
II	1,300
III	334
IV	3,487
V	414
VI	77
VII	51
VIII	963
IX	5
X	369
Total Words	19,356
Unique Words	1,475

B. Relation of Verb families to its Family I Root Verb [اَلْفِعْلُ الثلاثي الْمُجَرَّد]

All of the higher Verb Families (II through X) are related by meaning to its Root three-letter Verb (Family I). The Roman Numerals, which denote these Verb Families, were originally designated by Orientalists. They are very helpful in notation of Verb Families, perhaps more than the traditional notation of using the Verbal Noun to identify the Verb Families. We also prefer the the Roman Numeral classification due to its ease of notation.

These Families are derived from a respective 3-letter root, and further give rise to several additional nouns related by meaning. This is one important reason to pay close attention to nouns and their verb roots. This allows one to connect several different words based on a single verb root with one-another.

Although there can theoretically be ten derived verbs from a given 3-letter root, this does not occur in reality. We briefly mentioned that there are only certain specific Verb Families that exist for any respective 3-letter root. For example, verbs [عَلِمَ] and [سَلِمَ] derive all higher Verb Families except VII, and IX, but not others. Please note that depending on the depth of the Arabic Dictionary used, the exact number of conjugated families from a certain root will also vary. This also varies between Hans Wehr and Lane's Lexicon, where one will find more derived Verb Families in the latter. For our purposes, we should focus on the verbs found in the Qur'ān on a frequent basis.

II. Verb Family II [يُفَعِّلُ/فَعَّلَ]

Verb Family II along with Family IV are the most frequently found higher Verb Families in the Qur'ān. In terms of meaning, the Verb II form is usually **the intensive meaning of its Verb I root. In other words, it is the action done onto others. Thus, Verb Family II is generally transitive or** [مُتَعَدِّى]. The verb [نَزَلَ] means "to go down" and is intransitive. Its Verb Family II derivative [نَزَّلَ] means, "to send down". Another example of Family II meaning and its relation to its Root verb can be seen with the verb [عَلِمَ], which means, "to know". The Family II Verb [عَلَّمَ] means to "apply knowing on others" or simply "to teach". The Present Tense of [عَلَّمَ] would be [يُعَلِّمُ]. Sometimes, Verb Family II can impart a more intense form of the verb compared to its root. For example, the verb [قَتَلَ] means "to kill", while its Verb II Family derivative [قَتَّلَ] means "to massacre".

Conjugation of Verb Family II in the Past and Present Tense is identical to the scheme of the Verb I Family. The same principle holds for the other Higher Families as well. Unlike in the Verb I Family, there is no variability of the [ع] vowel in the past or Present Tense. The stem in the Past Tense and the Present Tense is the same. For Past Tense, just like in Family I Verbs, extra letters are added to the end of the 4-letter Past Tense **stem** [فَعَّلَ]. In the

Present Tense, extra letters are added to the front and end of the 5-letter stem [يُفَعِّلُ]. Remember the sign for Raf' is the Ḍammah, which the Present Tense ends with. Please look at the following conjugations from the verb [عَلَّمَ].

عَلَّمُوا → They (men) taught.

يُعَلِّمُونَ → They (men) teach.

أُعَلِّمُ → I teach.

عَلِّمْ → Teach (command).

A. Conjugation of Family II Verbs [يُفَعِّلُ/فَعَّلَ]

Table 44: Conjugation of Family II Verbs [يُفَعِّلُ/فَعَّلَ]						
اَلْفِعْلُ الْمُضارِعِ			اَلْفِعْلُ الماضي			[فَسَّرَ] to explain
جَمْع	مُثَنَّى	مُفْرَد	جَمْع	مُثَنَّى	مُفْرَد	
يُفَسِّرُونَ	يُفَسِّرَانِ	يُفَسِّرُ	فَسَّرُوا	فَسَّرَا	فَسَّرَ	غائِب مُذَكَّر
يُفَسِّرْنَ	تُفَسِّرَانِ	تُفَسِّرُ	فَسَّرْنَ	فَسَّرَتَا	فَسَّرَتْ	غائِب مُؤَنَّث
تُفَسِّرُونَ	تُفَسِّرَانِ	تُفَسِّرُ	فَسَّرْتُم	فَسَّرْتُمَا	فَسَّرْتَ	مُخاطَب مُذَكَّر
تُفَسِّرْنَ	تُفَسِّرَانِ	تُفَسِّرِينَ	فَسَّرْتُنَّ	فَسَّرْتُمَا	فَسَّرْتِ	مُخاطَب مُؤَنَّث
نُفَسِّرُ	نُفَسِّرُ	أُفَسِّرُ	فَسَّرْنا	فَسَّرْنا	فَسَّرْتُ	مُتَكَلِّم

- Please note that for Verb Families II, III, and IV, the Present Tense letter will always have a Ḍammah on the first letter; all other Present Tense forms have a Fatḥah on the first letter (with the exception of Passive Tense).

B. Family II Conjugations for Advanced Forms [فَعَّلَ]

	Table 45: Family II Conjugations for Advanced Forms [فَعَّلَ]								
Verbal Noun المَصْدَر	Verbal Doer اسم الفاعل	Passive Noun اسم المفعول	Present Passive المُضَارِع المَجْهُول	Past Passive المَاضِي المَجْهُول	Forbidding لا النَّهْيَّة	Command الْفِعْلُ الأَمْر	Present المُضَارِع	Past المَاضِي	Verb Family II Stem [فَعَّلَ]
تَعْلِيمٌ	مُعَلِّمٌ	مُعَلَّمٌ	يُعَلَّمُ	عُلِّمَ	لا تُعَلِّمْ	عَلِّمْ	يُعَلِّمُ	عَلَّمَ	عَلَّمَ

1. Please note that for Doer Noun [اسم الفاعل] forms, each of the families with more than three letters will have [مُ] as its first letter; For example, [مُعَلِّمٌ] is a teacher, while [مُعَلَّمٌ] is a student. It is just one vowel, which makes this big distinction.

2. You will notice in the other Verb Families including Family II that a Kasrah before the last letter denotes the Doer Noun. However, as for the Passive Noun, it has a Fatḥah vowel before its last letter. Thus, this sharp difference in meaning stems from a single vowel. Please also note that both the Doer and Passive Nouns take the Proper Plural pattern, like those from the Verb I Family,

3. Conjugation of the Command Tense is also simpler than that of Family I Verbs. From the bare [مُضَارِع] Present Tense stem, the first letter is removed and the last letter is made Sākin (from vowel to a Sukūn). For example, the Present Tense [يُعَلِّمُ] that means, "he is learning" is converted to [عَلِّمْ], which means, "learn!". This is indeed simpler.

4. The conjugation of the Verbal Noun is also simpler than that of the Verb I Family forms. Higher Families have **one set pattern** unlike the Verb I Family, which has several variable patterns. Family III of note has two Verbal Noun patterns.

5. The conjugation of the Passive Tense does not change for the Past and Present Tenses respectively. The Past Tense morphology is that the first stem letter takes a Ḍammah and the second stem letter takes a Kasrah. Because the morphology of a respective Higher Family verb may not allow this to always occur, the general rule applies. For Present Tense Passive Verbs, the first stem letter takes a Ḍammah while the [ع] letter takes a Fatḥah.

6. Please also note there can be Irregular forms (just like Form I) in each Verb Family II through X containing one of the vowel letters [و / ي / ا / أ] or a letter with a Shadda. Examples include the following verbs: [أَقَامَ / اِسْتِقَام / اِسْتَحَقَّ].

C. Verb Family II examples from the Qur'ān

1. ﴿... قَالُوٓاْ أَتَجْعَلُ فِيهَا مَن يُفْسِدُ فِيهَا وَيَسْفِكُ ٱلدِّمَآءَ وَنَحْنُ نُسَبِّحُ بِحَمْدِكَ وَنُقَدِّسُ لَكَ...﴾
"..They said, "Will You place upon it one who causes corruption therein and sheds blood, while we declare Your praise and sanctify You?".....(2:30) [فعل مُضارع]

2. ﴿ يَا بَنِي إِسْرَآئِيلَ ٱذْكُرُواْ نِعْمَتِيَ ٱلَّتِي أَنْعَمْتُ عَلَيْكُمْ وَأَنِّي فَضَّلْتُكُمْ عَلَى ٱلْعَالَمِينَ ﴾
"O Children of Israel, remember My favor that I have bestowed upon you and that I preferred you over the worlds." (2:47) [فعل ماضٍ]

3. ﴿...وَٱذْكُر رَّبَّكَ كَثِيرًا وَسَبِّحْ بِٱلْعَشِيِّ وَٱلْإِبْكَارِ ﴾
"...And remember your Lord much and praise [Him] in the evening and the morning." (3:41) [اَلْفِعْلُ الأَمر]

4. ﴿... وَلَهُمْ فِيهَا أَزْوَاجٌ مُّطَهَّرَةٌ وَهُمْ فِيهَا خَالِدُونَ ﴾
"..And they will have therein purified spouses, and they will abide therein eternally. (2:25) [اسم المَفعول]

III. Verb Family III [يُفاعِل/فَاعَلَ]

Verb Family III in meaning compared to its root is often related to doing an action against others. Therefore, it is typically Transitive or [مُتَعَدِّي]. It often expresses an attempt to do something. An example is [قَاتَلَ], which means, "fighting with others". It can also be defined as "an attempt to kill", since [قَتَلَ] means, "to kill". The verb [سَبَقَ] means to precede or be ahead. Its Verb III derivative [سَابَقَ] means an attempt to precede, or to compete with one another. The conjugation patterns for the Past and Present Tense stems are respectively [فاعَلَ] and [يُفاعِلُ] while its Command form is [فاعِلْ].

A. Verb Family III Conjugations

Table 46 – Verb Family III Conjugations

Verbal Noun المَصْدَر	Doer Noun اسم الفاعل	Passive Noun اسم المفعول	Present Passive المُضارِع المَجْهُول	Past Passive الماضي المَجْهُول	Forbidding لا النَّهِيَّة	Command اَلْفِعْلُ الأَمر	Present المُضارِع	Past الماضِي	Verb Family Stem [فاعَلَ]
مُجاهَدَةٌ جِهَادٌ	مُجاهِدٌ	مُجاهَدٌ	يُجاهَدُ	جُوهِدَ	لا تُجاهِدْ	جَاهِدْ	يُجَاهِدُ	جَاهَدَ	جَاهَدَ

B. Verb Family III examples from the Qur'ān

1. ﴿ قَدْ سَمِعَ ٱللَّهُ قَوْلَ ٱلَّتِي تُجَادِلُكَ فِي زَوْجِهَا وَتَشْتَكِي إِلَى ٱللَّهِ وَٱللَّهُ يَسْمَعُ تَحَاوُرَكُمَا...﴾

"..Allah indeed has heard the plea of her who pleads with thee about her husband and complains to Allah; and Allah hears the contentions of both of you." (58:1) [اَلْفِعْلُ الْمُضارِع]

2. ﴿ إِذَا جَاءَكَ ٱلْمُنَافِقُونَ قَالُوا نَشْهَدُ إِنَّكَ لَرَسُولُ ٱللَّهِ ...﴾

"When the hypocrites come to you, they say, "We testify that you are the Messenger of Allah"..." (63:1) [إسم الفاعل]

3. ﴿ ...وَيَقُولُونَ يَا وَيْلَتَنَا مَالِ هَذَا ٱلْكِتَابِ لاَ يُغَادِرُ صَغِيرَةً وَلاَ كَبِيرَةً إِلاَّ أَحْصَاهَا ...﴾

"They will say: "Woe to us! What sort of Book is this that leaves neither a small thing nor a big thing, but has recorded it (with numbers)!"" (18:49) [اَلْفِعْلُ الْمُضارِع]

4. ﴿ يَا أَيُّهَا ٱلنَّبِيُّ جَاهِدِ ٱلْكُفَّارَ وَٱلْمُنَافِقِينَ وَٱغْلُظْ عَلَيْهِمْ...﴾

"O Prophet, fight against the disbelievers and the hypocrites and be harsh upon them..." (9:73) [اَلْفِعْلُ الْأَمر][102]

IV. Verb Family IV [يُفعِلُ/أَفعَلَ]

The general meaning of Verb Family IV is related **to forcing or doing an action on others**. Thus, it is generally [مُتَعَدِّى]. Its meaning is similar to that of the Transitive Verb Family II and is very commonly used. For example, the verb [دَخَلَ] means "to enter", while [أَدْخَلَ] means to "make others enter", i.e. the action on others. The verb [نَزَلَ] means, "to go down" while [أَنْزَلَ] means "to bring down" similar to [نَزَّلَ].

In terms of structure, this is the **only** Verb Family where a Hamzah [أ] is used at the beginning of its Command form. The Verbal Noun pattern for Verb Family IV is on the pattern of [إفْعَال]. The Verbal Noun for [أَسْلَمَ] which means "to submit", is [إِسْلاَمٌ], which means submission. One interesting thing to note regarding the Present **Passive** Tense conjugation of Family IV [يُنْزَلُ] is that it is identical to the Present Passive Tense of Family I. In these rare cases, context clarifies the identity of the verb.

---

102 Please note that the Kasrah on the last letter of [اجاهِد] is added onto the Sukūn and original word [اجاهِدْ]. This Kasrah is necessary because without it, there would be two consecutive Sukūn, which are grammatically impossible in Arabic.

A. Verb Family IV Conjugations

Table 47 – Verb Family IV Conjugations									
Verbal Noun المَصْدَر	**Doer Noun** اسم الفاعل	**Passive Noun** اسم المفعول	**Present Passive** المُضارِع المَجْهول	**Past Passive** الماضي المَجْهول	**Forbidding** لا النَّهِيَّة	**Command** اَلْفِعْلُ الأَمْر	**Present** المُضارِع	**Past** الماضِي	**Verb Family IV Stem** [أَفْعَلَ]
إِنْزالٌ	مُنْزِلٌ	مُنْزَلٌ	يُنْزَلُ	أُنْزِلَ	لا تُنْزِلْ	أَنْزِلْ	يُنْزِلُ	أَنْزَلَ	أَنْزَلَ

B. Verb Family IV examples from the Qur'ān

1. ﴿...وَأَعْلَمُ مَا تُبْدُونَ وَمَا كُنتُمْ تَكْتُمُونَ﴾

   "..and I know what you reveal and what you have been concealing."(2:33) [فعل مُضارع]

2. ﴿وَإِذْ فَرَقْنَا بِكُمُ ٱلْبَحْرَ فَأَنجَيْنَاكُمْ وَأَغْرَقْنَا آلَ فِرْعَوْنَ وَأَنتُمْ تَنظُرُونَ﴾

   "And [recall] when We parted the sea for you and saved you and drowned the people of Pharaoh while you were looking on..." (2:50) [اَلْفِعْلُ الماضي]

3. ﴿وَإِن كُنتُنَّ تُرِدْنَ ٱللَّهَ وَرَسُولَهُ وَٱلدَّارَ ٱلْآخِرَةَ فَإِنَّ ٱللَّهَ أَعَدَّ لِلْمُحْسِنَاتِ مِنكُنَّ أَجْرًا عَظِيمًا﴾

   "But if you desire Allah and His Messenger, and the home of the Hereafter, then verily, Allah has prepared for the righteous (women) amongst you an enormous reward" (33:29). [اسمُ الفاعل]

4. ﴿إِنَّا أَرْسَلْنَا نُوحًا إِلَىٰ قَوْمِهِ أَنْ أَنذِرْ قَوْمَكَ مِن قَبْلِ أَن يَأْتِيَهُمْ عَذَابٌ أَلِيمٌ﴾

   "Indeed, We sent Nūḥ to his people, [saying], "Warn your people before there comes to them a painful punishment." (71:1). [اَلْفِعْلُ الأَمْر/اَلْفِعْلُ الماضي]

V. Method for Analyzing Verbal Sentences

After the student becomes familiar with verbs, its conjugations, and the basic structure of Verbal Sentences, it is useful to be systematic when reading and analyzing Verbal Sentences. If a specific methodology is not used, things can be missed, and subsequently the translation becomes deficient. Using the following methodology is useful in extracting an appropriate meaning when analyzing a respective Verbal Sentence from the Qur'ān or Ḥadīth.

1. The First step in analyzing a Verbal Sentence similar to the methodology of analyzing Nominal Sentences is Word Analysis. Specifically, this involves fully identifying and characterizing nouns and particles involved in the Verbal Sentence. The analysis of verbs occurs in the next step.
2. The Second step is Verb Analysis. **First,** identify the Verb Family of the verb in question (Family I through X). If the specific family is identified first, it will easier to identify the specific tense that the verb is taking, whether Past, Present, or Command. After identifying the Family, then identify its tense (Past, Present, Command, Passive) and then its conjugation (pronoun in terms of gender, plurality, and person).
3. The Third step is to identify the Doer. Remember, the Doer is Rafʿ if it is explicitly mentioned. If it is present explicitly, it is usually found immediately after the verb, but can be found elsewhere within the sentence.
4. The Fourth step is to identify the Direct Object if present. This may be attached to the verb itself, or be present sequentially after the Doer or Verb. When present, it is always Naṣb. If not present, check to see if there is an indirect Object (Jarr Construction), as the verb may be [لازم]. After screening for the Direct Object, there may be additional details noted in the Verbal Sentence. Also, note that not every noun in the Naṣb state is a Direct Object. The discussion on other nouns that are Naṣb in Verbal Sentences is presented in detail in Volume 2. The final step is putting everything together and deriving an appropriate translation/meaning.

➢ Example of Analyzing a Verbal Sentence

﴿وَإِذْ يَرْفَعُ إِبْرَاهِيمُ ٱلْقَوَاعِدَ مِنَ ٱلْبَيْتِ وَإِسْمَاعِيلُ...﴾ (2:127)

	إِسْمَاعِيلُ	وَ	الْبَيْتِ	مِنَ	الْقَوَاعِدَ	إِبْرَاهِيمُ	يَرْفَعُ	وَإِذْ
Step #1 Word Analysis	noun male singular Definite (Partially-flexible) Raf'	Ḥarf [عَطْف] Connecting particle	noun male singular Definite Jarr	Ḥarf Jarr	noun feminine Definite singular (Broken Plural) Naṣb	noun male singular Definite (Partially-flexible) Raf'	verb	[و] is a particle [إِذْ] is an Adverb particle
Step #2 Verb Analysis	[يَرْفَعُ]= Verb family I → Present tense [فعل مضارع] on conjugation [هُوَ].							
Step #3 ID the Doer	[إِسْمَاعِيلُ] Doer through [و]					[إِبْرَاهِيمُ] Doer		
Step #4 ID object and rest			[مِنَ الْبَيْتِ] Jarr Construction		[القَواعِد] Direct Object			
Put things together and translate	And remember when **Ibrāhīm was raising the foundations of the house and (with him) Ismaīl...**							

Lesson 13: Verb Families V through X - اَلْفِعْلُ الثُّلاثِي الْمَزِيدُ فيهِ

The same rules that applied to Verb Families II, III, and IV also apply to these Families V through X as previously discussed. The most frequently used Families in the Qur'ān from here are Families V, VIII, and X. Family IX is rarely used. The Verb Families VII through X all start with the letter Alif.

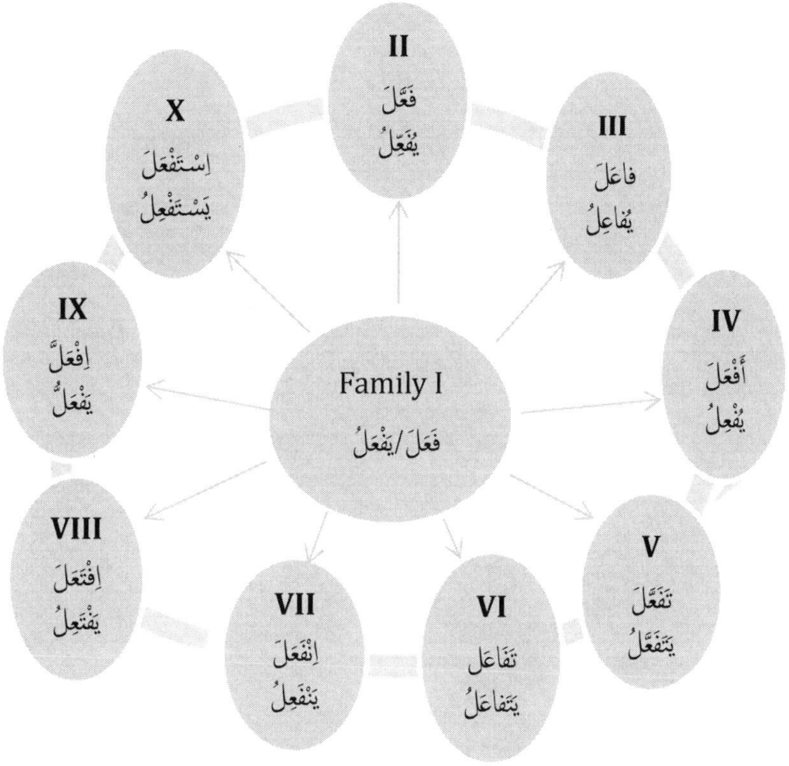

I. Verb Family V [تَفَعَّلَ/يَتَفَعَّلُ]

This Family is essentially a Tā attached to the Verb Family II pattern in the Past Tense. This Verb Family can be [لازِم] or [مُتَعَدِّى]. In terms of meaning, it is also closely tied to Family II, and is its reflexive form (the action done on oneself). For example, the Verb II [عَلَّمَ] means "to teach", while the Verb V [تَعَلَّمَ] from the same root means "to teach oneself" or "to learn". Similarly, [فَرَّقَ] means "to separate", while [تَفَرَّقَ] means to separate oneself.

In terms of structure, Verb Families V through X differ from the Present Tense stems of Verbs II, III, and IV as their first stem letter takes a Fatḥah. Verb V is also different from these three Verb families in that it's [ع] or next to last stem letter takes a Fatḥah (not a Kasrah). The Verbal Noun of Family V (and VI) is a bit different from the rest. Its structure is [تَفَعُّل] pattern, which is essentially the Past Tense stem form [تَفَعَّل] with its [ع] letter carrying the Ḍammah vowel. Another way in which Families V through X differ from the rest is in their conjugation of the Past **Passive** Tense. These Verb Families with stems of five letters or more contain **two Ḍammahs** in their Past Passive Tense conjugation. For example, the verb [اِسْتَغْفَرَ] becomes [أُسْتُغْفِرَ] whereas [اِجْتَنَبَ] becomes [أُجْتُنِبَ]. Here, in these cases, a Kasrah follows the second Ḍammah in keeping with the original conjugation found in Family I Verbs.

A. Verb Family V Conjugations

Table 48 – Verb Family V Conjugations

Verbal Noun المَصْدَر	Verbal Doer اسم الفاعل	Passive Noun اسم المفعول	Present Passive المُضارِع المَجْهول	Past Passive الماضي المَجْهول	Forbidding لا النَّهْيَة	Command اَلْفِعْلُ الْأَمْر	Present المُضارِع	Past الماضِي	Verb Family V Stem [تَفَعَّل]
تَكَبُّر	مُتَكَبِّر	مُتَكَبَّر	يُتَكَبَّر	تُكُبِّرَ	لا تَتَكَبَّرْ	تَكَبَّرْ	يَتَكَبَّرُ	تَكَبَّرَ	تَكَبَّرَ

B. Verb Family V examples from the Qur'ān and Ḥadīth

1. ﴿ ...وَإِنَّ مِنَ ٱلْحِجَارَةِ لَمَا يَتَفَجَّرُ مِنْهُ ٱلْأَنْهَارُ... ﴾
"...And indeed, there are stones out of which rivers gush forth ..." (2:74) [اَلْفِعْلُ الْماضي]

2. ﴿ ...فَيَتَعَلَّمُونَ مِنْهُمَا مَا يُفَرِّقُونَ بِهِ بَيْنَ ٱلْمَرْءِ وَزَوْجِهِ.. ﴾
"...And they learned from these two (angels) by what causes separation between man and his wife...." (2:102) [اَلْفِعْلُ الْماضي]

3. ﴿ يَا أَيُّهَا ٱلَّذِينَ آمَنُوا إِذَا قِيلَ لَكُمْ تَفَسَّحُوا فِي ٱلْمَجَالِسِ فَٱفْسَحُوا يَفْسَحِ ٱللَّهُ لَكُمْ... ﴾
"O you who have believed, when you are told, "Space yourselves" in assemblies, then make space; Allah will make space for you..." (2:102) [اَلْفِعْلُ الْأَمْر]

4. ﴿ خَيْرُكُمْ مَنْ تَعَلَّمَ الْقُرآنَ وَ عَلَّمَهُ ﴾
"The best of you is one who learns the Qur'ān and teaches it". (Bukhāri)[103] [اَلْفِعْلُ الْماضي]

5. ﴿ ...كَذَٰلِكَ يَطْبَعُ ٱللَّهُ عَلَىٰ كُلِّ قَلْبِ مُتَكَبِّرٍ جَبَّارٍ ﴾
"Thus does Allah seal over every heart [belonging to] an arrogant tyrant." (40:35) [اِسْمُ الْفاعِل]

---

103 Ṣaḥīḥ al-Bukhāri, Chapter on the Bounties of the Qur'ān: كتاب فضائل القرآن, Ḥadīth #4739.

C. Omission of Consecutive Tā from Verb Family V Conjugates

Please note that in the Present Tense or noun derivatives from Family V, one of the consecutive Tā's may be deleted. This usually occurs in conjugations of Second Person (which start with Tā).

➢ **Qur'ānic Examples**

1. ﴿ وَلَا بِقَوْلِ كَاهِنٍ قَلِيلًا مَّا تَذَكَّرُونَ ﴾
   "Nor the word of a soothsayer; little do you remember." (69:42)

Please note that the full conjugation of the underlined verb should have been [تَتَذَكَّرُونَ] without the omission of the beginning Tā.

2. ﴿ وَإِن كَانَ ذُو عُسْرَةٍ فَنَظِرَةٌ إِلَىٰ مَيْسَرَةٍ وَأَن تَصَدَّقُوا۟ خَيْرٌ لَّكُمْ إِن كُنتُمْ تَعْلَمُونَ ﴾
   "And if someone is in hardship, then [let there be] postponement until [a time of] ease. But if you give charity, then it is better for you, if you only knew." (2:280)

Please note that the full conjugation of the underlined verb should have been [تَتَصَدَّقوا] without the omission of the beginning Tā.

II. Verb Family VI [تَفاعَلَ/يَتَفاعَلُ]

Family VI is the reflexive of Family III, which represents the action done to oneself or the action done within. For example, Verb III [قاتَلَ] means "to fight" while Verb VI [تَقاتَلَ] means "to fight with one another". Likewise, Verb I [سَأَلَ] means "to ask", while the Verb VI [تَساءَلَ] means "to ask each other".

Family VI structure is essentially a Tā added to the beginning of the Family III Verb pattern [فاعَلَ]. However, unlike Family III, the Present Tense first letter stem in Family VI takes a Fatḥah. Thus, Family VI is similar to Family V in this regard. As a point of contrast with the other higher Verb Families, Verb Families V, VI, and IX maintain an [ع] Fatḥah (on second to last stem letter) instead of a Kasrah in their Present Tense conjugations. The Verbal Noun of Family V (like VI) is its stem Past Tense [تَفاعَلَ] pattern with a Ḍammah on its [ع] letter to form [تَفاعُلٌ].

A. Verb Family VI Conjugations

Table 49 – Verb Family VI Conjugations									
Verbal Noun المَصْدَر	Doer Noun اسم الفاعل	Passive Noun اسم المفعول	Present Passive المُضارِع المَجْهول	Past Passive الماضي المَجْهول	Forbidding لا النَّهِيَّة	Command اَلْفِعْلُ الْأَمْر	Present المُضارِع	Past الماضِي	Verb Family VI Stem [تَقاتَلَ]
تَكاثُرٌ	مُتَكاثِرٌ	مُتَكاثَرٌ	يُتَكاثَرُ	تُكُوثِرَ	لا تَتَكاثَرْ	تَكاثَرْ	يَتَكاثَرُ	تَكاثَرَ	تَكاثَرَ

B. Verb Family VI Examples from the Qur'ān

1. ﴿... وَلَا تَلْمِزُوا أَنفُسَكُمْ وَلَا تَنَابَزُوا بِٱلْأَلْقَابِ ...﴾

"...and do not defame one another, nor insult another by nicknames..." (49:11). [اَلْفِعْلُ الْماضي المَجْزوم]

2. ﴿... وَإِنْ تَعَاسَرْتُمْ فَسَتُرْضِعُ لَهُ أُخْرَى﴾

"...But if you disagree, then some other woman may suckle for him (65:6). [اَلْفِعْلُ الْماضي المجزوم]

3. ﴿... فَمَن لَّمْ يَجِدْ فَصِيَامُ شَهْرَيْنِ مُتَتَابِعَيْنِ تَوْبَةً مِّنَ ٱللّٰهِ...﴾

"....And whoso finds this beyond his means, he must fast for two consecutive months in order to seek repentance from Allah" (4:92). [اسم الفاعل]

III. Verb Family VII [يَنْفَعِلُ/اِنْفَعَلَ]

Verb Family VII represents Passive or intransitive actions that are done. Thus, verbs from this family are [لازِم], or Intransitive. For example, for the verb [كَسَرَ] that means, "to break", its VII derived form is [اِنْكَسَرَ], which means, "to be broken".

In terms of structure, the first two letters of the verb are [اِنْ]. Please note that this verb begins with Alif (not Hamzah) similar to Verb families VIII, IX, and X. Due to this, the Command Tense also begins with an Alif. In terms of the Verbal Noun pattern for this family, it is on the pattern of [اِنْفِعالٌ]. This pattern is obtained by taking the Past Tense stem pattern [اِنْفَعَلَ] and adding an Alif on the [ع] letter along with adding a Kasrah to the letter before the [ع]. This pattern is actually not a new pattern and perhaps you may recall that Verb Family IV also used this pattern as its Verbal Noun. The verb [أَفْعَلَ] becomes the Maṣdar [إِفْعالٌ]. This same Verbal Noun pattern is seen in Verb Families VIII, IX, and X respectively as we will inshā Allah soon see. Another variance that may be noted is Family VI Passive Past Tense structure. Here, the Past Tense stem [تَفَاعَلَ] becomes [تُفُوعِلَ]. The Alif becomes a Wāw because of Morphology (Ṣarf) rules.

A. Verb Family VII Conjugations

Table 50 – Verb Family VII Conjugations									
Verbal Noun المَصْدَر	Doer Noun اسم الفاعل	Passive Noun اسم المفعول	Present Passive المُضارِع المَجْهُول	Past Passive الماضي المَجْهُول	Forbidding لا النَّهِيَّة	Command اَلْفِعْلُ الْأَمْر	Present المُضارِع	Past الماضِي	Verb Family VII Stem [اِنْفَعَلَ]
اِنْكِسارٌ	مُنْكَسِرٌ	مُنْكَسَرٌ	يُنْفَطَرَ	أُنْكُسِرَ	لا تَنْكَسِرْ	اِنْكَسِرْ	يَنْكَسِرُ	اِنْكَسَرَ	اِنْكَسَر

B. Verb Family VII examples from the Qur'ān

1. ﴿... فَٱنۡفَجَرَتۡ مِنۡهُ ٱثۡنَتَا عَشۡرَةَ عَيۡنًا...﴾
"...then gushed forth therefrom twelve springs..." (2:60). [فعل ماضٍ]

2. ﴿ٱنطَلِقُوٓاْ إِلَىٰ مَا كُنتُم بِهِۦ تُكَذِّبُونَ﴾
"[They will be told], "Proceed to that which you used to deny" (77:29) [فعل أمر]

3. ﴿فَٱنطَلَقَا حَتَّىٰٓ إِذَا رَكِبَا فِي ٱلسَّفِينَةِ خَرَقَهَا...﴾
"So they both proceeded, till, when they embarked the ship, he (Khidr) scuttled it..." (18:71) [فعل ماضٍ]

IV. Verb Family VIII [يَفْتَعِلُ/اِفْتَعَلَ]

In this Verb Family, there is an Alif at the beginning, and there is a Tā is placed **between the [ف] and [ع] letters.** In terms of meaning, this family of verbs often is related to actions done for oneself. For example, the verb [كَسَبَ] means "to earn", while [اِكْتَسَبَ] means "to gain". In terms of Verbal Noun pattern, the Past Tense stem [اِفْتَعَلَ] is converted to [اِفْتِعَالٌ], which is similar to the pattern of Family VII.

A. Verb Family VIII Conjugations

Table 51 – Verb Family VIII Conjugations									
Verbal Noun المَصْدَر	Verbal Doer اسم الفاعل	Passive Noun اسم المفعول	Present Passive المُضارع المَجْهُول	Past Passive الماضي المَجْهُول	Forbidding لا النَّهْيَة	Command الْفِعْلُ الأَمْر	Present المُضارِع	Past الماضِي	Verb Family VIII Stem [اِفْتَعَلَ]
اِجْتِنابٌ	مُجْتَنِبٌ	مُجْتَنَبٌ	يُجْتَنَبُ	أُجْتُنِبَ	لا تَجْتَنِبْ	اِجْتَنِبْ	يَجْتَنِبُ	اِجْتَنَبَ	اِجْتَنَبَ

B. Verb Family VIII examples from the Qur'ān

1. ﴿وَإِذِ ٱعۡتَزَلۡتُمُوهُمۡ وَمَا يَعۡبُدُونَ إِلَّا ٱللَّهَ فَأۡوُۥٓاْ إِلَى ٱلۡكَهۡفِ...﴾
And when you withdraw from them, and that which they worship, except Allah, then seek refuge in the Cave... (18:16). [اَلْفِعْلُ الْماضِي]

2. ﴿..قِيلَ ٱرۡجِعُواْ وَرَآءَكُمۡ فَٱلۡتَمِسُواْ نُورٗا...﴾
"...It will be said, "Go back behind you and seek light..." (57:13). [اَلْفِعْلُ الأَمْر]

3. ﴿ إِنَّ ٱلْمُتَّقِينَ فِي جَنَّٰتٍ وَنَهَرٍ ۝ فِي مَقْعَدِ صِدْقٍ عِندَ مَلِيكٍ مُّقْتَدِرٍ ﴾

"Verily, the righteous will be in the midst of Gardens and Rivers. In a seat of truth, near the Omnipotent Sovereign (54:54-55). [اسم الفاعل]

V. Verb Family IX [يَفْعَلُّ/افْعَلَّ]

This form is used rarely in Arabic. It is often used to express colors and defects. Its structure is different from the rest of the Verb Family stems since it has a Shadda on its last letter.

A. Verb Family IX Conjugations

Table 52- Verb Family IX Conjugations									
Verbal Noun المَصْدَر	Verbal Doer اسم الفاعل	Passive Noun اسم المفعول	Present Passive المُضارِع المَجْهول	Past Passive الماضي المَجْهول	Forbidding لا النَّهِيَّة	Command[104] اَلْفِعْلُ الأَمْر	Present المُضارِع	Past الماضِي	Verb Family IX Stem [افْعَلَّ]
اِخْضِرارٌ	مُخْضَرٌّ	--	يُخْضَرُّ	أُخْضُرَّ	لا تَخْضَرَّ	اِخْضَرَّ	يَخْضَرُّ	اِخْضَرَّ	اِخْضَرَّ

B. Verb Family IX examples from the Qur'ān

﴿ يَوْمَ تَبْيَضُّ وُجُوهٌ وَتَسْوَدُّ وُجُوهٌ فَأَمَّا ٱلَّذِينَ ٱسْوَدَّتْ وُجُوهُهُمْ أَكَفَرْتُم بَعْدَ إِيمَٰنِكُمْ فَذُوقُوا۟ ٱلْعَذَابَ بِمَا كُنتُمْ تَكْفُرُونَ ﴾

"On the Day faces will turn white and [some] faces will turn black. As for those whose faces turn black, [to them it will be said], "Did you disbelieve after your belief? Then taste the punishment for what you used to reject.""(3:106) [اَلْفِعْلُ المُضارِع]

VI. Verb Family X [يَسْتَفْعِلُ/اِسْتَفْعَلَ]

Family X is frequently found in the Qur'ān and has six base letters in its stem Past Tense Third Person male form. This family contains the starting letters [اِسْت]. It often has the meaning of asking, or "to ask for". For example, [عَلِمَ] means to have knowledge, where [اِسْتَعْلَمَ] means to "ask for information" or in a sense to "ask for knowledge". The verb [غَفَرَ] means to forgive, while [اِسْتَغْفَرَ] means to "ask for forgiveness".

[104] There are three possible conjugations for the Command form due to the doubled last letter (with Shadda). The three possible conjugations are [اِخْضَرَّ], [اِخْضَرِّ], and [اِخْضَرِرْ].

A. Verb Family X Conjugations

Table 53 – Verb Family X Conjugations

المَصْدَر	اسم الفاعل	اسم المفعول	المُضارِع المَجْهُول	الماضي المجْهُول	لا النَّهِيَّة	اَلْفِعْلُ الأَمْر	المُضارِع	الماضِي	**Verb Family X** [اِسْتَفْعَلَ]
اِسْتِغْفارٌ	مُسْتَغْفِر	مُسْتَغْفَر	يُسْتَغْفَرُ	أُسْتُغْفِرَ	لا تَسْتَغْفِرْ	اِسْتَغْفِرْ	يَسْتَغْفِرُ	اِسْتَغْفَرَ	اِسْتَغْفَرَ

B. Verb Family X examples from the Qur'ān

1. ﴿ ...قَالَ أَتَسْتَبْدِلُونَ ٱلَّذِي هُوَ أَدْنَىٰ بِٱلَّذِي هُوَ خَيْرٌ...﴾

   ".....he said, "Would you exchange that which is better for that which is lower?..." (2:61). [اَلْفِعْلُ الْمُضارِع]

2. ﴿ .. وَقَالَ ٱلْمَلِكُ ٱئْتُونِي بِهِۦٓ أَسْتَخْلِصْهُ لِنَفْسِي...﴾

   "And the king said: "Bring him to me that I may appoint him for myself..." (12:54). [المَجْزوم اَلْفِعْلُ الْمُضارِع]

3. ﴿ آمِنُوا بِٱللَّهِ وَرَسُولِهِۦ وَأَنفِقُوا مِمَّا جَعَلَكُم مُّسْتَخْلَفِينَ فِيهِ ﴾

   "Believe in Allah and His Messenger, and spend of that whereof He has made you trustees..." (57:7) [اسم المفعول]

4. ﴿وَإِنِّي كُلَّمَا دَعَوْتُهُمْ لِتَغْفِرَ لَهُمْ جَعَلُوا أَصَابِعَهُمْ فِي آذَانِهِمْ وَٱسْتَغْشَوْا ثِيَابَهُمْ وَأَصَرُّوا وَٱسْتَكْبَرُوا ٱسْتِكْبَارًا ﴾

   "And indeed, every time I invited them that You may forgive them, they put their fingers in their ears, covered themselves with their garments, persisted, and were arrogant with [great] arrogance." (71:7)
   [فعل ماضٍ/فعل ماضٍ/المَصْدَر]

VII. Future Topics Covered in Volume Two of "Essentials of Qur'ānic Arabic"

All of what has been presented here in this Volume represents the core of Qur'ānic Arabic. Before the student goes further, it is paramount for them to review and master the grammar principles of this Volume. It is also important the the selected high yield vocabulary from the Qur'ān be memorized. The Second Volume of this series builds upon this knowledge, and teaches other principles that are essential to Qur'ānic Arabic studies. These include but are not limited to the following:

> **The Irregular Verbs, The Incomplete Verbs [كان / كاد / لَيْسَ], Important points from Morphology [الصرف], Review of Particles, the Naṣb Nouns [المَنْصُوبات], Exceptions [الإستثناء] and Negation, Methodology of Grammatically Analyzing Āyāt from the Qur'ān and Ḥadīth, Numbers and Warnings, and Examples of Qur'ānic Eloquence [البلاغة].**

Table 54 – Conjugation of the Ten Families

إِسْم المَفعول	إِسْم الفاعِل	المَصْدَر	مضارع مَجْهول	ماضي مَجْهول	لا النَّاهِيَّة	اَلْفِعْلُ الْأَمْر	الفِعْلُ المُضارِع	الفعلُ الماض	نَوْعُ الأَفْعال **Verb Family**
مَنْصُورٌ	ناصِرٌ	نَصْرٌ	يُنْصَرُ	نُصِرَ	لا تَنْصُرْ	أُنْصُرْ	يَنْصُرُ	نَصَرَ	فَعَلَ **I**
مُعَلَّمٌ	مُعَلِّمٌ	تَعْلِيمٌ	يُعَلَّمُ	عُلِّمَ	لا تُعَلِّمْ	عَلِّمْ	يُعَلِّمُ	عَلَّمَ	فَعَّلَ **II**
مُجاهَدٌ	مُجاهِدٌ	مُجاهَدَةٌ جِهَادٌ	يُجاهَدُ	جُوهِدَ	لا تُجاهِدْ	جَاهِدْ	يُجَاهِدُ	جَاهَدَ	فَاعَلَ **III**
مُنْزَلٌ	مُنْزِلٌ	إِنْزالٌ	يُنْزَلُ	أُنْزِلَ	لا تُنْزِلْ	أَنْزِلْ	يُنْزِلَ	أَنْزَلَ	أَفْعَلَ **IV**
مُتَكَبَّرٌ	مُتَكَبِّرٌ	تَكَبُّرٌ	يُتَكَبَّرُ	تُكُبِّرَ	لا تَتَكَبَّرْ	تَكَبَّرْ	يَتَكَبَّرُ	تَكَبَّرَ	تَفَعَّلَ **V**
مُتَكاثَرٌ	مُتَكاثِرٌ	تَكاثُرٌ	يُتَكاثَرُ	تُكُوثِرَ	لا تَتَكاثَرْ	تَكاثَرْ	يَتَكاثَرُ	تَكاثَرَ	تَفاعَلَ **VI**
--	مُنْكَسِرٌ	اِنكِسارٌ	يُنْكَسَرُ	أُنْكُسِرَ	لا تَنْكَسِرْ	اِنْكَسِرْ	يَنْكَسِرُ	اِنْكَسَرَ	اِنْفَعَلَ **VII**
مُجْتَنَبٌ	مُجْتَنِبٌ	اِجْتِنابٌ	يُجْتَنَبُ	أُجْتُنِبَ	لا تَجْتَنِبْ	اِجْتَنِبْ	يَجْتَنِبُ	اِجْتَنَبَ	اِفْتَعَلَ **VIII**
--	مُبْيَضٍّ	اِبْيِضاضٌ	يُبْيَضُّ	أُبْيِضَّ	لا تَبْيَضّ	اِبْيَضِضْ	يَبْيَضُّ	اِبْيَضَّ	اِفْعَلَّ **IX**
مُسْتَغْفَرٌ	مُسْتَغْفِرٌ	اِسْتِغْفارٌ	يُسْتَغْفَرُ	أُسْتُغْفِرَ	لا تَسْتَغْفِرْ	اِسْتَغْفِرْ	يَسْتَغْفِرُ	اِسْتَغْفَرَ	اِسْتَفْعَلَ **X**

Required Vocabulary Assignments for Qur'ānic Arabic

1. **Alongside each lesson, "high-yield" vocabulary from the Qur'ān listed on the vocabulary sheet "80% of Qur'ānic Vocabulary" should be memorized. It is available for free access on the website** http://emuslim.com/quran/English80.asp. **Here, it has been adapted on pages 152 - 165 and pages 170-182.**
2. **Another supplementary vocabulary list is detailed on pages 166-169 and on page 183 that need to be learned along with the former mentioned list.**
3. **Memorization of high-yield Qur'ānic vocabulary is essential for understanding the Qur'ān.**

Table 55: Qur'ānic Vocabulary Assignments		
Required Vocabulary	80% of Qur'ānic Vocabulary Handout	Supplemental Qur'ānic Vocabulary (pgs. 166-169, 183)
Lesson 1 (a- b) ***NOUNS***	pgs. 152-153	----
Lesson 2 (a-d)	pgs. 154-157	pg. 166
Lesson 3 (a- b)	pgs. 158-159	pg. 167
Lesson 4 (a- d)	pgs. 160-163	pg. 168
Lesson 5 (a-b)	pgs. 164-165	pg. 169
Lesson 6	Review pgs. 152 - 159	review pg. 166-167
Lesson 7	Review pgs. 160 - 165	review pg. 168-169
Lesson 8 (a-b) ***VERBS***	pgs. 170-171 (focus on the two right columns)	---
Lesson 9 (a-d)	pgs. 172-175 (focus on the two right columns)	---
Lesson 10	Review pgs. 170 - 175	---
Lesson 11	pgs. 170 - 175 (focus on the two left columns)	---
Lesson 12 (a-d)	pgs. 176 – 179	---
Lesson 13 (a-d)	pgs. 180 - 182	pg. 183

I. Qur'ānic Vocabulary – Nouns

A. Lesson 1 Vocabulary (part a)

Prophets and ...			Allah's Signs...		
Messenger	(pl رُسُل) رَسُول	332	sign	(pl آيَات) آيَة	382
Prophet	(أَنبِيَاء) نَبِيّ	75	evidence	(pl بَيِّنَات) بَيِّنَة	71
Prophets	نَبِيُّون، نَبِيِّين، أَنْبِيَاء		Qur'an; reading, recitation	قُرْآن	70
	آدَم نُوح إِبْرَاهِيم	137	cattle	أَنْعَام	32
	لُوط إِسْمَاعِيل إِسْحَاق	56	mountain	(pl جِبَال) جَبَل	39
	يَعْقُوب (إِسْرَائِيل) يُوسُف	86	sea; large river	(بِحَار/أَبْحُر) بَحْر	38
	هُود شُعَيْب صَالِح	30	sun	(شُمُوس) شَمْس	33
	مُوسَى عِيسَى ابنُ مَرْيَم	195	moon	(أَقْمَار) قَمَر	33
Satan (pl	شَيَاطِين) شَيْطَان	88	night	(لَيَال) لَيْل	80
Pharaoh	(فَرَاعِنَة) فِرْعَوْن	74	day	(أَنْهُر) نَهَار	57
People of Hud (pbuh)	عَاد	24	earth	(أَرَاضٍ) أَرْض	461
People of Salih (pbuh)	ثَمُود	26	sky (pl	سَمَاوَات) سَمَاء	310

Adapted from "80% of Quranic Vocabulary", page 9 by 'Abdul-Raḥeem 'Abdul-'Azeez available for free download at http://emuslim.com/quran/english80.asp.

B. Lesson 1 Vocabulary (part b)

Last day, ...					
companion, fellow	صَاحِب (أَصْحَاب)	94	forever; ever	أَبَدًا	28
end	عَاقِبَة (عواقِب)	32	reward	أَجْر (أُجُور *pl*)	105
torment	عَذَاب (عَذابات)	322	term	أَجَل (آجال)	52
chastisement (as a result of sin)	عِقَاب	20	the Hereafter	اَلْآخِرَة	115
Resurrection	قِيَامَة	70	painful	أَلِيم	72
meeting	لِقَاء (لِقاءات)	24	reward	ثَوَاب	13
fixed	مُسَمًّى (مُسَمَّات)	21	hellfire	جَحِيم	26
fire	نَار (نيران)	145	reward	جَزَاء	42
river	نَهَر (أَنْهَار *pl*)	54	garden	جَنَّة (جَنَّات *pl*)	147
woe unto ...	وَيْل	40	the Hell	جَهَنَّم	77
day	يَوْم (أَيَّام *pl*)	393	reckoning	حِسَاب (حِسابات)	39
that day	يَوْمَئِذٍ	70	hour (day of resurrection)	سَاعَة (ساعات)	47

Adapted from "80% of Quranic Vocabulary", page 10 by 'Abdul-Raḥeem 'Abdul-'Azeez available for free download at http://emuslim.com/quran/english80.asp.

C. Lesson 2 Vocabulary (part a)

Deen, …			Faith, …		
matter; affair	أَمْر (أُمُور *pl*)	*13*	one	أَحَد (إِحْدَى *fg*)	85
piety; fear; protection	تَقْوَى	17	god; deity	إِله (آلِهَة *pl*)	*34*
truth, true; right	حَقّ (حُقوق)	247	partner, associate	شَرِيك(شُرَكَاء *pl*)	40
falsehood	بَاطِل	26	witness	شَهَادَة (شَهادات)	26
wisdom	حِكْمَة (حِكَم)	20	throne	عَرْش (عُرُوش)	26
praise	حَمْد	43	unseen, hidden	عَهْد (عُهُود)	29
religion; law; judgement	دِين (أَدْيان)	92	unseen	غَيْب (غُيُوب)	49
poor-due, charity	زَكَاة (زَكَوَات)	32	book	كِتَاب (كُتُب *pl*)	261
witness, present	شَهِيد (شُهَدَاء *pl*)	56	word	كَلِمَة (كَلِمات)	42
prayer	صَلَاة (صَلَوَات)	83	angel	مَلَك (مَلَائِكَة *pl*)	88
clear, self-expressive	مُبِين	119	covenant, treaty	مِيثَاق (مَوَاثِيق)	25
light	نُور (أَنْوَار)	43	one	وَاحِد (وَاحِدَة *fg*)	61

*Adapted from "80% of Quranic Vocabulary", page 11 by 'Abdul-Raḥeem 'Abdul-'Azeez
available for free download at http://emuslim.com/quran/english80.asp.*

D. Lesson 2 Vocabulary (part b)

Deeds, …			Blessings, …		
actions, deeds, works	أَعْمَال *pl* (عَمَل)	41	favors	آلَاء *pl*	34
good (deed)	حَسَنَة (*pl* حَسَنَات)	31	authority; warrant	سُلْطَان (سَلاطِين)	37
evil, bad	سَيِّئَة (*pl* سَيِّئَات)	68	grace	فَضْل (فُضُول)	84
good, better	خَيْر (خِيَار)	186	water	مَاء (مِيَاه)	63
evil, bad, worse	شَرّ (شُرُور)	29	dominion, reign	مُلْك	48
sin	إِثْم (آثَام)	35	favor	نِعْمَة (نِعَم)	37
sin	ذَنْب (*pl* ذُنُوب)	37	all	أَجْمَعُون، أَجْمَعِين	26
sin	جُنَاح	25	permission	إِذْن (أُذُون)	39
unlawful	حَرَام (حُرُم)	26	punishment; power; adversity	بَأْس	25
name	اِسْم (*pl* أَسْمَاء)	27	all, everybody	جَمِيع	53
discourse; speech	حَدِيث (أَحَادِيث)	23	same; equal; level; fair	سَوَاء	27
good	طَيِّبَة (*pl* طَيِّبَات)	30	party, group	فَرِيق (فُرَقَاء)	33

Adapted from "80% of Quranic Vocabulary", page 12 by 'Abdul-Raḥeem 'Abdul-'Azeez available for free download at http://emuslim.com/quran/english80.asp.

E. Lesson 2 Vocabulary (part c)

Relatives, ...			Self (body parts ...)		
mother	أُمّ (pl أُمَّهَات)	35	face	وَجْه (pl وُجُوه)	72
father	أَب، أَبَت (pl آبَاء)	117	eye; spring	عَيْن (pl أَعْيُن عُيُون)	47
wife; husband	زَوْج (pl أَزْوَاج)	76	sights	أَبْصَار pl (بَصَر)	38
man	رَجُل (pl رِجَال)	57	mouths	أَفْوَاه pl (فَم)	21
woman	امْرَأَة (pl نِسَاء)	83	tongue; language	لِسَان (pl أَلْسِنَة)	25
child	وَلَد (pl أَوْلَاد)	56	heart	قَلْب (pl قُلُوب)	132
father	وَالِد (dl وَالِدَيْن)	20	breast	صَدْر (pl صُدُور)	44
descendants; children	ذُرِّيَّة (ذُرِّيَّات)	32	hand	يَد (pl أَيْدِي)	118
son	ابْن	41	foot	رِجْل (pl أَرْجُل)	15
sons	(pl. بَنُون، بَنِين، أَبْنَاء	22	soul	نَفْس (pl أَنْفُس)	293
brother	أَخ (أَخُو، أَخَا، أَخِي	67	soul; spirit	رُوح (أَرْوَاح)	21
brothers	إِخْوَان pl	22	power, strength	قُوَّة (قُوًى)	28

Adapted from "80% of Quranic Vocabulary", page 13 by 'Abdul-Raḥeem 'Abdul-'Azeez available for free download at http://emuslim.com/quran/english80.asp.

F. Lesson 2 Vocabulary (part d)

World, ...				People, ...			
house	(pl بُيُوت)	بَيْت	64	community	(pl أُمَم)	أُمَّة	64
abode	(pl دِيَار)	دَار	48	people	(أَقْوَام)	قَوْم	383
world	(دُنًى)	دُنْيَا	115	man		اِنْسَان	65
way	(pl سُبُل)	سَبِيل	176	men, people		نَاس	248
path	(صُرُط)	صِرَاط	46	male	(pl ذُكُور)	ذَكَر	16
world	(pl عَالَمِين)	عَالَم	73	female	(pl إِنَاث)	أُنْثَى	30
trial; persecution	(فِتَن)	فِتْنَة	34	slave	(pl عِبَاد)	عَبْد	126
town	(pl قُرًى)	قَرْيَة	57	enemy	(pl أَعْدَاء)	عَدُوّ	44
wealth	(pl أَمْوَال)	مَال	86	disbelievers	(كَافِر)sg pl	كُفَّار	21
provision; enjoyment	(أَمْتِعَة)	مَتَاع	34	criminal	(مُجْرِمُون)	مُجْرِم	52
mosque	(pl مَسَاجِد)	مَسْجِد	28	chiefs, leaders		مَلَأ	22
place; abode	(مَكَانَة)	مَكَان	32	protecting friend; guardian	(أَوْلِيَاء)	وَلِيّ	86

Adapted from "80% of Quranic Vocabulary", page 14 by 'Abdul-Raḥeem 'Abdul-'Azeez available for free download at http://emuslim.com/quran/english80.asp.

G. Lesson 3 Vocabulary (part a)

This, that...!			No, No!!!		
this	(هَٰؤُلاء) *mg*	هٰذَا	(There is) no god		لَا إِلٰهَ
that	(أُلائِكَ) *mg*	ذٰلِكَ	except Allah		إِلَّا اللهُ
this	(هَٰؤُلاء) *fg*	هٰذِهِ	never, certainly not		كَلَّا
that	*fg*	تِلْكَ	not	*(for future)*	لَنْ
these	*mg/fg*	هٰؤُلَاءِ	not	*(for past)*	لَمْ
those	*mg/fg*	أُولٰئِكَ	not		مَا
he who	(الَّذِينَ) *mg*	الَّذِي	not	*(fg* (لَيْسَتْ)	لَيْسَ
she who	(الَّتِي) *fg*	الَّتِي	yes, indeed		بَلَى
those who	*mg*	الَّذِينَ	not, other than		غَيْرَ
these	*(for br.pl)*	هٰذِهِ	besides, less than		دُونَ
those	*(for br.pl)*	تِلْكَ	except, unless, if not		إِلَّا
those who	*(for br.pl)*	الَّتِي	yes		نَعَمْ

Adapted from "80% of Quranic Vocabulary", page 1 by 'Abdul-Raḥeem 'Abdul-'Azeez available for free download at http://emuslim.com/quran/english80.asp.

H. Lesson 3 Vocabulary (part b)

Whose? ←Pronouns→ Who?					
his	*mg*	...هٗ	He	*mg*	هُوَ
their	*mg*	...هُمْ	Them	*mg*	هُمْ
your	*mg*	...كَ	you	*mg*	أَنْتَ
Yours truly,	*mg*	...كُمْ	you all	*mg*	أَنْتُم
my	(me نِي) for verbs only	...يْ	I	*mg/fg*	أَنَا
us	for verbs only *mg/fg*	...نَا	We	*mg/fg*	نَحْنُ
her	*fg*	...هَا	She	*fg*	هِيَ
their	*fg*	...هُنَّ	They	*fg*	هُنَّ
Yours truly,	*fg*	...كِ	you	*fg*	أَنْتِ
their	*(for br.pl)*	...هَا	they	*(for br.pl)*	هِيَ
their	*dl*	...هُمَا	those two	*dl*	هُمَا
your	*dl*	...كُمَا	you two	*dl*	أَنْتُمَا

Adapted from "80% of Quranic Vocabulary", page 2 by 'Abdul-Raḥeem 'Abdul-'Azeez available for free download at http://emuslim.com/quran/english80.asp.

I. Lesson 4 Vocabulary (part a)

Where?		Questions!?	
above, up	فَوْقَ	what?, that which	مَا
under	تَحْتَ	who?, the one who	مَنْ
in front of	بَيْنَ أَيْدَي، بَيْنَ يَدَيْ	when?, the time when	مَتَى
back, after	خَلْفَ	where?	أَيْنَ
in front of	أَمَامَ	how?	كَيْفَ
behind	وَرَاء	how many?	كَمْ
right; oath	يَمِين (أَيْمَان *pl*)	which?	أَيٌّ
left	شِمَال (شَمَائِل *pl*)	wherefrom?, why?	أَنَّى
between	بَيْنَ	Is? Am? Are? Do? Have?	أَ، هَل
around	حَوْلَ	what?	مَاذَا
wherever	حَيْثُ	why?	لِمَ، لِمَاذَا
wherever	أَيْنَمَا	if not, why not	لَوْ لَا

Adapted from "80% of Quranic Vocabulary", page 3 by 'Abdul-Raḥeem 'Abdul-'Azeez available for free download at http://emuslim.com/quran/english80.asp.

J. Lesson 4 Vocabulary (part b)

Miscellaneous		When?, …	
endowed with; owner *mg*	ذُو، ذَا، ذِي	before (in terms of time)	قَبْلَ
endowed with; owner *fg*	ذَاتُ	after (in terms of time)	بَعْدَ
people of; owners of	أُوْلُوا، أُوْلِي	time, period, at the time of	حِينَ
people of; relatives (أهالٍ)	أَهْلٌ	when *(for past)*	إِذْ
family, relatives, people	آلٌ	when *(for future)*	إِذَا
lo!; do not…, will not…	أَلَا	then	ثُمَّ
what an excellent	نِعْمَ	then, thus, therefore	فَ
what an evil	بِئْسَ	nay, -- rather, but, however	بَلْ
evil is that which	بِئْسَمَا	near, with	عِنْدَ، لَدى، لَدُنْ
sth similar	مِثْلٌ	nothing but	إِنْ … إِلَّا
similitude (*pl* أَمْثَالٌ)	مَثَلٌ	nothing but	مَا … إِلَّا
than the one who; from those who (مِنْ+مَنْ)	مِمَّنْ	that..not; so as not to (أَنْ+لَا)	أَلَّا

Adapted from "80% of Quranic Vocabulary", page 4 by 'Abdul-Raḥeem 'Abdul-'Azeez available for free download at http://emuslim.com/quran/english80.asp.

K. Lesson 4 Vocabulary (part c)

	Prepositions	←Ḥarf Jarr→	Prepositions	
	with what; because	بِمَا	with, in, from,…	بِ
	about what	عَمَّا	about	عَنْ
	in what	فِيمَا	in	فِي
	as, just as	كَمَا	as, like	كَ
	for what / that which	لِمَا	for	لِ، لَ
	out of what	مِمَّا	from	مِنْ
	as to, as for	أَمَّا	towards	إِلَى
	if; either / or	إِمَّا	by (of oath)	تَ (بِ)
	that	أَنَّمَا	until	حَتَّى
Not from Ḥarf	verily; is but/only	إِنَّمَا	on	عَلَى
	as if	كَأَنَّمَا	with	مَعَ
	whenever	كُلَّمَا	and; by (of oath)	وَ

Adapted from "80% of Quranic Vocabulary", page 5 by 'Abdul-Raḥeem 'Abdul-'Azeez available for free download at http://emuslim.com/quran/english80.asp.

L. Lesson 4 Vocabulary (part d)

Prefix for verb, ...		Inna ...	
has (with مَاضِي); surely (with مضارع)	قَدْ (فعل+)	verily, truly	إِنَّ
will (for near future)	سَ (فعل+)	that	أَنَّ
will (for future)	سَوْفَ (فعل+)	as if	كَأَنَّ
will surely	لَ+فعل+نَّ	but, however	لٰكِنَّ (لٰكِنْ)
indeed	لَقَدْ (فعل+)	perhaps, may be	لَعَلَّ
indeed, surely	لَ	that/to (Ḥarf Naṣb for Verbs)	أَنْ
let sb do (imperative) (Harf Jazm for Verbs)	لِ، لْ (أَمْر)	if (Ḥarf Jazm for Verbs)	إِنْ
the	الْ	alone/only (attached to a pronoun)	إِيَّا
or?	أَمْ	possibly /perhaps	عَسَى
or	أَوْ	when	لَمَّا (مَتَى)
some of	بَعْض	if	لَوْ
everyone; all	كُلّ (كِلا both)	O! (Particle of Calling)	يَا، يَاأَيُّهَا

Lām of Emphasis (left side label)   *Inna and its Sisters* (right side label)

Adapted from "80% of Quranic Vocabulary", page 6 by 'Abdul-Raḥeem 'Abdul-'Azeez
available for free download at http://emuslim.com/quran/english80.asp.

M. Lesson 5 Vocabulary (part a)

Superlative Adjectives Transitive[105]	Derived Adjectives Intransitive[106]

صِيغَة مُبالَغة & صِفَة مُشَبَّهَة (of Allah and others')					
knowing, ever aware	خَبِير	45	first	أَوَّل (أُولَى *fg*)	82
Nice, gentle, gracious	لَطِيف		last	آخِر (آخِرَة *fg*)	40
Compassionate	رَحْمن	57	other	آخَر (أُخْرَى *fg*)	65
peace	سَلَام	42	trustworthy	أَمِين	14
one who listens	سَمِيع	47	one who sees clearly	بَصِير	53
grateful	شَكُور	24	far	بَعِيد	25
mighty	عَزِيز	99	most forgiving	تَوَّاب	11
most forgiving	غَفُور	91	protector	حَفِيظ	26
All-powerful	قَدِير	45	wise	حَكِيم	97
warner	نَذِير	44	forbearing	حَلِيم	15
strong helper	نَصِير	24	praiseworthy	حَمِيد	17
one who takes care of a thing for another	وَكِيل	24	warm (friend); boiling water	حَمِيم	20

Adapted from "80% of Quranic Vocabulary", page 7 by 'Abdul-Raḥeem 'Abdul-'Azeez
available for free download at http://emuslim.com/quran/english80.asp

105 This intensive derivative called [صِفَةُ المُبالَغة] indicates excess, or intensive meaning of an action. Here, the excess meaning is limited to itself without taking others into consideration unlike [إسْمُ التَّفْضِيل].

106 The [الصِفَة المُشَبَّهَة] is different from the Doer noun [إسْمُ الفاعل] in that it is more permanent, and is a fixed attribute. There are several stem patterns of [الصِفَة المُشَبَّهَة], the most common is the stem [فَعِيلٌ]. This topic is discussed in more detail in Volume 2.

N. Lesson 5 Vocabulary (part b)

				Derived Adjectives Intransitive		**Superlative Adjectives Transitive**	
Superlative/ Comparative Nouns	**اسم تَفْضِيل**			**صِفَة مُشَبَّهَة & صِيغَة مُبالَغة**			
most severe	أَشَدّ	31	severe; strong		شَدِيد	52
higher, superior	أَعْلَى	11	high, exalted		عَلِيّ	11
better-knowing, more informed	أَعْلَم	49	knower		عَلِيم	162
nearer	أَقْرَب	19	near		قَرِيب	26
bigger	أَكْبَر	23	big	(fg كَبِيرَة)	كَبِير	44
more; most	أَكْثَر	80	plenty; much	(fg كَثِيرَة)	كَثِير	74
better	أَحْسَن	36	quick; swift; fast		سَرِيع	10
more entitled; more worthy	أَحَقّ	10	merciful		رَحِيم	182
nearer; more likely; lower; less	أَدْنَى	12	supreme		عَظِيم	107
more unjust	أَظْلَم	16	little	(fg قَلِيلَة)	قَلِيل	71
better guided	أَهْدَى	7	noble; honorable; generous		كَرِيم	27
nearer, closer; woe	أَوْلَى	11				

Adapted from "80% of Quranic Vocabulary", page 8 by 'Abdul-Raḥeem 'Abdul-'Azeez available for free download at http://emuslim.com/quran/english80.asp.

O. Supplementary Vocabulary - Part A

مُفْرَد	جَمْع	مُفْرَد	جَمْع	مُفْرَد	جَمْع	مُفْرَد	جَمْع
خُطْوَة	خُطُوات	خَطِيئَة	خَطايا/خَطِيئات	قَرِين	قُرَناء	كَلْب	كِلاب
footstep		fault, sin		close friend		dog	
كَوْكَب	كَواكِب	مِيقات	مَواقِيت	كَسْلان	كُسالَى	رَأْس	رُؤُوس
star		appointment; meeting point		lazy		head	
ثَمْرَة	ثَمَرات	رَجاء	----	قَلَم	أَقْلام	قَرن	قُرون
fruit		hoping		pen		generation	
فِئَة	فِئات	قَدَم	أَقْدام	شَهْر	أَشْهُر	ظِلّ	ظِلال
group		step; foot		month		shade	
أَذًى	----	لَهْو	----	لَعِب	----	رِجْس	----
injury, harm		entertainment		play; amusement		filth, impure	
مِحْراب	مَحارِيب	نِداء	----	صادِق	صادِقون	مَصِير	مَصائِر
private chamber		call		truthful person		destination	
مَدِينَة	مُدُن/مَدائِن	صَيْحَة	صَيْحات	فَرِيضَة	فَرائِض	مُخْلِص	مُخْلِصُون
city		shout		requirement		sincere	
نَخْلَة	نَخْل/نَخِيل	رَحْل	رِحال	سَعْيًا/السَّعْي	--	ضَرّ	أَضْرار
date-palm		bag		effort		injury; harm	
مِيزان	مَوازِين	مَرَّة	مَرّات	يَتِيم	يَتامَى	شَأْن	شُؤُون
balance; scale		one time		orphan		matter; affair	

P. Supplementary Vocabulary - Part B

مُفرَد	جَمْع		مُفرَد	جَمْع		مُفرَد	جَمْع		مُفرَد	جَمْع	
فاسِق	فاسِقون	open sinner	كَيْل	أَكْيال	measure	سَبَب	أَسْباب	course, means, way	مِرارًا	----	repeatedly
فُؤَاد	أَفْئِدَة	heart	جديد	جُدُد	new	عِبْرَة	عِبَر	admonition	سِرّ	أَسْرار	happiness
مَوْعِظَة	مَواعِظ	admonition	صَعيد	صُعُد	earth, soil	نُسُك	----	sacrifice	أُذُن	آذان	ear
رَيب	---	doubt	نَبات	نَباتات	vegetation; plant	عَظْم	عِظام	bone	أُمْنِيَة	أَمانِيّ	false hope
هُدًى	---	guidance	أَعْمى	عُمْيٌ	blind	مَقْبَرَة	مَقابِر	grave	أَنْف	أُنوف	nose
جَمَل	جِمال / إبِل	camel	غالِب	غالِبُون	dominant/ victorious	بَرِيء	----	innocent	أَبْكَم	بُكْم	dumb
ذَهَب	--	gold	أَثَر	آثار	trace, footsteps, tracks	بَطْن	بُطُون	stomach	أُسْطورة	أَساطير	tale; story
بُرْهان	بَراهين	evidence	أَرِيكَة	أَرائِك	throne	طَعام	أَطْعِمَة	food	أَسْوَد/سَوداء	سُودٌ	black
مِسْكين	مَساكين	poor person	مَوْقِع	مَواقِع	place	غُلام	غِلْمان/غِلمَة	servant; boy	إِصْبَع	أَصابِع	finger
فِضَّة	---	silver	نِدّ	أَنْداد	partner	مَريض	مَرْضَى	sick person	راهِب	رُهْبان	monk

Q. Supplementary Vocabulary - Part C

مُفْرَد	جَمْع	Meaning	مُفْرَد	جَمْع	Meaning	مُفْرَد	جَمْع	Meaning	مُفْرَد	جَمْع	Meaning
نَذْر	نُذُور	vow	نَجْم	نُجوم	star	مُحضَر	مُحْضَرُون	one brought/presented	بَرّ	أَبْرار	righteous person
شَعْب	شُعوب	nation/people	حِزْب	أَحْزاب	party	مَلِك	مُلوك	king	غُرْفَة	غُرَف/غُرُفات	room; quarter
عَقِب	أَعْقاب	end	صَوْت	أَصْوات	voice	جِدار	جُدُر	wall	لُبّ	أَلْباب	intellect
مُخْتَلِف	مُخْتَلِفُوب	differing/varying	خَبَر	أَخْبار	news	جِسْم	أَجْسام	body	دابَّة	دَواب	creature (4-legged)
ثَوْب	ثِياب	clothes; garment	خَزانَة	خَزائِن	treasure	حُلم	أَحْلام	dream	دُبُر	أَدْبار	back
جِلد	جُلود	skin	خَفيف	خِفاف	light (in weight)	حِمار	حَمير / حُمُر	donkey	دَرَجَة	دَرَجات	level
جَنْب	جُنوب	side	خَليل	أَخِلَّاء	close friend	حَمْل	أَحْمال	load; burden	----	أَعْراب	nomad, bedouin
جُنْد	جُنود	army	دَمْع	دُموع	tear	حور	حَوراء	maiden of paradise	رَقَبَة	رِقاب	neck; slave
ثِقْل	أَثْقال	load; burden	دَم	دِماء	blood	حَبْل	حِبال	rope	رِيح	رِياح	wind; smell

R. Supplemental Vocabulary – Part D

مُفْرَد	جَمْع		مُفْرَد	جَمْع		مُفْرَد	جَمْع		مُفْرَد	جَمْع	
حَدّ	حُدود	limit	ظَهْر	ظُهور	back	سِبْط	أَسْباط	tribe	عَلِيم	عُلَماء	knowledgeable
نَجْوى	نَجاوى	secret talk/counsel	مُسْتَقَرّ	----	dwelling place, abode	سَرير	سُرُر	bed; couch	عَمّ	أَعْمام	paternal uncle
سِلسِلَة	سلاسِل	chain	نَخْلَة	نَخْل/نَخيل	date-palm	عُسْر	----	difficulty, hardship	عِماد	عَمَد	pillar
سُورة	سُوَر	chapter from al-Qur'ān	صَحيفَة	صُحُف	page	شَرْط	أَشْراط	condition; sign	عِنَب	أَعْناب	grape
فاكِهَة	فَواكِه	fruit	طَريقة	طَرائِق	way; path	بَغْيًا/البَغْيُ	----	envy, rebellion, oppression	عُنُق	أَعْناق	neck
شاعِر	شُعَراء	poet	عَقْد	عُقُود	covenant; pact	شَيْخ	شُيُوخ	old man	شِيعَة	شِيَع	sect
صَنَم	أَصْنام	idol	غَمامَة	غَمام	cloud	قِنطار	قَناطير	large amount (of gold)	كَنْز	كُنُوز	treasure
سَحابَة	سَحاب	cloud	شَفيع	شُفَعاء	intercessor	عام	أَعْوام	year	غُرور	----	deception

II. Qur'ānic Vocabulary – Verbs

A. Lesson 8 Vocabulary (part a)

	Verbal Noun	Doer Noun	Command tense	Present tense (fathah)	Past tense (fathah)	
to do	فِعْل	فَاعِل	اِفْعَلْ	يَفْعَلُ	فَعَلَ	105
to open, to give victory	فَتْح	فَاتِح	اِفْتَحْ	يَفْتَحُ	فَتَحَ	29
to raise; to resurrect	بَعْث	بَاعِث	اِبْعَثْ	يَبْعَثُ	بَعَثَ	65
to make, to place, to set up	جَعْل	جَاعِل	اِجْعَلْ	يَجْعَلُ	جَعَلَ	346
to gather, to collect	جَمْع	جَامِع	اِجْمَعْ	يَجْمَعُ	جَمَعَ	40
to go	ذَهَاب	ذَاهِب	اِذْهَبْ	يَذْهَبُ	ذَهَبَ	35
to raise	رَفْع	رَافِع	اِرْفَعْ	يَرْفَعُ	رَفَعَ	28
to enchant, to bewitch	سِحْر	سَاحِر	اِسْحَرْ	يَسْحَرُ	سَحَرَ	49
to act righteously	مَصْلَحَة	صَالِح	اِصْلَحْ	يَصْلَحُ	صَلَحَ	131
to curse	لَعْن	لَاعِن	اِلْعَنْ	يَلْعَنُ	لَعَنَ	27
to profit	نَفْع	نَافِع	اِنْفَعْ	يَنْفَعُ	نَفَعَ	42

Adapted from "80% of Quranic Vocabulary", page 15 by 'Abdul-Raḥeem 'Abdul-'Azeez available for free download at http://emuslim.com/quran/english80.asp.

B. Lesson 8 Vocabulary (part b)

	Verbal Noun	Doer Noun	Command tense	Present tense (dammah)	Past tense (fathah)	
	فِعْل	فَاعِل	اُفْعُلْ	يَفْعُلُ	فَعَلَ	
to help; to deliver	نَصْر	نَاصِر	اُنْصُرْ	يَنْصُرُ	نَصَرَ	92
to reach	بُلُوغ	بَالِغ	اُبْلُغْ	يَبْلُغُ	بَلَغَ	49
to leave	تَرْك	تَارِك	اُتْرُكْ	يَتْرُكُ	تَرَكَ	43
to gather; to bring together	حَشْر	حَاشِر	اُحْشُرْ	يَحْشُرُ	حَشَرَ	43
to judge; to rule	حُكْم	حَاكِم	اُحْكُمْ	يَحْكُمُ	حَكَمَ	80
to come out	خُرُوج	خَارِج	اُخْرُجْ	يَخْرُجُ	خَرَجَ	61
to live forever	خُلُود	خَالِد	اُخْلُدْ	يَخْلُدُ	خَلَدَ	83
to create out of nothing	خَلْق	خَالِق	اُخْلُقْ	يَخْلُقُ	خَلَقَ	248
to enter	دُخُول	دَاخِل	اُدْخُلْ	يَدْخُلُ	دَخَلَ	78
to remember	ذِكْر	ذَاكِر	اُذْكُرْ	يَذْكُرُ	ذَكَرَ	163
to provide	رِزْق	رَازِق	اُرْزُقْ	يَرْزُقُ	رَزَقَ	122

Adapted from "80% of Quranic Vocabulary", page 16 by 'Abdul-Raḥeem 'Abdul-'Azeez available for free download at http://emuslim.com/quran/english80.asp.

C. Lesson 9 Vocabulary (part a)

	Verbal Noun	Doer Noun	Command tense	Present tense (dammah)	Past tense (fathah)	
to prostrate	سُجُود	سَاجِد	اُسْجُدْ	يَسْجُدُ	سَجَدَ	49
to perceive	شُعُور	شَاعِر	اُشْعُرْ	يَشْعُرُ	شَعَرَ	29
to be grateful	شُكْر	شَاكِر	اُشْكُرْ	يَشْكُرُ	شَكَرَ	63
to be true; to say the truth	صِدْق	صَادِق	اُصْدُقْ	يَصْدُقُ	صَدَقَ	89
to worship; to serve	عِبَادَة	عَابِد	اُعْبُدْ	يَعْبُدُ	عَبَدَ	143
to transgress	فِسْق،	فَاسِق	اُفْسُقْ	يَفْسُقُ	فَسَقَ	54
to kill; to slay	قَتْل	قَاتِل	اُقْتُلْ	يَقْتُلُ	قَتَلَ	93
to sit; to remain behind	قُعُود	قَاعِد	اُقْعُدْ	يَقْعُدُ	قَعَدَ	23
to prescribe; to write	كِتَابَة	كَاتِب	اُكْتُبْ	يَكْتُبُ	كَتَبَ	56
to disbelieve; to be ungrateful	كُفْر	كَافِر	اُكْفُرْ	يَكْفُرُ	كَفَرَ	461
to plot	مَكْر	مَاكِر	اُمْكُرْ	يَمْكُرُ	مَكَرَ	43
to look; to wait	نَظَر	نَاظِر	اُنْظُرْ	يَنْظُرُ	نَظَرَ	*95*

Adapted from "80% of Quranic Vocabulary", page 17 by 'Abdul-Raḥeem 'Abdul-'Azeez available for free download at http://emuslim.com/quran/english80.asp.

D. Lesson 9 Vocabulary (part b)

	Verbal Noun	Doer Noun	Command tense	Present tense (kasrah)	Past tense (fathah)	
	فِعْل	فَاعِل	اِفْعِلْ	يَفْعِلُ	فَعَلَ	
to strike	ضَرْب	ضَارِب	اِضْرِبْ	يَضْرِبُ	ضَرَبَ	58
to carry; to bear	حَمْل	حَامِل	اِحْمِلْ	يَحْمِلُ	حَمَلَ	50
to bear with patience	صَبْر	صَابِر	اِصْبِرْ	يَصْبِرُ	صَبَرَ	94
to wrong	ظُلْم	ظَالِم	اِظْلِمْ	يَظْلِمُ	ظَلَمَ	266
to recognize	مَعْرِفَة	عارِف	اِعْرِفْ	يَعْرِفُ	عَرَفَ	59
to understand; to comprehend	عَقْل	عَاقِل	اِعْقِلْ	يَعْقِلُ	عَقَلَ	49
to forgive; to cover	مَغْفِرَة	غَافِر	اِغْفِرْ	يَغْفِرُ	غَفَرَ	95
to decree; to have power;	قَدْر،قُدْرَة	قَادِر	اِقْدِرْ	يَقْدِرُ	قَدَرَ	47
to lie	كَذِب	كاذِب	اِكْذِبْ	يَكْذِبُ	كَذَبَ	76
to earn	كَسْب	كاسِب	اِكْسِبْ	يَكْسِبُ	كَسَبَ	62
to possess	مِلْك	مَالِك	اِمْلِكْ	يَمْلِكُ	مَلَكَ	*49*

Adapted from "80% of Quranic Vocabulary", page 18 by 'Abdul-Raḥeem 'Abdul-'Azeez available for free download at http://emuslim.com/quran/english80.asp.

E. Lesson 9 Vocabulary (part c)

	Verbal Noun	Doer Noun	Command tense	Present tense (fathah)	Past tense (kasrah)	
	فِعْل	فَاعِل	اِفْعَلْ	يَفْعَلُ	فَعِلَ	
to hear	سَمَاعَة	سَامِع	اِسْمَعْ	يَسْمَعُ	سَمِعَ	100
to be grieved	حُزْن	حَازِن	اِحْزَنْ	يَحْزَنُ	حَزِنَ	30
to think; to consider	حَسْب	حاسِب	اِحْسَبْ	يَحْسَبُ	حَسِبَ	46
to guard; to protect	حِفْظ	حَافِظ	اِحْفَظْ	يَحْفَظُ	حَفِظَ	27
to lose	خُسْر	خَاسِر	اِخْسَرْ	يَخْسَرُ	خَسِرَ	51
to have mercy on someone	رَحْمَة	رَاحِم	اِرْحَمْ	يَرْحَمُ	رَحِمَ	148
to bear witness; to be present	شُهُود	شَاهِد	اِشْهَدْ	يَشْهَدُ	شَهِدَ	66
to know	عِلْم	عَالِم	اِعْلَمْ	يَعْلَمُ	عَلِمَ	518
to work; to do	عَمَل	عَامِل	اِعْمَلْ	يَعْمَلُ	عَمِلَ	318
to dislike; to detest	كُرْه	كَارِه	اِكْرَهْ	يَكْرَهُ	كَرِهَ	25
to watch; to see	بَصَر	بَاصِر	أُبْصُرْ	يَبْصُرُ	بَصُرَ	13

Adapted from "80% of Quranic Vocabulary", page 19 by 'Abdul-Raḥeem 'Abdul-'Azeez available for free download at http://emuslim.com/quran/english80.asp.

F. Lesson 9 Vocabulary (part d)

Harf Jarr that come with the verb & may change the meanings		*Focus on Verbs that are not Irregular (those without a Voweled Root Letter)	
to go forward, strive	ضَرَبَ فِي	to come	أَتَى
to mention	ضَرَبَ لِ	to bring	أَتَى بِ
to strike upon, overshadow	ضَرَبَ عَلَى	to seek	بَغَى
to give an example	ضَرَبَ مَثَلًا	to be unjust, to oppress	بَغَى عَلَى
to forgo, pardon	عَفَا	to repent	تَابَ، تَابَ إِلَى
to forgive	عَفَا عَنْ	to accept	تَابَ عَلَى
to decree, fulfill	قَضَى	to come	جَاءَ
to judge	قَضَى بَيْنَ	to bring	جَاءَ بِ
to kill	قَضَى عَلَى	to go	ذَهَبَ
to place, put down	وَضَعَ	to take away	ذَهَبَ بِ
to remove	وَضَعَ عَنْ	to go away	ذَهَبَ عَنْ
to turn, cause to turn	وَلَّى	to be pleased	رَضِيَ
turn to	وَلَّى إِلَى	to be pleased with	رَضِيَ عَنْ
turn away from	وَلَّى عَنْ	to strike, hit	ضَرَبَ

Adapted from "80% of Quranic Vocabulary", page 34 by 'Abdul-Raḥeem 'Abdul-'Azeez available for free download at http://emuslim.com/quran/english80.asp.

G. Lesson 12 Vocabulary (part a)

Verb Family II	Verbal Noun	Doer Noun	Command tense	Present tense	Past tense	
	تَفْعِيل	مُفَعِّل	فَعِّل	يُفَعِّل	فَعَّل	
to change	تَبْدِيل	مُبَدِّل	بَدِّلْ	يُبَدِّلُ	بَدَّلَ	33
to give good news	تَبْشِير	مُبَشِّر	بَشِّرْ	يُبَشِّرُ	بَشَّرَ	48
to make clear	تَبْيِين	مُبَيِّن	بَيِّنْ	يُبَيِّنُ	بَيَّنَ	35
to adorn / make to seem fair	تَزْيِين	مُزَيِّن	زَيِّنْ	يُزَيِّنُ	زَيَّنَ	26
to glorify; to praise	تَسْبِيح	مُسَبِّح	سَبِّحْ	يُسَبِّحُ	سَبَّحَ	48
to bring under control	تَسْخِير	مُسَخِّر	سَخِّرْ	يُسَخِّرُ	سَخَّرَ	26
to pronounce to be true	تَصْدِيق	مُصَدِّق	صَدِّقْ	يُصَدِّقُ	صَدَّقَ	31
to punish; to torment	تَعْذِيب	مُعَذِّب	عَذِّبْ	يُعَذِّبُ	عَذَّبَ	49
to teach	تَعْلِيم	مُعَلِّم	عَلِّمْ	يُعَلِّمُ	عَلَّمَ	42
to send forward	تَقْدِيم	مُقَدِّم	قَدِّمْ	يُقَدِّمُ	قَدَّمَ	27
to accuse of falsehood	تَكْذِيب	مُكَذِّب	كَذِّبْ	يُكَذِّبُ	كَذَّبَ	198
to send down	تَنْزِيل	مُنَزِّل	نَزِّلْ	يُنَزِّلُ	نَزَّلَ	79
to deliver; to rescue	تَنْجِيَة	مُنَجِّي	نَجِّ	يُنَجِّي	نَجَّى	39

Adapted from "80% of Quranic Vocabulary", page 25 by 'Abdul-Raḥeem 'Abdul-'Azeez available for free download at http://emuslim.com/quran/english80.asp.

H. Lesson 12 Vocabulary (part b)

Verb Family III	Verbal Noun	Doer Noun	Command tense	Present tense	Past tense	
	مُفَاعَلَة /فِعال	مُفَاعِل	فَاعِلْ	يُفَاعِلُ	فَاعَلَ	
to struggle; to strive	مُجَاهَدَ /جِهاد	مُجَاهِد	جَاهِدْ	يُجَاهِدُ	جَاهَدَ	31
to fight	مُقَاتَلَة/قِتال	مُقَاتِل	قَاتِلْ	يُقَاتِلُ	قَاتَلَ	54
to call out; to cry unto	مُنَادَاة، نِدَاء	مُنَادٍ	نَادِ	يُنَادِي	نَادَى	44
to be a hypocrite	مُنَافَقَة /نِفاق	مُنَافِق	نَافِقْ	يُنَافِقُ	نَافَقَ	34
to migrate	مُهَاجَرَة	مُهَاجِر	هَاجِرْ	يُهَاجِرُ	هَاجَرَ	24

Adapted from "80% of Quranic Vocabulary", page 26 by 'Abdul-Raḥeem 'Abdul-'Azeez available for free download at http://emuslim.com/quran/english80.asp.

I. Lesson 12 Vocabulary (part c)

Verb Family IV	Verbal Noun	Doer Noun	Command tense	Present tense	Past tense	
	إِفْعَال	مُفْعِل	أَفْعِلْ	يُفْعِلُ	أَفْعَلَ	
to see; to watch	إِبْصَار	مُبْصِر	أَبْصِرْ	يُبْصِرُ	أَبْصَرَ	36
to do good; to do excellently	إِحْسَان	مُحْسِن	أَحْسِنْ	يُحْسِنُ	أَحْسَنَ	72
to bring forth	إِخْرَاج	مُخْرِج	أَخْرِجْ	يُخْرِجُ	أَخْرَجَ	108
to make to enter	إِدْخَال	مُدْخِل	أَدْخِلْ	يُدْخِلُ	أَدْخَلَ	45
to send back; to take back	إِرْجَاع	مُرْجِع	أَرْجِعْ	يُرْجِعُ	أَرْجَعَ	33
to send	إِرْسَال	مُرْسِل	أَرْسِلْ	يُرْسِلُ	أَرْسَلَ	135
to exceed; to be extravagant	إِسْرَاف	مُسْرِف	أَسْرِفْ	يُسْرِفُ	أَسْرَفَ	23
to submit; to surrender	إِسْلَام	مُسْلِم	أَسْلِمْ	يُسْلِمُ	أَسْلَمَ	72
to ascribe a partner	إِشْرَاك	مُشْرِك	أَشْرِكْ	يُشْرِكُ	أَشْرَكَ	120
to become	إِصْبَاح	مُصْبِح	أَصْبِحْ	يُصْبِحُ	أَصْبَحَ	34
to become good; to make good	إِصْلَاح	مُصْلِح	أَصْلِحْ	يُصْلِحُ	أَصْلَحَ	40

Adapted from "80% of Quranic Vocabulary", page 27 by 'Abdul-Raḥeem 'Abdul-'Azeez available for free download at http://emuslim.com/quran/english80.asp.

J. Lesson 12 Vocabulary (part d)

Verb Family IV (contd.)	Verbal Noun	Doer Noun	Command tense	Present tense	Past tense	
to turn away; to backslide	إِعْرَاض	مُعْرِض	أَعْرِضْ	يُعْرِضُ	أَعْرَضَ	53
to drown	إِغْرَاق	مُغْرِق	أَغْرِقْ	يُغْرِقُ	أَغْرَقَ	21
to spread corruption	إِفْسَاد	مُفْسِد	أَفْسِدْ	يُفْسِدُ	أَفْسَدَ	36
to be successful	إِفْلَاح	مُفْلِح	أَفْلِحْ	يُفْلِحُ	أَفْلَحَ	40
to make to grow; to cause to grow	إِنْبَات	مُنْبِت	أَنْبِتْ	يُنْبِتُ	أَنْبَتَ	16
to warn	إِنْذَار	مُنْذِر	أَنْذِرْ	يُنْذِرُ	أَنْذَرَ	70
to send down; to reveal	إِنْزَال	مُنْزِل	أَنْزِلْ	يُنْزِلُ	أَنْزَلَ	190
to produce create;	إِنْشَاء	مُنْشِئ	أَنْشِئْ	يُنْشِئُ	أَنْشَأَ	22
to favor; to bestow grace	إِنْعَام	مُنْعِم	أَنْعِمْ	يُنْعِمُ	أَنْعَمَ	17
to spend	إِنْفَاق	مُنْفِق	أَنْفِقْ	يُنْفِقُ	أَنْفَقَ	69
to not recognize; to deny	إِنْكَار	مُنْكِر	أَنْكِرْ	يُنْكِرُ	أَنْكَرَ	25
to destroy	إِهْلَاك	مُهْلِك	أَهْلِكْ	يُهْلِكُ	أَهْلَكَ	*58*

Adapted from "80% of Quranic Vocabulary", page 28 by 'Abdul-Raḥeem 'Abdul-'Azeez available for free download at http://emuslim.com/quran/english80.asp.

K. Lesson 13 Vocabulary (part a)

Verb Family V	Verbal Noun	Doer Noun	Command tense	Present tense	Past tense	
	تَفَعُّل	مُتَفَعِّل	تَفَعَّلْ	يَتَفَعَّلُ	تَفَعَّلَ	
to think over; to reflect	تَفَكُّر	مُتَفَكِّر	تَفَكَّرْ	يَتَفَكَّرُ	تَفَكَّرَ	17
to receive admonition	تَذَكُّر	مُتَذَكِّر	تَذَكَّرْ	يَتَذَكَّرُ	تَذَكَّرَ	51
to put one's trust	تَوَكُّل	مُتَوَكِّل	تَوَكَّلْ	يَتَوَكَّلُ	تَوَكَّلَ	44
to become clear	تَبَيُّن	مُتَبَيِّن	تَبَيَّنْ	يَتَبَيَّنُ	تَبَيَّنَ	18
to wait & watch for opportunity	تَرَبُّص	مُتَرَبِّص	تَرَبَّصْ	يَتَرَبَّصُ	تَرَبَّصَ	17

Verb Family VI	Verbal Noun	Doer Noun	Command tense	Present tense	Past tense	
	تَفَاعُلْ	مُتَفَاعِل	تَفَاعَلْ	يَتَفَاعَلُ	تَفَاعَلَ	
to be blessed or exalted	تَبَارُك	مُتَبَارِك	تَبَارَكْ	يَتَبَارَكُ	تَبَارَكَ	9
to ask each other	تَسَاءُل	مُتَسَاءِل	تَسَاءَلْ	يَتَسَاءَلُ	تَسَاءَلَ	9

Adapted from "80% of Quranic Vocabulary", page 31 by 'Abdul-Raḥeem 'Abdul-'Azeez available for free download at http://emuslim.com/quran/english80.asp.

L. Lesson 13 Vocabulary (part b)

Verb Family VII	Verbal Noun	Doer Noun	Command tense	Present tense	Past tense	
	انْفِعَال	مُنْفَعِل	اِنْفَعِلْ	يَنْفَعِلُ	اِنْفَعَلَ	
to turn around; to return	اِنْقِلَاب	مُنْقَلِب	اِنْقَلِبْ	يَنْقَلِبُ	اِنْقَلَبَ	20

Verb Family VIII	Verbal Noun	Doer Noun	Command tense	Present tense	Past tense	
	اِفْتِعَال	مُفْتَعِل	اِفْتَعِلْ	يَفْتَعِلُ	اِفْتَعَلَ	
to differ	اِخْتِلَاف	مُخْتَلِف	اِخْتَلِفْ	يَخْتَلِفُ	اِخْتَلَفَ	52
to follow	اِتِّبَاع	مُتَّبِع	اِتَّبِعْ	يَتَّبِعُ	اِتَّبَعَ	140
to take; to adopt	اِتِّخَاذ	مُتَّخِذ	اِتَّخِذْ	يَتَّخِذُ	اِتَّخَذَ	128

Adapted from "80% of Quranic Vocabulary", page 32 by 'Abdul-Raḥeem 'Abdul-'Azeez available for free download at http://emuslim.com/quran/english80.asp.

M. Lesson 13 Vocabulary (part c)

Verb Family IX	Verbal Noun	Doer Noun	Command tense	Present tense	Past tense	
	اِفْعِلَال	مُفْعَلٌّ	اِفْعَلَّ	يَفْعَلُّ	اِفْعَلَّ	
to become black	اِسْوِدَاد	مُسْوَدٌّ	اِسْوَدَّ	يَسْوَدُّ	اِسْوَدَّ	3
to become white	اِبْيِضَاض	مُبْيَضٌّ	اِبْيَضَّ	يَبْيَضُّ	اِبْيَضَّ	3

Verb Family X	Verbal Noun	Doer Noun	Command tense	Present tense	Past tense	
to seek to hasten	اِسْتِعْجَال	مُسْتَعْجِل	اِسْتَعْجِلْ	يَسْتَعْجِلُ	اِسْتَعْجَلَ	20
to ask forgiveness	اِسْتِغْفَار	مُسْتَغْفِر	اِسْتَغْفِرْ	يَسْتَغْفِرُ	اِسْتَغْفَرَ	42
to act arrogantly	اِسْتِكْبَار	مُسْتَكْبِر	اِسْتَكْبِرْ	يَسْتَكْبِرُ	اِسْتَكْبَرَ	48
to mock at	اِسْتِهْزَاء	مُسْتَهْزِئ	اِسْتَهْزِئْ	يَسْتَهْزِئُ	اِسْتَهْزَأَ	23

Adapted from "80% of Quranic Vocabulary", page 33 by 'Abdul-Raḥeem 'Abdul-'Azeez available for free download at http://emuslim.com/quran/english80.asp.

N. Lesson 13 Vocabulary - Part d

الآلْفِعْلُ الْماضي	الآلْفِعْلُ الْمُضارِع	الآلْفِعْلُ الْماضي	الفعل المضارع	الآلْفِعْلُ الْماضي	الفعل المضارع	الآلْفِعْلُ الْماضي	الفعل المضارع
نَبَأَ	يَنْبَأُ	صَنَعَ	يَصْنَعُ	سَخِرَ	يَسْخَرُ	أَعْلَنَ	يُعْلِنُ
to inform (ـَ)		to make; to construct (ـَ)		to ridicule; to mock		to announce; to reveal (IV)	
سَكَنَ	يَسْكُنُ	غَلَبَ	يَغْلِبُ	عَرَضَ	يَعْرِضُ	أَنْظَرَ	يُنْظِرُ
to live; to rest (ـُ)		to overcome (ـِ)		to display; to turn away		to give respite (IV)	
شَرِبَ	يَشْرَبُ	عَدَلَ	يَعْدِلُ	مَتَّعَ	يُمَتِّعُ	أَقْسَمَ	يُقْسِمُ
to drink		to be just (ـِ)		to grant ; to bestow (II)		to swear (IV)	
فَتَنَ	يَفْتِنُ	كَشَفَ	يَكْشِفُ	حَرَّمَ	يُحَرِّمُ	أَمْسَكَ	يُمْسِكُ
to persecute; to test (ـِ)		to uncover (ـِ)		to forbid (II)		to retain; to withhold (IV)	
كَتَمَ	يَكْتُمُ	زَعَمَ	يَزْعُمُ	أَخَّرَ	يُؤَخِّرُ	أَسْمَعَ	يُسْمِعُ
to conceal; hide (ـُ)		to claim (ـُ)		to delay; to give respite (II)		to make listen (IV)	
سَبَقَ	يَسْبِقُ	نَكَحَ	يَنْكِحُ	ذَكَّرَ	يُذَكِّرُ	أَطْعَمَ	يُطْعِمُ
to precede (ـِ)		to marry (ـِ)		to remind (II)		to feed (IV)	
أَفِكَ	يَأْفَكُ	صَرَفَ	يَصْرِفُ	كَلَّمَ	يُكَلِّمُ	أَتْبَعَ	يُتْبِعُ
to delude; to turn away		to turn; to divert (ـِ)		to speak (II)		to follow (IV)	
بَسَطَ	يَبْسُطُ	حَلَفَ	يَحْلِفُ	كَفَّرَ	يُكَفِّرُ	أَخْلَفَ	يُخْلِفُ
to extend; to stretch (ـُ)		to swear (ـِ)		to remove (II)		to break; to fail (IV)	
فَقِهَ	يَفْقَهُ	حَبِطَ	يَحْبَطُ	قَدَّرَ	يُقَدِّرُ	أَعْتَدَ	يُعْتِدُ
to understand (ـَ)		to become worthless		to determine; to plot (II)		to prepare (IV)	
نَفَخَ	يَنْفُخُ	حَذِرَ	يَحْذَرُ	عاهَدَ	يُعاهِدُ	تَرَبَّصَ	يَتَرَبَّصُ
to breathe (ـُ)		to beware; to fear (ـَ)		to make a covenant (III)		to await (V)	
فَرِحَ	يَفْرَحُ	سَلَكَ	يَسْلُكُ	جادَلَ	يُجادِلُ	اِسْتَمَعَ	يَسْتَمِعُ
to rejoice		to make enter; to insert (ـُ)		to argue; to dispute (III)		to listen (VIII)	

Glossary of Arabic Grammar Terms [ا - س]

إِسْتِقْبال	Future	جَمْعُ الْمُذَكَّرِ السَّالِم	Masculine Sound Plural
إِسْم/أَسْماء	Noun	الْجِنْس	Gender
الأَسْمَاءُ الْخَمْسَة	The Five Special Nouns (أبو, أخ , حَمُو فُو, ذُو)	جَمْعُ التَّكْسِير	Broken Plural
إِسمُ الْإِشارَة	Pointing Noun	جُمْلَة إِسْمِيَّة	Nominal Sentence
اسمُ الصِّلَة	Relative Pronoun	جُمْلَة فِعْلِيَّة	Verbal Sentence
إِسْمُ الْفاعِل	Active Participle; Doer Noun	جَواب الشرط	Response Statement after a condition
إِسمُ الْمَفْعول	Passive Participle; Passive noun	حَرَكَة / حَرَكات	Vowel(s) Ḍammah, Kasrah, and Fatḥah
اَلْإِضافَة	Possession Construction	حَرْف/حُرُوف	Particle(s); these include those causing a change in Iʿrāb, or those that do not.
إِعْراب	Inflected state or Case of a Noun or Verb: either Rafʿ, Naṣb, Jarr, or Jazm	حُروف الاسْتِفْهام	Particles of Interrogation
إِنَّ وَ أَخَواتُها	Inna and its Sisters: Ḥarf Naṣb Particles	حروف الجَرّ	Particles that cause Jarr such as [مِن / بِ / إِلى] etc.
البَلَاغَة	The study of rhetoric and eloquence	حُرُوفُ الْجَزْم	Particles that cause verbs to be in Jazm
تاء الْمَرْبُوتَة	The Tā of femininity: ة	حُروف العِلَّة	A vowel letter such as [ا / ي / و / ّ / أ]
الْجَارُّ وَ الْمَجْرور	Jarr Construction	خَبَر	Predicate
الجزم/مَجْزُومٌ	Jazm Iʿrāb (with verbs)	سَاكِنٌ / سُكُون	Mark of stopping on a letter; Sukūn; also known as Jazm
جَمْع الْمُؤَنَّث السّالم	Feminine Sound Plural		

Glossary of Arabic Grammar Terms [ش - ل]

شِبْهُ الجُمْلَة	Predicate [خَبَر] which is essentially a Jarr Construction	اَلْفِعْلُ الْأَمْر	Command Tense verb
الشَّرط	Condition in a Conditional Statement that is denoted by a Condition Particle	فِعْلُ الثلاثي المُجَرَّدِ	Family I Verb; the "root verb"
صِفَة/صِفات	adjective(s)	فِعْلُ الثلاثي المُزيد فِيهِ	Higher Verb families which are derived from the Verb I Family
ضَمِير / ضَمَائِر	pronoun(s)	الفِعْلُ الرُّباعي	Four-letter root verb
ضَمِير مُتَّصِل	Connected Pronoun	فعل لازِم	Intransitive Verb: it does not take a Direct Object
ضَمِير مُنْفَصِل	Detached Pronoun	فعل ماضٍ	Verb in the Past Tense
ظَرْفُ الزَّمان	Noun in Naṣb that indicates the time when an action occurs	فِعْلٌ مُتَعَدِّي	Transitive verb.
ظَرْفُ الْمَكان	Noun in Naṣb that indicates the place when an action occurs	فِعلٌ مَجْهول	Passive Verb
عائِد	A pronoun that connects the [صِلَة] to the word it is describing	فِعْلٌ مُضَارِع	Present or Future Tense verb.
غائِب	Third Person	القِسْم	Definiteness of a word
غَيْرُ مُنْصَرِف	Partially Flexible word	لا النَّافِيَة	Lā of Negation negation particle
الفُصْحى	The original Classical Arabic language	لا النَّهِيَّة	Forbidding done by a Lā (negative command)

Glossary of Arabic Grammar Terms (م - ي)

المُؤَنَّث	Feminine	مَصْدَر /مصادِر	verbal noun(s)
مُبْتَدَأ	Subject (Nominal sentence)	مُضَاف	1st Particle of the Iḍāfah Construction
مَبْنِي	Inflexible; when used for verbs, it means they cannot take I'rāb	المُضَاف إلَيْهِ	Second Particle of the Iḍāfah Construction; it is always in the Jarr state
مُثَنَّى	Dual	مُعْرَب	Verb or noun that is Flexible; its vowel(s) adapt fully according to its I'rāb.
مَجْرُور	Noun that is in the Jarr state	المَعْرِفَة	Definite (noun)
مَجْهُول	Passive Tense	مُفْرَد	Singular; also used to indicate a type of (خَبَر)
مُخاطَب	Second Person	مَفْعُول بِهِ	Direct Object of a verb
المُذَكَّر	Masculine	مَوْصُوف	Word being described
مُرَكَّب / مُرَكَّبات	Word Construction(s)	نَائِبُ الفاعِل	Deputy Doer, substitutes the Doer in Passive Verbal Sentences
مُرَكَّب إضافِيّ	Possession Construction	النَّحو	Science of grammar
مُرَكَّب تَوصيفِيّ	Describing Construction	النَّكِرَة	Indefinite (noun)
المُصْحَف	Al-Qur'ān in book form preserved according to Uthmāni script		

Review Questions for Essentials of Qur'ānic Arabic

Instructions: Questions from each lesson should be done after a thorough study of the respective lesson and without looking at any of the notes. This will benefit the student by allowing them to realize areas of deficiency, etc. Exercises should be checked with the Answers provided on pgs. 203-213.

Lesson 1 Review Questions

True/False:

1. Tajwīd is not that important in when learning Arabic grammar.
2. Most Arabic words are derived from one single Arabic root verb.
3. Adjectives and Verbal nouns are not considered nouns.
4. Rafʿ state is denoted by a Ḍammah at the end of the noun.
5. A noun is considered feminine by default unless there is a reason for it to be masculine.

Short Answer:

6. Briefly discuss how a Hamzah is different from an Alif when it is at the beginning of a word
7. What are the names of three types of Words in Arabic?
8. What four characteristics do nouns have?
9. What are the two endings that can occur on Dual nouns?
10. What is the most common sign on a noun to indicate that it is feminine?

Vocabulary Review: translate the underlined words in the following Qur'ānic Āyāt.

11-12. ﴿ آمَنَ ٱلرَّسُولُ بِمَا أُنْزِلَ إِلَيْهِ مِنْ رَبِّهِ وَٱلْمُؤْمِنُونَ ﴾ [2:285]

13-14. ﴿ جَزَاءً مِنْ رَبِّكَ عَطَاءً حِسَابًا ﴾ [78:36]

15-16. ﴿ وَٱلَّذِينَ آمَنُواْ وَعَمِلُواْ ٱلصَّالِحَاتِ سَنُدْخِلُهُمْ جَنَّاتٍ تَجْرِي مِن تَحْتِهَا ٱلْأَنْهَارُ خَالِدِينَ فِيهَا أَبَدًا... ﴾ [4:57]

17-20. ﴿ أَلَمْ تَرَ أَنَّ ٱللَّهَ يَسْجُدُ لَهُ مَنْ فِي ٱلسَّمَاوَاتِ وَمَنْ فِي ٱلْأَرْضِ وَٱلشَّمْسُ وَٱلْقَمَرُ ﴾ [22:18]

Lesson 2 Review Questions

True/False

1. Some feminine words are [شَمْس / حَرْب / نَفْس / خَمْر].
2. Most plurals of nouns are on a specific Broken Plural pattern.
3. The regular plural pattern ending can only be of two specific endings.
4. All nouns have an I'rāb even if they cannot change their endings.
5. The sign of a Partially Flexible noun in the Jarr state is Ḍammah.

6. You can have Tanwīn with words that have "Al" on them.

Short Answer:

7. What are the two possible endings for plural of [مُسْلِمَة] ?

8. Briefly describe the difference between nouns that are Partially Flexible and Inflexible.

9. Name one noun that is Partially Flexible and one noun that is Inflexible.

For each highlighted noun in the following Qur'ānic Āyāt, determine its four qualities (plurality, gender, definiteness, and I'rāb) and its Flexibility. Include all possible I'rāb that the noun may take if used outside the respective Āyah.

10. ﴿...وَأَنَّا مِنَّا ٱلْمُسْلِمُونَ وَمِنَّا ٱلْقَاسِطُونَ...﴾ [72:14]

11. ﴿إِنَّ ٱلْمُسْلِمِينَ وَٱلْمُسْلِمَاتِ وَٱلْمُؤْمِنِينَ وَٱلْمُؤْمِنَاتِ...﴾ [33:35]

12. ﴿قَالَ مُوسَىٰ لِقَوْمِهِ ٱسْتَعِينُوا بِٱللَّهِ وَٱصْبِرُوا...﴾ [7:128]

13. ﴿قُلْ صَدَقَ ٱللَّهُ فَٱتَّبِعُواْ مِلَّةَ إِبْرَاهِيمَ حَنِيفًا وَمَا كَانَ مِنَ ٱلْمُشْرِكِينَ﴾ [3:95]

14. ﴿أَوْ كَظُلُمَاتٍ فِي بَحْرٍ لُّجِّيٍّ يَغْشَاهُ مَوْجٌ مِّن فَوْقِهِ مَوْجٌ مِّن فَوْقِهِ سَحَابٌ ظُلُمَاتٌ بَعْضُهَا فَوْقَ بَعْضٍ..﴾ [24:40]

15. ﴿...وَلَوْلَا دَفْعُ ٱللَّهِ ٱلنَّاسَ بَعْضَهُم بِبَعْضٍ لَّهُدِّمَتْ صَوَامِعُ وَبِيَعٌ وَصَلَوَاتٌ وَمَسَاجِدُ يُذْكَرُ فِيهَا ٱسْمُ ٱللَّهِ كَثِيرًا...﴾ [22:40]

<u>Vocabulary Review: translate the underlined words in the following Qur'ānic Āyāt.</u>

16-18. ﴿..وَأَقَامُواْ ٱلصَّلَاةَ وَأَنفَقُواْ مِمَّا رَزَقْنَاهُمْ سِرًّا وَعَلَانِيَةً وَيَدْرَؤُونَ بِٱلْحَسَنَةِ ٱلسَّيِّئَةَ أُوْلَٰئِكَ لَهُمْ عُقْبَى ٱلدَّارِ﴾ [13:22]

19-20. ﴿لَيْسَ عَلَيْكُمْ جُنَاحٌ أَنْ تَبْتَغُوا فَضْلًا مِنْ رَبِّكُمْ...﴾ [2:198]

21-22. ﴿ٱلَّذِينَ يَنْقُضُونَ عَهْدَ ٱللَّهِ مِنْ بَعْدِ مِيثَاقِهِ...﴾ [2:27]

23-30. Please fill in the blank spaces with the appropriate noun with the appropriate I'rāb.

	Single	Dual (Naṣb)	Plural
23.	مُسْلِمَةٌ	مُسْلِمَتَانِ	
24.		بَيْتَيْنِ	بُيُوتٍ
25.	مُسْلِمًا	مُسْلِمَيْنِ	
26.		كَلِمَتَانِ	كَلِمَاتٌ
27.	مُجَاهِدٍ	مُجَاهِدَيْنِ	

	Raf'	Naṣb	Jarr
28.	مُحَمَّدٌ		مُحَمَّدٍ
29.	عِيسٰى	عِيسٰى	
30.	مَرْيَمُ	مَرْيَمَ	

Lesson 3 Review Questions

True/False:

1. All pronouns are Partially Inflexible.
2. Pronouns are of two types, attached and detached.
3. When Pronouns are attached they can be in the Raf' state.
4. Detached pronouns are typically in the Naṣb state.
5. In Verbal sentences, the Doer (Subject) is in the Raf' state.
6. Pointing nouns and Relative pronouns are nouns that are always Definite.
7. Pointing nouns are of three types: near, far, and very far.
8. [ثَمَّ / هُنا / هُناك] are Pointing Nouns.
9. [ما] and [مَنْ] are Pointing Nouns.
10. Words like [الَّذِي] function to describe the Definite word that precedes it.

11-15. Without looking at the notes, Complete the table below:

Plural	Dual	Single	
هُمْ		هُوَ	3rd Person masculine
	هُما	هِيَ	3rd Person feminine
	أَنْتُما		2nd Person masculine
أَنْتُنَّ		أَنْتِ	2nd Person feminine
	نَحْنُ	أَنا	1st Person

15-19. Without looking at the notes, complete the table: use [كِتاب] as the Noun in the Jarr state. Write the words properly in the blank spaces with the appropriate pronoun.

	Plural	Dual	Single	
15.		كِتابِهِما	كِتابِهِ	3rd Person masculine
16.				3rd Person feminine
17.			كِتابِكَ	2nd Person masculine
18.	كِتابِكُنَّ			2nd Person feminine
19.		كِتابِنا		1st Person

<u>Short answer:</u>

20. How would the meaning of the following Āyah change if [إِيَّاكَ] was omitted and replaced with [كَ] after the verb:

﴿إِيَّاكَ نَعْبُدُ وَإِيَّاكَ نَسْتَعِينُ﴾

21. What is the feminine counterpart to [هٰذا]?

22. What is the masculine counterpart to [تِلْكَ]?

23. What is plural of [هٰذا]?

Vocabulary Review from the Qur'ān: Translate the highlighted word(s). <u>For the Nouns that are underlined, identify whether it is **a pointing noun (near), pointing noun (far)**, or **Relative Pronoun**.</u>

24. ﴿...يَجْعَلُونَ أَصَابِعَهُمْ فِي آذَانِهِمْ مِنَ الصَّوَاعِقِ حَذَرَ الْمَوْتِ...﴾ [2:19]

25. ﴿وَاللَّهُ خَلَقَ كُلَّ دَابَّةٍ مِنْ مَاءٍ فَمِنْهُمْ مَنْ يَمْشِي عَلَىٰ بَطْنِهِ وَمِنْهُمْ مَنْ يَمْشِي عَلَىٰ رِجْلَيْنِ وَمِنْهُمْ مَنْ يَمْشِي عَلَىٰ أَرْبَعٍ يَخْلُقُ اللَّهُ مَا يَشَاءُ إِنَّ اللَّهَ عَلَىٰ كُلِّ شَيْءٍ قَدِيرٌ﴾ [24:45]

26. ﴿إِنَّ الَّذِينَ يَغُضُّونَ أَصْوَاتَهُمْ عِنْدَ رَسُولِ اللَّهِ أُولَٰئِكَ الَّذِينَ امْتَحَنَ اللَّهُ قُلُوبَهُمْ لِلتَّقْوَىٰ﴾ [49:3]

27. ﴿وَقُلْ لِلْمُؤْمِنَاتِ يَغْضُضْنَ مِنْ أَبْصَارِهِنَّ وَيَحْفَظْنَ فُرُوجَهُنَّ وَلَا يُبْدِينَ زِينَتَهُنَّ إِلَّا مَا ظَهَرَ مِنْهَا...﴾ [24:31]

Lesson 4 Review Questions

<u>True/False:</u>

1. Typically, any noun followed by a Ḥarf will change its I'rāb to Naṣb or Jarr.
2. Ḥarf cannot act on Verbs.
3. Sometimes Isms act as Ḥarf Jarr like [حَوْل], [بَعْض], or [تَحْتَ].
4. Ḥarf Jarr can sometimes cause the noun before it to be in Jarr.
5. Ḥarf Jarr can never be attached to a noun.
6. Verbs cannot be in the Jarr state.
7. [إنَّ/لَعلَّ/لكِن] cause the word after it to be in the Jarr state.
8. The following act as Ḥarf Jarr: [تَحْتَ/عَلى/بِ/قَبْل].
9. [أفعال] and [فعُول] and [مَساجِد] are very common Broken Plural patterns.
10. Nouns can sometimes be in the Jazm state.

<u>11-21. Translate the following highlighted Ḥarf along with its corresponding Noun in the following Qur'ānic Āyāt:</u>

11. ﴿...كُلَّمَا رُزِقُوا مِنْهَا مِنْ ثَمَرَةٍ رِزْقًا قَالُوا هَٰذَا الَّذِي رُزِقْنَا مِنْ قَبْلُ...﴾ [2:25]

12. ﴿...وَلَا يَحِلُّ لَكُمْ أَنْ تَأْخُذُوا مِمَّا آتَيْتُمُوهُنَّ شَيْئًا...﴾ [2:229]

13. ﴿وَٱلَّذِينَ كَفَرُوا وَكَذَّبُوا بِآيَاتِنَا أُولَٰئِكَ أَصْحَابُ ٱلنَّارِ هُمْ فِيهَا خَالِدُونَ﴾ [2:39]

14. ﴿...يَقُولُونَ بِأَفْوَاهِهِمْ مَا لَيْسَ فِي قُلُوبِهِمْ وَٱللَّهُ أَعْلَمُ بِمَا يَكْتُمُونَ﴾ [3:167]

15. ﴿ثُمَّ بَعَثْنَاكُمْ مِنْ بَعْدِ مَوْتِكُمْ لَعَلَّكُمْ تَشْكُرُونَ﴾ [2:56]

16. ﴿..ٱلَّذِينَ إِذَا أَصَابَتْهُمْ مُصِيبَةٌ قَالُوا إِنَّا لِلَّهِ وَإِنَّا إِلَيْهِ رَاجِعُونَ﴾ [2:156]

17. ﴿إِنْ هُوَ إِلَّا رَجُلٌ بِهِ جِنَّةٌ فَتَرَبَّصُوا بِهِ حَتَّىٰ حِينٍ﴾ [23:25]

18. ﴿يَسْأَلُونَكَ عَنِ ٱلسَّاعَةِ أَيَّانَ مُرْسَاهَا قُلْ إِنَّمَا عِلْمُهَا عِندَ رَبِّي لَا يُجَلِّيهَا لِوَقْتِهَا إِلَّا هُوَ ثَقُلَتْ فِي ٱلسَّمَاوَاتِ وَٱلْأَرْضِ لَا تَأْتِيكُمْ إِلَّا بَغْتَةً يَسْأَلُونَكَ كَأَنَّكَ حَفِيٌّ عَنْهَا قُلْ إِنَّمَا عِلْمُهَا عِندَ ٱللَّهِ وَلَٰكِنَّ أَكْثَرَ ٱلنَّاسِ لَا يَعْلَمُونَ﴾ [7:187]

19-25. **In the following Qur'ānic Āyāt, the Broken Plural stem pattern is given for the highlighted noun. <u>If the highlighted noun is singular, convert it to its plural; if plural change it to its singular form.</u>**

19. ﴿وَقَالَ نِسْوَةٌ فِي ٱلْمَدِينَةِ ٱمْرَأَتُ ٱلْعَزِيزِ تُرَاوِدُ فَتَاهَا عَنْ نَفْسِهِ...﴾ [12:30; {فُعُل}]

20. ﴿...وَلَمْ يَتَّخِذْ وَلَدًا وَلَمْ يَكُنْ لَهُ شَرِيكٌ فِي ٱلْمُلْكِ...﴾ [25:2; {فُعَلاء}]

21. ﴿وَإِذَا ٱلْبِحَارُ سُجِّرَتْ﴾ [81:6; {فِعال}]

22. ﴿قَالَتْ إِنَّ ٱلْمُلُوكَ إِذَا دَخَلُوا قَرْيَةً أَفْسَدُوهَا...﴾ [27:34; {فُعُول}]

23. ﴿مَا نَنْسَخْ مِنْ آيَةٍ أَوْ نُنْسِهَا نَأْتِ بِخَيْرٍ مِنْهَا أَوْ مِثْلِهَا..﴾ [81:6; {أَفْعال}]

24. ﴿...كَأَنَّهَا كَوْكَبٌ دُرِّيٌّ يُوقَدُ مِنْ شَجَرَةٍ مُبَارَكَةٍ..﴾ [24:35; {فَواعِل}]

25. ﴿قُلْ إِنْ تُخْفُوا مَا فِي صُدُورِكُمْ أَوْ تُبْدُوهُ يَعْلَمْهُ ٱللَّهُ...﴾ [3:29; {فُعُول}]

Lesson 5 Review Questions

<u>True/False:</u>

1. The Muḍāf is the object belonging to the noun that follows it.
2. The Muḍāf can never have (ال-) and does not have Tanwīn.
3. The Muḍāf I'laih can be in the Raf', Naṣb, or Jarr state.
4. The Iḍāfah is typically Definite except when the Muḍāf I'laih is common without (ال-).
5. When describing a word, the descriptive word can come before or after the word.
6. The (صِفَة) (adjective) has all four characteristics of the noun described.
7. Nothing comes between the Mawṣūf and Ṣifah.
8. Broken Plural is considered Feminine Singular.

9. A noun attached to a Pronoun is really an Iḍāfah Construction.

10. In Plural and Dual Nouns with a ان ending, this is chopped off when it is a Muḍāf.

11. A Word Construction in many respects acts as a single word or unit in a sentence.

12. Different Constructions can be merged together forming a single larger construction.

Translate the following highlighted Constructions in the following Qur'ānic Āyāt (be exact as possible).

13. ﴿ إِلَّا مَنْ أَتَى ٱللَّهَ بِقَلْبٍ سَلِيمٍ ﴾ [26:89]

14. ﴿ إِنَّكَ لَمِنَ ٱلْمُرْسَلِينَ ۝ عَلَى صِرَاطٍ مُّسْتَقِيمٍ ۝ تَنزِيلَ الْعَزِيزِ الرَّحِيمِ ﴾ [36:3-5]

15. ﴿ وَٱضْرِبْ لَهُم مَّثَلًا أَصْحَابَ ٱلْقَرْيَةِ إِذْ جَاءَهَا ٱلْمُرْسَلُونَ ﴾ [36:13]

16. ﴿ وَإِذْ قُلْنَا ٱدْخُلُوا هَٰذِهِ ٱلْقَرْيَةَ فَكُلُوا مِنْهَا حَيْثُ شِئْتُمْ رَغَدًا... ﴾ [2:58]

17. ﴿ فَطَوَّعَتْ لَهُ نَفْسُهُ قَتْلَ أَخِيهِ فَقَتَلَهُ فَأَصْبَحَ مِنَ ٱلْخَاسِرِينَ ﴾ [5:30]

Identify all constructions in the following Qur'ānic Āyāt (Possession, Describing, Pointing, and Jarr Constructions. **Underline Jarr Constructions with one line, Possession Constructions with two lines, and Describing Constructions with dotted lines, and Pointing Constructions with wavy lines**. Constructions that are merged should be highlighted.

18. ﴿ وَإِنَّكَ لَعَلَى خُلُقٍ عَظِيمٍ ﴾ [68:4]

19. ﴿ تَبَارَكَ ٱلَّذِي بِيَدِهِ ٱلْمُلْكُ وَهُوَ عَلَى كُلِّ شَيْءٍ قَدِيرٌ ﴾ [67:1]

20. ﴿ وَلِلَّذِينَ كَفَرُوا بِرَبِّهِمْ عَذَابُ جَهَنَّمَ وَبِئْسَ ٱلْمَصِيرُ ﴾ [67:6]

21. ﴿ ...و وَهَٰذَا ٱلْبَلَدِ ٱلْأَمِينِ ﴾ [95:3]

22. ﴿ وَلَمَّا جَاءَهُمْ رَسُولٌ مِّنْ عِندِ ٱللَّهِ مُصَدِّقٌ لِّمَا مَعَهُمْ نَبَذَ فَرِيقٌ مِّنَ ٱلَّذِينَ أُوتُوا ٱلْكِتَابَ كِتَابَ ٱللَّهِ وَرَاءَ ظُهُورِهِمْ كَأَنَّهُمْ لَا يَعْلَمُونَ ﴾ [2:101]

23. ﴿ وَ لِلَّذِينَ كَفَرُوا بِرَبِّهِمْ عَذَابُ جَهَنَّمَ وَبِئْسَ ٱلْمَصِيرُ ﴾ [78:40]

Lesson 6 Review Questions

True/False:

1. In a Nominal Sentence, the Subject [مُبْتَدَأ] and Predicate [خَبَر] are Raf'.

2. The Predicate or [خَبَر] is generally Definite.

3. The [مُبْتَدَأ] and [خَبَر] typically match in all qualities except definiteness.

4. The [خَبَر] can only be a single word.

5. A Nominal Sentence can have within it a Verbal Sentence or another Nominal Sentence.
6. Interrogative particles work by acting at the beginning of a sentence.
7. [أَيُّ] as an interrogative particle acts as a Muḍāf unlike other interrogatives.
8. In a Nominative Sentence, the word "is" is implied.
9. A Ḥarf Jarr Construction cannot be part of a Nominative Sentence.
10. Pointing nouns can act as [مُبْتَدَأ] or [خَبَر].

Write the following in Arabic:

11. I am a Muslim.
12. That is a house.
13. That Masjid is big.
14. Your house is big
15. You are in the city.

In the following parts from the Qur'ānic Āyāt, the Nominal Sentence has been extracted.

(1) Identify the Subject [مُبْتَدَأ] by underlining it and (2) translate the highlighted word with its respective plural or singular.

16. ﴿..وَتِلْكَ حُدُودُ اللَّهِ...﴾ [65:1]
17. ﴿..إِنَّ ٱللَّهَ بَالِغُ أَمْرِهِ..﴾ [65:3]
18. ﴿..ذَٰلِكَ أَمْرُ ٱللَّهِ..﴾ [65:4]
19. ﴿ذَٰلِكَ ٱلْيَوْمُ ٱلَّذِي كَانُوا يُوعَدُونَ﴾ [70:44]
20. ﴿...وَٱللَّهُ عَلِيمٌ بِذَاتِ ٱلصُّدُورِ﴾ [64:4]
21. ﴿فَهُوَ فِي عِيشَةٍ رَّاضِيَةٍ﴾ [69:21]
22. ﴿..هَٰذَا سِحْرٌ مُّبِينٌ﴾ [61:5]
23. ﴿...أَنِّي رَسُولُ ٱللَّهِ إِلَيْكُمْ﴾ [61:5]
24. ﴿...مَنْ أَنصَارِي إِلَى ٱللَّهِ..﴾ [61:14]

Lesson 7 Review Questions

True/False:

1. In a Nominative Sentence, the [خَبَر] is always Indefinite.
2. Iḍāfah construction can sometimes be Indefinite.
3. [مُبْتَدَأ] can be a word construction such as an Iḍāfah or a Describing Construction.
4. When [مُبتَدَأ] and [خَبَر] are Definite, a pronoun is usually used to prevent it from becoming a Describing Construction.

Translate the following into Arabic:

5. messenger of the king
6. messenger of a king
7. the Muslim king
8. The king is a Muslim.
9. the Muslim teacher of the city.
10. This Muslim teacher is a king.
11. This Muslim is the king.
12. This is the teacher of the king.
13. this teacher of the king

From the following Qur'ānic Āyāt, translate the highlighted words with their respective plural/singular if possible.

14-15. ﴿ قَالَ قَرِينُهُ رَبَّنَا مَا أَطْغَيْتُهُ وَلَٰكِنْ كَانَ فِي ضَلَالٍ بَعِيدٍ ﴾ [50:27]

16-17. ﴿ إِنَّ ٱلَّذِينَ ٱتَّخَذُوا ٱلْعِجْلَ سَيَنَالُهُمْ غَضَبٌ مِنْ رَبِّهِمْ ﴾ [7:152]

18-19. ﴿ قَالُوا يَا قَوْمَنَا إِنَّا سَمِعْنَا كِتَابًا أُنزِلَ مِن بَعْدِ مُوسَى مُصَدِّقًا لِّمَا بَيْنَ يَدَيْهِ يَهْدِي إِلَى ٱلْحَقِّ وَإِلَى طَرِيقٍ مُّسْتَقِيمٍ ﴾ [46:30]

20-21. ﴿ وَأَمَّا مَنْ أُوتِيَ كِتَابَهُ وَرَاءَ ظَهْرِهِ ۝ فَسَوْفَ يَدْعُواْ ثُبُورًا ﴾ [84:10-11]

22-23. ﴿ قُلْ أَنَدْعُواْ مِن دُونِ ٱللَّهِ مَا لاَ يَنفَعُنَا وَلاَ يَضُرُّنَا وَنُرَدُّ عَلَى أَعْقَابِنَا بَعْدَ إِذْ هَدَانَا ٱللَّهُ.. ﴾ [6:71]

Lesson 8 Review Questions

True/False:

1. The Arabic root verb is 3rd Person single Present Tense.
2. The Present Tense verb by default ends in Ḍammah if in its single form.
3. Each verb comes with its own verbal noun.
4. Verbs in Family I can derive other verbs in different families.
5. For a Past Tense verb with a Fatḥah on the middle letter, any vowel may be present on the same letter in the Present Tense form of the verb.
6. For a Past Tense verb with a Ḍammah on the middle letter, any vowel may be present on the same letter in the Present Tense form of the verb.

7. For a Past Tense verb with a Kasrah on the middle letter, a Kasrah is usually present on the same letter in the Present Tense form of the verb.

8. Only verbs in the Present Tense state take I'rāb.

9. If the verb has a Fatḥah in the middle letter, and if its last two letters is one of the letters of the throat, then the vowel on the middle letter in the Present Tense gets a Fatḥah.

10-14. Fill in the empty spaces with the appropriately conjugated verb (قَرَأَ) with the attached pronoun (هَا) at its end.

Plural	*Dual*	*Single*	
	قَرَآ	قَرَأَ	3rd Person Masculine
	قَرَأَتَا		3rd Person Feminine
	قَرَأْتُمَا		2nd Person masculine
		قَرَأْتِ	2nd Person feminine
	قَرَأْنَا		1st Person

15-19. Fill in the empty spaces with the appropriately conjugated verb (يَضْرِبُ) with the attached pronoun (هُمْ) at its end.

Plural	**Dual**	**Single**	
		يَضْرِبُ	3rd Person Masculine
	تَضْرِبَانِ	تَضْرِبُ	3rd Person Feminine
تَضْرِبُونَ			2nd Person masculine
	تَضْرِبَانِ		2nd Person feminine
	نَضْرِبُ		1st Person

Qur'ānic Vocabulary: For the following highlighted verbs, (1) convert them into the Root verb form (3rd Person past, male singular) (2) Translate them, and (3) identify their conjugation referring to the detached pronoun they represent.

20-21. ﴿ وَإِذَا جَآؤُوكُمْ قَالُوٓاْ آمَنَّا وَقَد دَّخَلُواْ بِٱلْكُفْرِ وَهُمْ قَدْ خَرَجُواْ بِهِ ﴾ [5:61]

22. ﴿...وَمَا ظَلَمَهُمُ ٱللَّهُ وَلَٰكِنْ أَنْفُسَهُمْ يَظْلِمُونَ ﴾ [3:117]

23. ﴿ فَوَيْلٌ لَهُمْ مِمَّا كَتَبَتْ أَيْدِيهِمْ وَوَيْلٌ لَهُمْ مِمَّا يَكْسِبُونَ ﴾ [2:79]

24-25. ﴿..فَإِذَا بَلَغْنَ أَجَلَهُنَّ فَلَا جُنَاحَ عَلَيْكُمْ فِيمَا فَعَلْنَ فِي أَنْفُسِهِنَّ...﴾ [2:234]

Qur'ānic Vocabulary: For the following highlighted verbs, (1) convert them into their Present Tense form in the same exact conjugation (2) Translate them, and (3) identify their conjugation referring to the detached pronoun they represent.

26. ﴿ وَإِنْ حَكَمْتَ فَاحْكُمْ بَيْنَهُمْ بِٱلْقِسْطِ ﴾ [5:42]

25. ﴿ وَإِذَا مَا أُنْزِلَتْ سُورَةٌ نَظَرَ بَعْضُهُمْ إِلَىٰ بَعْضٍ.. ﴾ [9:127]

26. ﴿ فَغَفَرْنَا لَهُ ذَٰلِكَ وَإِنَّ لَهُ عِنْدَنَا لَزُلْفَىٰ وَحُسْنَ مَآبٍ ﴾ [38:25]

27. ﴿ وَأَمَّا ٱلَّذِينَ فَسَقُوا فَمَأْوَاهُمُ ٱلنَّارُ.. ﴾ [32:20]

Lesson 9 Review Questions

True/False:

1. The Doer and Direct Object in a (الجملَةُ الفِعْلِيَّةُ) take the Raf' state.
2. A (الجملَةُ الفِعْلِيَّةُ) starts with a verb.
3. A verb can be in the dual or plural state if the Subject is not explicitly mentioned.
4. If the Doer is not mentioned in a Verbal Sentence then there is no Doer.
5. The term for Direct Object acted on by a verb is called (مَفْعُول بِهِ).
6. In a (الجملَةُ الفِعْلِيَّةُ) with the mentioned Doer is (المُسلمون), the verb (نَصَرَ) would be conjugated as (نَصَرُوا) at the beginning of the sentence.
7. An Indirect Object is the same as a (مَفْعُول بِهِ).
8. A pronoun attached to a verb is always a (مَفْعُول بِهِ) and is Naṣb.
9. A Transitive verb is typically associated with a Ḥarf Naṣb.
10. In verbs that cannot take a (مَفْعُول بِهِ), a Jarr Construction is used and acts similar to a Direct Object.

In the following Qur'ānic Āyāt below (1), underline all verbs (Family I). Then (2) identify their Doer (فاعِل) by underlining twice. If Doer not explicitly mentioned, then write the implied doer (pronoun).

11. ﴿ ...فَأَخَذَتْكُمُ ٱلصَّاعِقَةُ وَأَنْتُمْ تَنظُرُونَ ﴾ [2:55]

12. ﴿ ...بَل لَّعَنَهُمُ ٱللَّهُ بِكُفْرِهِمْ فَقَلِيلاً مَّا يُؤْمِنُونَ ﴾ [2:88]

13. ﴿ وَلَمَّا جَاءَهُمْ رَسُولٌ مِّنْ عِندِ ٱللَّهِ مُصَدِّقٌ لِّمَا مَعَهُمْ نَبَذَ فَرِيقٌ مِّنَ ٱلَّذِينَ أُوتُوا ٱلْكِتَابَ كِتَابَ ٱللَّهِ وَرَاءَ ظُهُورِهِمْ كَأَنَّهُمْ لاَ يَعْلَمُونَ ﴾ [2:101]

14. ﴿ ..وَمَا كَفَرَ سُلَيْمَانُ وَلَكِنَّ ٱلشَّيَاطِينَ كَفَرُوا.. ﴾ [2:102]

15. ﴿ وَإِذْ يَرْفَعُ إِبْرَاهِيمُ ٱلْقَوَاعِدَ مِنَ ٱلْبَيْتِ... ﴾ [2:127]

<u>In the following Qur'ānic Āyāt below (1), underline all verbs (Family I). Then (2) identify the Direct Object [مَفْعُول بِهِ] Doer by underlining twice. If the respective verb does not have a Direct object, check to see if it has an Indirect object underline it with dots.</u>

16. ﴿وَٱلَّذِينَ إِذَا فَعَلُواْ فَاحِشَةً أَوْ ظَلَمُواْ أَنْفُسَهُمْ ذَكَرُواْ ٱللَّهَ...﴾ [3:135]

17. ﴿يَجْعَلُونَ أَصَابِعَهُمْ فِي آذَانِهِم مِّنَ ٱلصَّوَاعِقِ حَذَرَ ٱلْمَوْتِ﴾ [2:19]

18. ﴿..تَقْتُلُونَ أَنفُسَكُمْ وَتُخْرِجُونَ فَرِيقاً مِّنْكُمْ مِّنْ دِيَارِهِمْ..﴾ [2:85]

19. ﴿هُوَ ٱلَّذِي خَلَقَ ٱلسَّمَاوَاتِ وَٱلْأَرْضَ فِي سِتَّةِ أَيَّامٍ ثُمَّ ٱسْتَوَى عَلَى ٱلْعَرْشِ﴾ [57:4]

20. ﴿قَالَ رَبِّ إِنِّي ظَلَمْتُ نَفْسِي فَٱغْفِرْ لِي فَغَفَرَ لَهُ﴾ [28:16]

<u>**Vocabulary (Verbs):** Translate into Past and Present Tense verb (3rd Person Masculine single).</u>

21. To remember
22. To provide/sustain
23. To hit/ strike
24. To carry
25. To lie

Lesson 10 Review Questions

<u>True/False</u>

1. Past tense verbs can go into one of three states.
2. [مضارع] Verbs go into Raf', Naṣb, and Jarr states.
3. If a verb is in Naṣb or Jazm, there is Ḥarf acting on it.
4. Nouns can only go into the Jarr state due to a Ḥarf.
5. Nouns can go into Naṣb because of a Ḥarf or a Verb.
6. The Feminine Nūn is cut off if the verb is in the Naṣb or Jazm state.
7. [إِنْ] and [لَمْ] are two Ḥarf Jazm
8. [لَكِنَّ] and [لَعَلَّ] are two Ḥarf Naṣb for verbs.
9. There is a Sukūn instead of Ḍammah on single verbs if in Jazm state.
10. The most important information that can be used in conjugating the [أَمْر] of a verb is its vowel on the middle letter in the Past Tense.

<u>Short Answer.</u>

11. What are the two particles that can be used to put verbs in the Future Tense?
12. What are the similarities in terms of verb structure between the Command state and when the Lām of Forbidding acts on the verb?
13. Name one particle that functions in conditional statements.
14. Name two particles of Jazm and two Particles of Naṣb that act on verbs.
15. Name two particles in Arabic that are structurally identical but have completely different grammatical functions and roles.

In the following Āyāt, state the I'rāb of the highlighted Verb below, and underline the Ḥarf if applicable.

16. ﴿ يَهْدِي إِلَى الرُّشْدِ فَآمَنَّا بِهِ وَلَن نُّشْرِكَ بِرَبِّنَا أَحَدًا ﴾ [72:2]

17. ﴿ وَلَا يَزَالُونَ يُقَاتِلُونَكُمْ حَتَّىٰ يَرُدُّوكُمْ عَن دِينِكُمْ إِنِ اسْتَطَاعُوا ﴾ [2:217]

18. ﴿ وَإِذْ قَالَ مُوسَىٰ لِقَوْمِهِ إِنَّ اللَّهَ يَأْمُرُكُمْ أَن تَذْبَحُوا بَقَرَةً قَالُوا أَتَتَّخِذُنَا هُزُوًا قَالَ أَعُوذُ بِاللَّهِ أَنْ أَكُونَ مِنَ الْجَاهِلِينَ ﴾ [2:67]

19. ﴿ فَمَن يَكْفُرْ بِالطَّاغُوتِ وَيُؤْمِن بِاللَّهِ فَقَدِ اسْتَمْسَكَ بِالْعُرْوَةِ الْوُثْقَىٰ ﴾ [2:256]

20. ﴿ وَيُعَلِّمُكُم مَّا لَمْ تَكُونُوا تَعْلَمُونَ ﴾ [2:151]

In the following Āyāt, convert the highlighted verb in the Command Tense (الْفِعْلُ الْأَمْر) in the same conjugation.

21. ﴿ إِلَّا تَنصُرُوهُ فَقَدْ نَصَرَهُ اللَّهُ ... ﴾ [9:40]

22. ﴿ إِذْ قَالَ لِأَبِيهِ يَا أَبَتِ لِمَ تَعْبُدُ مَا لَا يَسْمَعُ وَلَا يُبْصِرُ وَلَا يُغْنِي عَنكَ شَيْئًا ﴾ [19:42]

23. ﴿ مَّا يَفْعَلُ اللَّهُ بِعَذَابِكُمْ إِن شَكَرْتُمْ وَآمَنتُمْ وَكَانَ اللَّهُ شَاكِرًا عَلِيمًا ﴾ [4:147]

24. ﴿ ... وَإِذَا ذَكَرْتَ رَبَّكَ فِي الْقُرْآنِ وَحْدَهُ وَلَّوْا عَلَىٰ أَدْبَارِهِمْ نُفُورًا ﴾ [17:46]

25. ﴿ وَمِنْ حَيْثُ خَرَجْتَ فَوَلِّ وَجْهَكَ شَطْرَ الْمَسْجِدِ الْحَرَامِ وَإِنَّهُ لَلْحَقُّ مِن رَّبِّكَ وَمَا اللَّهُ بِغَافِلٍ عَمَّا تَعْمَلُونَ ﴾ [2:149]

LESSON 11 REVIEW QUESTIONS

True/False:

1. Every verb in the Passive Tense takes a Deputy Doer or (نائِبُ الفاعِل).
2. Every verb can take a Passive Tense.
3. The beginning Vowel in either Passive Present or Past Tense Verb is a Ḍammah.
4. (اسمُ الفاعِل) and (اسم المفعول) can be derived from most verbs.
5. Only a few verbs have associated Maṣdars that come in a few patterns.
6. Verbs can be either (لازِم) or (مُتَعَدِّي).
7. A verb that is Intransitive cannot take a (مَفْعول بِهِ).
8. (المصدر) and (اسم الفاعل) are similar to verbs in that they relate to a particular action.
9. The I'rāb of the Deputy Doer is Naṣb since there is no Doer present.
10. A very common Maṣdar pattern for Family I verbs are (فَعْل).

In the following Qur'ānic Āyāt below, convert the highlighted verbs to the Passive tense.

11. ﴿ ...وَكَرِهُوا أَن يُجَاهِدُوا بِأَمْوَالِهِمْ وَأَنفُسِهِمْ فِي سَبِيلِ اللَّهِ ﴾ [9:81]

12. ﴿ الَّذِينَ يَذْكُرُونَ اللَّهَ قِيَامًا وَقُعُودًا وَعَلَىٰ جُنُوبِهِمْ... ﴾ [3:191]

13. ﴿ وَلَقَدْ عَلِمْتُمُ الَّذِينَ اعْتَدَوْا مِنكُمْ فِي السَّبْتِ... ﴾ [2:65]

14. ﴿.. مَا ظَلَمَهُمُ ٱللَّهُ وَلَٰكِنْ أَنْفُسَهُمْ يَظْلِمُونَ﴾ [3:117]

15. ﴿...فَإِذَا بَلَغْنَ أَجَلَهُنَّ فَلَا جُنَاحَ عَلَيْكُمْ فِيمَا فَعَلْنَ فِي أَنْفُسِهِنَّ﴾ [2:234]

In the following Qur'ānic Āyāt below, convert the highlighted verbs into the Doer Noun (اِسْمُ الفَاعِلِ), match the gender and plurality.

16. ﴿وَٱلَّذِينَ إِذَا فَعَلُواْ فَاحِشَةً أَوْ ظَلَمُواْ أَنْفُسَهُمْ ذَكَرُواْ ٱللَّهَ...﴾ [3:135]

17. ﴿وَلَوْ دُخِلَتْ عَلَيْهِم مِّنْ أَقْطَارِهَا ثُمَّ سُئِلُوا ٱلْفِتْنَةَ لَآتَوْهَا وَمَا تَلَبَّثُوا بِهَا إِلَّا يَسِيرًا﴾ [33:14]

18. ﴿...فَإِذَا بَلَغْنَ أَجَلَهُنَّ فَلَا جُنَاحَ عَلَيْكُمْ فِيمَا فَعَلْنَ فِي أَنْفُسِهِنَّ﴾ [2:234]

19. ﴿هُوَ ٱلَّذِي خَلَقَ ٱلسَّمَاوَاتِ وَٱلْأَرْضَ فِي سِتَّةِ أَيَّامٍ ثُمَّ ٱسْتَوَىٰ عَلَى ٱلْعَرْشِ﴾ [57:4]

20. ﴿وَلَا تَقْرَبَا هَٰذِهِ ٱلشَّجَرَةَ فَتَكُونَا مِنَ ٱلظَّالِمِينَ﴾ [2:35]

In the following Qur'ānic Āyāt below, convert the highlighted verbs into the Passive Noun (اِسْمُ المَفْعُول), match the gender and plurality.

21. ﴿وَٱلَّذِينَ إِذَا فَعَلُواْ فَاحِشَةً أَوْ ظَلَمُواْ أَنْفُسَهُمْ ذَكَرُواْ ٱللَّهَ...﴾ [3:135]

22. ﴿وَلَوْ دُخِلَتْ عَلَيْهِم مِّنْ أَقْطَارِهَا ثُمَّ سُئِلُوا ٱلْفِتْنَةَ لَآتَوْهَا وَمَا تَلَبَّثُوا بِهَا إِلَّا يَسِيرًا﴾ [33:14]

23. ﴿...فَإِذَا بَلَغْنَ أَجَلَهُنَّ فَلَا جُنَاحَ عَلَيْكُمْ فِيمَا فَعَلْنَ فِي أَنْفُسِهِنَّ﴾ [2:234]

24. ﴿هُوَ ٱلَّذِي خَلَقَ ٱلسَّمَاوَاتِ وَٱلْأَرْضَ فِي سِتَّةِ أَيَّامٍ ثُمَّ ٱسْتَوَىٰ عَلَى ٱلْعَرْشِ﴾ [57:4]

25. ﴿وَلَا تَقْرَبَا هَٰذِهِ ٱلشَّجَرَةَ فَتَكُونَا مِنَ ٱلظَّالِمِينَ﴾ [2:35]

LESSON 12 REVIEW QUESTIONS

True/False:

1. The rules for verb conjugation for Families II through X do not change.
2. The Maṣdar patterns to conjugate Verb Families II through X are based on many different patterns.
3. All Verb Families from II through X are somehow related to its Family I verb in meaning.
4. Verb Families II through IV are typically (مُتَعَدِّى).
5. In terms of meaning Verb Families II through IV typically relate to doing an action on the self.
6. The (مصدر), (اِسْمُ الفَاعِل), or (اِسْمُ المَفْعُول) from Verb Families II and above begin with the letter (م).
7. The (اِسْمُ الفَاعِل) has a Kasrah on the (ع) letter.
8. The (اِسْمُ المَفْعُول) has a Fatḥah on the (ع) letter from Verb Families II and above.
9. Form IV is the only verb type that actually has a Hamzah in its Command form.
10. For Command State in Forms II and above, it is formed by simply replacing the (ي) of Present Tense verbs with Alif like in the Verb I Families.

For the following highlighted verbs, <u>(1) identify its Verb Family (I, II, III, or IV)</u>, and <u>(2) Identify its tense (Past, Present, Command, or Passive). If there is an associated Ḥarf, identify the I'rāb of the Verb.</u>

11. ﴿فَأْتِيَاهُ فَقُولَا إِنَّا رَسُولَا رَبِّكَ فَأَرْسِلْ مَعَنَا بَنِي إِسْرَائِيلَ وَلَا تُعَذِّبْهُمْ...﴾ [20:47]

12. ﴿إِنَّمَا يُؤْمِنُ بِآيَاتِنَا ٱلَّذِينَ إِذَا ذُكِّرُوا بِهَا خَرُّوا سُجَّدًا وَسَبَّحُوا بِحَمْدِ رَبِّهِمْ...﴾ [32:15][107]

13. ﴿...وَأَنْزَلَ مِنَ ٱلسَّمَاءِ مَاءً فَأَخْرَجَ بِهِ مِنَ ٱلثَّمَرَاتِ رِزْقًا لَكُمْ...﴾ [2:22]

14. ﴿قَالُواْ يَا نُوحُ قَدْ جَادَلْتَنَا فَأَكْثَرْتَ جِدَالَنَا فَأْتِنَا بِمَا تَعِدُنَا إِن كُنتَ مِنَ ٱلصَّادِقِينَ﴾ [11:32]

15. ﴿...يَعْبُدُونَنِي لَا يُشْرِكُونَ بِي شَيْئًا...﴾ [24:55]

16. ﴿...وَقَاتِلُواْ ٱلْمُشْرِكِينَ كَآفَّةً كَمَا يُقَاتِلُونَكُمْ كَآفَّةً وَٱعْلَمُواْ أَنَّ ٱللهَ مَعَ ٱلْمُتَّقِينَ﴾ [9:36]

17. ﴿إِنَّا سَخَّرْنَا ٱلْجِبَالَ مَعَهُ يُسَبِّحْنَ بِٱلْعَشِيِّ وَٱلْإِشْرَاقِ﴾ [38:18]

18. ﴿سَوَاءٌ عَلَيْهِمْ أَأَنْذَرْتَهُمْ أَمْ لَمْ تُنْذِرْهُمْ لَا يُؤْمِنُونَ﴾ [2:6]

19. ﴿سَنُلْقِي فِي قُلُوبِ ٱلَّذِينَ كَفَرُوا ٱلرُّعْبَ بِمَا أَشْرَكُوا بِٱللهِ مَا لَمْ يُنَزِّلْ بِهِ سُلْطَانًا﴾ [3:151]

20. ﴿وَأَدْخَلْنَاهُمْ فِي رَحْمَتِنَا إِنَّهُمْ مِنَ ٱلصَّالِحِينَ﴾ [21: 86]

For the following highlighted nouns, <u>(1) identify the category to which it belongs (Verbal Noun, Doer Noun, or Passive Doer, (2) Identify its Verb Family (I, II, III, or IV)</u>

21. ﴿قَالُواْ يَا نُوحُ قَدْ جَادَلْتَنَا فَأَكْثَرْتَ جِدَالَنَا فَأْتِنَا بِمَا تَعِدُنَا إِن كُنتَ مِنَ ٱلصَّادِقِينَ﴾ [11:32]

22. ﴿وَقُلْ رَبِّ أَدْخِلْنِي مُدْخَلَ صِدْقٍ وَأَخْرِجْنِي مُخْرَجَ صِدْقٍ﴾ [17:80]

23. ﴿...وَإِن مِّن شَيْءٍ إِلاَّ يُسَبِّحُ بِحَمْدِهِ وَلَكِن لاَّ تَفْقَهُونَ تَسْبِيحَهُمْ إِنَّهُ كَانَ حَلِيمًا غَفُورًا﴾ [17:44]

24. ﴿وَمَا نُرْسِلُ ٱلْمُرْسَلِينَ إِلاَّ مُبَشِّرِينَ وَمُنذِرِينَ...﴾ [6:48]

25. ﴿قُلْ لَوْ أَنْتُمْ تَمْلِكُونَ خَزَائِنَ رَحْمَةِ رَبِّي إِذًا لَأَمْسَكْتُمْ خَشْيَةَ ٱلْإِنْفَاقِ...﴾ [17:100]

<u>Convert the highlighted verbs or derived nouns into its identical counterpart from the Verb I Family. Please retain the respective conjugation, plurality, gender, etc. if applicable.</u>

26. ﴿...وَيُنَزِّلُ عَلَيْكُمْ مِنَ ٱلسَّمَاءِ مَاءً لِيُطَهِّرَكُمْ بِهِ...﴾ [8:11]

27. ﴿وَأَدْخَلْنَاهُ فِي رَحْمَتِنَا إِنَّهُ مِنَ ٱلصَّالِحِينَ﴾ [21:75]

28. ﴿كُتِبَ عَلَيْكُمُ ٱلْقِتَالُ وَهُوَ كُرْهٌ لَكُمْ...﴾ [2:216]

29. ﴿رَبَّنَا فَٱغْفِرْ لَنَا ذُنُوبَنَا وَكَفِّرْ عَنَّا سَيِّئَاتِنَا وَتَوَفَّنَا مَعَ ٱلْأَبْرَارِ﴾ [3:193]

30. ﴿قَالَ ٱللهُ إِنِّي مُنَزِّلُهَا عَلَيْكُمْ فَمَن يَكْفُرْ بَعْدُ مِنكُمْ فَإِنِّي أُعَذِّبُهُ عَذَابًا لاَّ أُعَذِّبُهُ أَحَدًا مِّنَ ٱلْعَالَمِينَ﴾ [5:115]

---

107 Please note that the verb (يُؤْمِنُ) comes from (آمَنَ) an Irregular verb in Verb Family IV.

Lesson 13 Review Questions

For the following highlighted verbs, __(1) identify its Verb Family (V-X), and (2) Identify its tense (Past, Present, Command, or Passive). If there is an associated Ḥarf, identify the Iʿrāb of the Verb__

1. ﴿وَأَنْزَلْنَا إِلَيْكَ ٱلذِّكْرَ لِتُبَيِّنَ لِلنَّاسِ مَا نُزِّلَ إِلَيْهِمْ وَلَعَلَّهُمْ يَتَفَكَّرُونَ﴾ [16:44]
2. ﴿وَقَالَ ٱلَّذِينَ ٱتَّبَعُوا۟ لَوْ أَنَّ لَنَا كَرَّةً فَنَتَبَرَّأَ مِنْهُمْ كَمَا تَبَرَّؤُوا۟ مِنَّا كَذَٰلِكَ يُرِيهِمُ ٱللَّهُ أَعْمَالَهُمْ حَسَرَاتٍ عَلَيْهِمْ وَمَا هُم بِخَارِجِينَ مِنَ ٱلنَّارِ﴾ [2:167]
3. ﴿وَيَسْتَعْجِلُونَكَ بِٱلْعَذَابِ وَلَنْ يُخْلِفَ ٱللَّهُ وَعْدَهُ...﴾ [22:47]
4. ﴿قَالَ سَلَامٌ عَلَيْكَ سَأَسْتَغْفِرُ لَكَ رَبِّي إِنَّهُ كَانَ بِي حَفِيًّا﴾ [19:47]
5. ﴿فَٱنطَلَقَا حَتَّىٰ إِذَا لَقِيَا غُلَامًا فَقَتَلَهُ قَالَ أَقَتَلْتَ نَفْسًا زَكِيَّةً بِغَيْرِ نَفْسٍ لَّقَدْ جِئْتَ شَيْئًا نُّكْرًا﴾ [18:74]
6. ﴿...وَمَنْ يَسْتَنْكِفْ عَنْ عِبَادَتِهِ وَيَسْتَكْبِرْ فَسَيَحْشُرُهُمْ إِلَيْهِ جَمِيعًا﴾ [4:172]
7. ﴿وَلَقَدِ ٱسْتُهْزِئَ بِرُسُلٍ مِنْ قَبْلِكَ فَحَاقَ بِٱلَّذِينَ سَخِرُوا مِنْهُمْ مَا كَانُوا بِهِ يَسْتَهْزِئُونَ﴾ [21:41]
8. ﴿...إِلَى ٱللَّهِ مَرْجِعُكُمْ جَمِيعًا فَيُنَبِّئُكُمْ بِمَا كُنْتُمْ فِيهِ تَخْتَلِفُونَ﴾ [5:48]
9. ﴿تَبَارَكَ ٱلَّذِي نَزَّلَ ٱلْفُرْقَانَ عَلَىٰ عَبْدِهِ لِيَكُونَ لِلْعَالَمِينَ نَذِيرًا﴾ [25:1]
10. ﴿يُجَادِلُونَكَ فِي ٱلْحَقِّ بَعْدَمَا تَبَيَّنَ كَأَنَّمَا يُسَاقُونَ إِلَى ٱلْمَوْتِ﴾ [8:6]

For the following highlighted nouns, __(1) identify the category to which it belongs (Verbal Noun, Doer Noun, or Passive Doer, (2) Identify its Verb Family (V - X)__

11. ﴿فَأَعْرِضْ عَنْهُمْ وَٱنْتَظِرْ إِنَّهُمْ مُنْتَظِرُونَ﴾ [32:30]
12. ﴿يَسْمَعُ آيَاتِ ٱللَّهِ تُتْلَىٰ عَلَيْهِ ثُمَّ يُصِرُّ مُسْتَكْبِرًا كَأَنْ لَمْ يَسْمَعْهَا فَبَشِّرْهُ بِعَذَابٍ أَلِيمٍ﴾ [45:8]
13. ﴿...وَمِنَ ٱلنَّخْلِ مِنْ طَلْعِهَا قِنْوَانٌ دَانِيَةٌ وَجَنَّاتٍ مِنْ أَعْنَابٍ وَٱلزَّيْتُونَ وَٱلرُّمَّانَ مُشْتَبِهًا وَغَيْرَ مُتَشَابِهٍ...﴾ [6:99]
14. ﴿وَنَزَعْنَا مَا فِي صُدُورِهِمْ مِنْ غِلٍّ إِخْوَانًا عَلَىٰ سُرُرٍ مُتَقَابِلِينَ﴾ [15:47]
15. ﴿يَا صَاحِبَيِ ٱلسِّجْنِ أَأَرْبَابٌ مُتَفَرِّقُونَ خَيْرٌ أَمِ ٱللَّهُ ٱلْوَاحِدُ ٱلْقَهَّارُ﴾ [12:39]

__16-23. Identify the Verb Family (I to X) and the tense (past, present, or command)__

16	17	18	19	20	21	22	23
تَخْتَلِفِينَ	أَسْتَغْفِرُ	أَسْلِمْ	يُنْزِلُونَ	يُسَبِّحُونَ	جَاهِدْ	يَخْرُجُ	أَنْزِلْ

24. The 10 Family Table: Complete the empty boxes below without referring to the book.

مَصْدَر	اسم الفاعل	Present Passive	Past Passive	Forbidding	الأمر	المُضارِع	الماضِي	الفِعْل	
		يُضْرَبُ	ضُرِبَ	لا تَضْرِبْ	اِضْرِبْ	يَضْرِبُ		فَعَلَ	I
تَكْذِيب	مُكَذِّبٌ		كُذِّبَ		كَذِّبْ		كَذَّبَ	فَعَّلَ	II
قِتَال		يُقَاتَلُ	قُوتِلُ	لا تُقَاتِلْ			قَاتَلَ	فَاعَلَ	III
		يُسْلَمُ		لا تُسْلِمْ		يُسْلِمُ		أَفْعَلَ	IV
تَعَلُّمٌ			تُعُلِّمَ		تَعَلَّمْ	يَتَعَلَّمُ	تَعَلَّمَ	تَفَعَّلَ	V
	مُتَفَاخِرٌ		تُفُوخِرَ	لا تَتَفَاخَرْ	تَفَاخَرْ	يَتَفَاخَرُ	تَفَاخَرَ		VI
اِنْقِلاب	مُنْقَلِبٌ	--	--	لا تَنْقَلِبْ	اِنْقَلِبْ	يَنْقَلِبُ	اِنْقَلَبَ	اِنْفَعَلَ	VII
		يُكْتَرَبُ	اُكْتُرِبَ	لا تَكْتَرِبْ			اِكْتَرَبَ	اِفْتَعَلَ	VIII
		يُسْتَقْبَلُ	اُسْتُقْبِلَ	لا تَسْتَقْبِلْ	اِسْتَقْبِلْ		اِسْتَقْبَلَ	اِسْتَفْعَلَ	X

Answer Key for Review Questions

Lesson 1 Answers

True/False:

1. F   2. T   3. F   4. T   5. F

Short Answer:

6. Hamzah is always pronounced, while an Alif is only pronounced when at the beginning of a sentence or from a pause.

7. Fi'l, Noun, Ḥarf.

8. Number, Gender, Definiteness, and I'rāb.

9. ﴾انِ﴿ and ﴾يْنِ﴿.

10. ة

Vocabulary Review: (from right to left as in the corresponding Āyah)

11-12. the Messenger....(his) Lord

13-14. a reward..... account/reckoning

15-16. the rivers.......forever

17-20. the heavens..... the earth..... the sun..... the moon

Lesson 2 Answers

True/False

1. T   2. T   3. T   4. T   5. F   6. F

Short Answer:

7. ﴾مُسْلِماتٌ﴿ or ﴾مُسْلِماتٍ﴿.

8. Inflexible Nouns do not change their endings, while partially Inflexible Nouns cannot take a Kasrah, nor can they have Tanwīn.

9. Partially Flexible: ﴾مَساجِد﴿ or ﴾مَكَّة﴿ Inflexible: ﴾أُوْلَـئِكَ﴿.

10. Plural, male, Definite, Raf', and Flexible.

11. ﴾اَلْمُسْلِمِينَ﴿ is plural, male, Definite, Naṣb or Jarr, and Flexible; ﴾اَلْمُسْلِمَاتِ﴿ is plural, female, Definite, Naṣb or Jarr, and Flexible.

12. Single, male, Definite, Raf', Naṣb, or Jarr, and Inflexible.

13. Single, male, Definite, Naṣb, or Jarr, and Partially Flexible.

14. Single, male, Indefinite, Jarr, and Flexible.

15. Single, female (Broken Plural), Indefinite, Raf', and Partially Flexible

16-18. the evil ..the good..........................the prayer

19-20. favor...sin

21-22. covenant (his).....treaty/pact

	Single	Dual	Plural
23.			مُسْلِمونَ
24.	بَيْتٍ		
25.			مُسْلِمِينَ
26.	كَلِمَةٌ		
27.			مُجاهِدِينَ
	Rafʿ	Naṣb	Jarr
28.		مُحَمَّدًا	
29.			عِيسٰى
30.			مَرْيَمَ

Lesson 3 Answers

True/False:

1. F 2. T 3. F 4. F 5. T

6. T 7. F 8. T 9. F 10. T

11-15.

Plural	Dual	Single
هُمْ	هُما	هُوَ
هُنَّ	هُما	هِيَ
أَنْتُم	أَنْتُما	أَنْتَ
أَنْتُنَّ	أَنْتُما	أَنْتِ
نَحْنُ	نَحْنُ	أَنا

	Plural	Dual	Single
15.	كِتابِهِمْ	---	---
16.	كِتابِهِنَّ	كِتابِهِما	كِتابِها
17.	كِتابِكُمْ	كِتابِكُما	---
18.	---	كِتابِكُما	كِتابِكِ
19.	كِتابِنا	---	كِتابِي

Short answer

20. The meaning would be "we worship You and we ask You for help" but it lacks exclusivity.
21. هَذِهِ
22. ذَلِكَ
23. هَؤُلاءِ
24. their fingers.... their ears
25. creature... from them.... <u>Relative Pronoun....</u> its belly.....two feet.... <u>Relative Pronoun</u>... <u>Relative Pronoun</u>
26. .... <u>Relative Pronoun</u> ...their voices.... <u>Pointing Noun (far)... Relative Pronoun...</u> their hearts
27. their sights (women)....Relative Pronoun

Lesson 4 Answers

True/False:

1. T	2. F	3. T	4. F	5. F
6. T	7. F	8. T	9. T	10. F

11. from it (feminine).... from fruit..... from before
12. to you (all)..... from what
13. with our signs... in it
14. in their hearts...... with what ....with their mouths
15. from after your death .... so that you
16. Indeed we..... to Allah..... Indeed we... to Him
17. with him.... until a time
18. regarding the hour... with my Lord.... with its time... in the heavens and earth.... as if you.... from it.... with Allah.... but most

19. المُدُنِ	20. شُرَكَاءُ	21. البِحْرُ	22. المَلِكَ	23. أَمْثالِها	24. كَواكِبُ	25. صَدْرِكُمْ

Lesson 5 Answers

True/False:

1. T	2. T	3. F	4. T	5. F	6. T
7. T	8. T	9. T	10. T	11. T	12. T

Translate the following highlighted Constructions in the following Qur'ānic Āyāt (be exact as possible).

13. a sound heart
14. a straight path…revelation from the Most Powerful, Most Merciful
15. people of the village/town
16. this tree
17. himself…killing of his brother….from the losers

18-23. Jarr Constructions have one line, Possession constructions have two lines, Describing Constructions have dotted lines and Pointing Constructions have wavy lines. Constructions that are merged are highlighted.

18. ﴿ وَإِنَّكَ لَعَلى خُلُقٍ عَظِيمٍ ﴾ [68:4]

19. ﴿ تَبَارَكَ ٱلَّذِي بِيَدِهِ ٱلْمُلْكُ وَهُوَ عَلَى كُلِّ شَيْءٍ قَدِيرٌ ﴾ [67:1]

20. ﴿ وَلِلَّذِينَ كَفَرُوا بِرَبِّهِمْ عَذَابُ جَهَنَّمَ وَبِئْسَ ٱلْمَصِيرُ ﴾ [67:6]

21. ﴿ وَهَذَا ٱلْبَلَدِ ٱلْأَمِينِ ﴾ [95:3]

22. ﴿ وَلَمَّا جَاءَهُمْ رَسُولٌ مِّنْ عِندِ ٱللَّهِ مُصَدِّقٌ لِّمَا مَعَهُمْ نَبَذَ فَرِيقٌ مِّنَ ٱلَّذِينَ أُوتُواْ ٱلْكِتَابَ كِتَابَ ٱللَّهِ وَرَاءَ ظُهُورِهِمْ كَأَنَّهُمْ لاَ يَعْلَمُونَ ﴾ [2:101]

23. ﴿ وَلِلَّذِينَ كَفَرُوا بِرَبِّهِمْ عَذَابُ جَهَنَّمَ وَبِئْسَ ٱلْمَصِيرُ ﴾ [78:40]

Lesson 6 Answers

True/False:

1. T	2. F	3. T	4. F	5. T
6. T	7. T	8. T	9. F	10. T

Write the following:

11. أَنَا مُسْلِمٌ	12. ذَلِكَ بَيْتٌ	13. ذَلِكَ الْمَسْجِدُ كَبِيرٌ
14. بَيْتُكَ كَبِيرٌ	15. أَنْتَ فِي الْمَدِينَةِ	

In the following parts from the Qur'ānic Āyāt, the Nominal Sentence has been extracted.
(1) Identify the Subject [مُبْتَدَأ] **by underlining it and (2) translate the highlighted word with its respective plural or singular.**

16. ﴿ ...وَتِلْكَ حُدُودُ اللَّهِ... ﴾ [limits/حَدّ]

17. ﴿ ...إِنَّ ٱللَّهَ بَالِغُ أَمْرِهِ... ﴾ [command/أُمُورِهِ]

18. ﴿ ...ذَٰلِكَ أَمْرُ ٱللَّهِ... ﴾ [that/أُولَئِكَ]

19. ﴿ ذَٰلِكَ ٱلْيَوْمُ ٱلَّذِي كَانُوا يُوعَدُونَ ﴾ [the day/ٱلْأَيَّام]

20. ﴿ ...وَٱللَّهُ عَلِيمٌ بِذَاتِ ٱلصُّدُورِ ﴾ [the chests/ٱلصَّدْر]

21. ﴿ فَهُوَ فِي عِيشَةٍ رَّاضِيَةٍ ﴾ [life/---]

22. ﴿...هَٰذَا سِحْرٌ مُّبِينٌ ﴾ [magic/--]

23. ﴿...أَنِّي رَسُولُ ٱللَّهِ إِلَيْكُمْ ﴾ [messenger/رُسُل]

24. ﴿...مَنْ أَنصَارِي إِلَى ٱللَّهِ.. ﴾ [{my}helpers/نَاصِر]

Lesson 7 Answers

True/False:

1. F 2. T 3. T 4. T

Translate the following into Arabic:

5. رَسُولُ الْمَلِكِ	6. رَسُولُ مَلِكٍ	7. الْمَلِكُ الْمُسلِمُ	8. الْمَلِكُ مُسْلِمٌ	9. مُعَلِّمُ الْمَدِينَةِ الْمُسْلِمُ
10. الْمُعَلِّمُ الْمُسْلِمُ مَلِكٌ	11. الْمُسلِمُ هُوَ الْمَلِكُ	12. هَذَا هُوَ مُعَلِّمُ الْمَلِكِ	13. مُعَلِّمُ الْمَلِكِ هَذَا	

14. close friend[قُرَناء]	**15.** far	**16.** calf [عُجُول]	**17.** anger	**18.** confirming
19. path [طُرُق/طَرائِق]	**20.** behind	**21.** back [ظُهور]	**22.** besides/--	**23.** heels [عَقِب]

Lesson 8 Answers

True/False:

1. F 2. T 3. T 4. T 5. T

6. F 7. F 8. T 9. T

10-14. Fill in the Spaces with [قَرَأَ] with the attached pronoun [هُ] at its end.

Plural	Dual	Single	
قَرَأُوهُ	---	---	3rd Person masculine
قَرَأْنَهُ	---	قَرَأَتْهُ	3rd Person feminine
قَرَأْتُمُوهُ	---	قَرَأْتَهُ	2nd Person masculine
قَرَأْتُنَّهُ	قَرَأْتُمَاهُ	---	2nd Person feminine
قَرَأْنَاهُ	---	قَرَأْتُهُ	1st Person (masculine/feminine)

15-19. Fill in the spaces with [يَضْرِبُ] with the attached pronoun [هُمْ] at its end.

Plural	Dual	Single	
يَضْرِبونَهُمْ	يَضْرِبانِهِمْ	---	3rd Person masculine
يَضْرِبْنَهُمْ	---	---	3rd Person feminine
---	تَضْرِبانِهِمْ	تَضْرِبُهُمْ	2nd Person masculine
تَضْرِبْنَهُمْ	---	تَضْرِبِينَهُم	2nd Person feminine
نَضْرِبُهُمْ	---	أَضْرِبُهُم	1st Person (masculine/feminine)

	Verb root	Translation	Conjugation [pronoun]
20.	دَخَلَ	To enter	هُم
21.	خَرَجَ	To exit/leave	هُم
22.	ظَلَمَ	To transgress	نَحْنُ
23.	كَتَبَ	To write	هِيَ
24.	بَلَغَ	To reach	هُنَّ
25.	فَعَلَ	To do	هُنَّ

	Present Tense form	Translation	Conjugation [pronoun]
26.	تَحْكُمُ	To judge	أَنْتَ
27.	يَنْظُرُ	To see	هُوَ
28.	نَغْفِرُ	To forgive	نَحْنُ
29.	يَفْسُقُونَ	To corrupt	هُمْ

Lesson 9 Answers

True/False:

1. F　2. T　3. T　4. F　5. T
6. F　7. F　8. F　9. F　10. T

11. ﴿...فَأَخَذَتْكُمُ ٱلصَّاعِقَةُ وَأَنتُمْ تَنظُرُونَ﴾

12. ﴿...بَلْ لَّعَنَهُمُ ٱللَّهُ بِكُفْرِهِمْ فَقَلِيْلاً مَّا يُؤْمِنُونَ﴾

13. ﴿وَلَمَّا جَاءَهُمْ رَسُولٌ مِّنْ عِندِ ٱللهِ مُصَدِّقٌ لِّمَا مَعَهُمْ نَبَذَ فَرِيقٌ مِّنَ ٱلَّذِينَ أُوتُواْ ٱلْكِتَابَ كِتَابَ ٱللهِ وَرَاءَ ظُهُورِهِمْ كَأَنَّهُمْ لاَ يَعْلَمُونَ﴾

|هُم → يَعْلَمُونَ|

14. ﴿..وَمَا كَفَرَ سُلَيْمَانُ وَلَكِنَّ ٱلشَّيَاطِينَ كَفَرُواْ..﴾　كَفَرُواْ　→ هُم

15. ﴿وَإِذْ يَرْفَعُ إِبْرَاهِيمُ ٱلْقَوَاعِدَ مِنَ ٱلْبَيْتِ...﴾

16. ﴿وَٱلَّذِينَ إِذَا فَعَلُواْ فَاحِشَةً أَوْ ظَلَمُواْ أَنْفُسَهُمْ ذَكَرُواْ ٱللَّهَ...﴾

17. ﴿يَجْعَلُونَ أَصَابِعَهُمْ فِي آذَانِهِم مِّنَ ٱلصَّوَاعِقِ حَذَرَ ٱلْمَوْتِ﴾

18. ﴿..تَقْتُلُونَ أَنفُسَكُمْ وَتُخْرِجُونَ فَرِيقاً مِّنْكُمْ مِّنْ دِيَارِهِمْ..﴾

19. ﴿هُوَ ٱلَّذِي خَلَقَ ٱلسَّمَاوَاتِ وَٱلْأَرْضَ فِي سِتَّةِ أَيَّامٍ ثُمَّ ٱسْتَوَى عَلَى ٱلْعَرْشِ﴾

20. ﴿قَالَ رَبِّ إِنِّي ظَلَمْتُ نَفْسِي فَٱغْفِرْ لِي فَغَفَرَ لَهُ﴾

Vocabulary (Verbs):

21	22	23	24	25
ذَكَرَ يَذْكُرُ	رَزَقَ يَرْزُقُ	ضَرَبَ يَضْرِبُ	حَمَلَ يَحْمِلُ	كَذَبَ يَكْذِبُ

Lesson 10 Answers

True/False:

1. F 2. F 3. T 4. F 5. T

6. F 7. T 8. F 9. T 10. F

Short Answer.

11. [سَ] and [سَوْفَ]

12. The verb structurally is changed in a similar fashion, either by adding a Sukūn on 1st Person or by dropping the Nūn at the end.

13. [أَيْنَ]/[ما]/[مَنْ]/ [إِنْ]/, or [مَتَى]

14. Jazm Particles = [لَم/إِنْ/مَنْ/لِ/لا/لَمَّا/ما]; Naṣb Particles =[كَيْ/حَتَّى/لَنْ/لَكِن/لِ/أَنْ]

15. [وَ]/[حَتَّى]/[لا]/[لِ]/[ما]/[مَنْ]

In the following Āyāt, state the I'rāb of the highlighted Verb below, and underline the Ḥarf if applicable.

16.	نُشْرِكَ Naṣb			
17.	يَزَالُونَ Raf'	يُقَاتِلُون Raf'	يَرُدُّو Naṣb	آسْتَطَاعُوا Jazm
18.	يَأْمُرُ Raf'	تَذْبَحُواْ Jazm	تَتَّخِذُ Raf'	أَكُونَ Naṣb
19.	يَكْفُرْ Jazm	يُؤْمِنُ Jazm		
20.	تَكُونُوا Jazm	تَعْلَمُونَ Raf'		

In the following Āyāt, convert the highlighted verb in the command tense [اَلْفِعْلُ الْأَمْر] in the same conjugation.

21	22	23	24	25
أنصُرُوا	أُعْبُدُ	أُشْكُرُوا	أُذْكُرْ	أُخْرُجْ إِعْمَلُوا

Lesson 11 Answers

True/False:

1. T 2. F 3. T 4. T 5. F

6. T 7. T 8. T 9. T 10. T

11	12	13	14	15	16	17	18	19	20
كُرِهُوا	يُذْكَرُونَ	عُلِمْتُمْ	ظُلِمَ يُظْلَمُونَ	بُلِغْنَ فُعِلْنَ	فاعِلُونَ ظَالِمُونَ ذَاكِرُونَ	دَاخِلَةٌ سَائِلُونَ	بَالِغَاتٌ فاعِلاتٌ	خَالِقٌ	قارِبانِ كائِنانِ

21	22	23	24	25
مَفْعولونَ مَظْلومونَ مَذْكُورونَ	مَدْخُولَةٌ مَسْأُولُونَ	مَبْلوغاتٌ مَفْعولاتٌ	مَخْلوقٌ	مَقْروبانِ ---

Lesson 12 Answers

True/False:

1. T	2. F	3. T	4. T	5. F
6. T	7. T	8. T	9. T	10. F

Question#	11		12		13		14	
Verb	أَرْسِلْ	لَا تُعَذِّبْ	ذُكِّرُوا	سَبَّحُوا	أَنْزَلَ	أَخْرَجَ	جَادَلْت	اَكْثَرْتَ
Verb Family	IV	II	II	II	IV	IV	III	IV
Tense	Command	Present /Jazm	Past Passive	Past	Past	Past	Past	Past
Question#	15		16			17		
Verb	يَعْبُدُونَ	يُشْرِكُونَ	قَاتِلُوا	يُقَاتِلُونَ	اَعْلَمُواْ	سَخَّرْنَا	يُسَبِّحْنَ	
Verb Family	I	IV	III	III	I	II	II	
Tense	Present	Present	Command	Present	Command	Past	Present	
Question#	18		19			20		
Verb	أَنْذَرْتَ	لَمْ تُنْذِرْ	كَفَرُوا	أَشْرَكُوا	لَمْ يُنَزِّلْ	أَدْخَلْنَا		
Verb Family	IV	IV	I	IV	II	IV		
Tense	Past	Present /Jazm	Past	Past	Present/ Jazm	Past		

Question#	21		22			23	
Noun	جِدَالَ	ٱلصَّادِقِينَ	مُدْخَلَ	صِدْقٍ	مُخْرَجَ	حَمْدِ	تَسْبِيحَ
Category	Verbal noun	Doer Noun	Passive noun	Verbal noun	Passive noun	Verbal noun	Verbal noun
Family	III	I	IV	I	IV	I	II

Question#	24			25	
Noun	ٱلْمُرْسَلِينَ	مُبَشِّرِينَ	مُنذِرِينَ	رَحْمَةِ	ٱلْإِنْفَاقِ
Category	Doer Noun	Doer Noun	Doer Noun	Verbal noun	Verbal noun
Family	IV	II	IV	I	IV

26	27	28	29	30
يَنْزِلُ	دَخَلْنا	القَتْلُ	أَكْفُرْ	نازِل

Lesson 13 Answers

Question #	1	2			3		4
Verb	يَتَفَكَّرُونَ	ٱتَّبَعُوا	نَتَبَرَّأَ	تَبَرَّؤُوا	يَسْتَعْجِلُونَ	يُخْلِفَ	أَسْتَغْفِرُ
Verb Family	V	VIII	V	V	X	IV	X
Tense	Present	Command	Present Naṣb	Past	Present	Present Naṣb	Present

Question #	5		6			7		
Verb	ٱنطَلَقَا	قَتَلْتَ	يَسْتَنْكِفْ	يَسْتَكْبِرْ	يَحْشُرُ	ٱسْتُهْزِئَ	سَخِرُوا	يَسْتَهْزِئُونَ
Verb Family	VII	I	X	X	I	X	I	X
Tense	Past	Past	Present Jazm	Present Jazm	Present	Past Passive	Past	Present

Question #	8		9		10	
Verb	يُنَبِّئُ	تَخْتَلِفُونَ	تَبَارَكَ	نَزَّلَ	يُجَادِلُونَ	تَبَيَّنَ
Verb Family	II	VIII	VI	II	III	V
Tense	Present	Present	Past	Past	Present	Past

Question#	11	12	13	14	15
Noun	مُنْتَظِرُونَ	مُسْتَكْبِرًا	مُتَشَابِهٍ	مُتَقَابِلِينَ	مُتَفَرِّقُونَ
Category	Doer Noun	Verbal Noun	Doer Noun	Doer Noun	Doer Noun
Family	VII	X	VI	VI	V

16. VII Present	17. X Present	18. IV Command	19. IV Present	20. II Present	21. III Command	22. I Present	23. IV Command

24. The 10 Family Table: Answers are highlighted.

مَصْدَر	اسم الفاعِل	Present Passive	Past Passive	Forbidding	الأمر	مُضارِع	الماضي	الفِعْل	
ضَرْبٌ	ضارِبٌ	يُضْرَبُ	ضُرِبَ	لا تَضْرِبْ	اِضْرِبْ	يَضْرِبُ	ضَرَبَ	فَعَلَ	**I**
تَكْذِيب	مُكَذِّبٌ	يُكَذَّبُ	كُذِّبَ	لا تُكَذِّبْ	كَذِّبْ	يُكَذِّبُ	كَذَّبَ	فَعَّلَ	**II**
قِتال	مُقاتِلٌ	يُقاتَلُ	قُوتِلَ	لا تُقاتِلْ	قاتِلْ	يُقاتِلُ	قاتَلَ	فاعَلَ	**III**
إِسْلامٌ	مُسْلِمٌ	يُسْلَمُ	أُسْلِمَ	لا تُسْلِمْ	أَسْلِمْ	يُسْلِمُ	أَسْلَمَ	أَفْعَلَ	**IV**
تَعَلُّم	مُتَعَلِّمٌ	يُتَعَلَّمُ	تُعُلِّمَ	لا تَتَعَلَّمْ	تَعَلَّمْ	يَتَعَلَّمُ	تَعَلَّمَ	تَفَعَّلَ	**V**
تَفاخُرٌ	مُتَفاخِرٌ	يُتَفاخَرُ	تُفُوخِرَ	لا تَتَفاخَرْ	تَفاخَرْ	يَتَفاخَرُ	تَفاخَرَ	تَفاعَلَ	**VI**
اِنْقِلاب	مُنْقَلِبٌ	--	--	لا تَنْقَلِبْ	اِنْقَلِبْ	يَنْقَلِبُ	اِنْقَلَبَ	اِنْفَعَلَ	**VII**
اِكْتِرابٌ	مُكْتَرِبٌ	يُكْتَرَبُ	اُكْتُرِبَ	لا تَكْتَرِبْ	اِكْتَرِبْ	يَكْتَرِبُ	اِكْتَرَبَ	اِفْتَعَلَ	**VIII**
اِسْتِقْبالٌ	مُسْتَقْبِلٌ	يُسْتَقْبَلُ	اُسْتُقْبِلَ	لا تَسْتَقْبِلْ	اِسْتَقْبِلْ	يَسْتَقْبِلُ	اِسْتَقْبَلَ	اِسْتَفْعَلَ	**X**

References

1. 'Abdul-Raḥeem, 'Abdul-'Azeez. 80% of Quranic Words, available for free download at: **http://emuslim.com/quran/english80.asp**.
2. Āl Ash-Sheikh, Ṣāliḥ bin 'Abdul 'Azīz bin Muḥammad bin Ibrāhīm [مَوقع الإسلام الدعوي و الإرشادي], Section on Ḥadīth **http://www.al-islam.com/.**
3. Al-Faṣeeḥ, [الفصيح لِعُلُوم اللغة العربيّة], **http://www.alfaseeh.com/vb/showthread.php?t=54331.**
4. Dukes, Kais, PhD. Qur'ānic Arabic Corpus. 2009-2011. Language Research Group, University of Leeds. **http://corpus.quran.com/**.
5. Encyclopaedia Britannica, Naskhi Script, 10/10/12, **http://www.britannica.com/EBchecked/topic/403972/naskhi-script**.
6. Reefnet, *Reefnet.com,* website: **http://www.reefnet.gov.sy/education/kafaf/index.html**.
7. Ḥassan, Iffath. Qur'ānic Language Made Easy: Basic Grammar Required to Understand the Qur'ān**.** Illinois: IQRA International Educational Foundation, 2002.
8. Jiyād, Moḥammed. A Hundred and One Rules! A Short Reference for Syntactic, Morphological, & Phonological rules for Novice and Intermediate Levels of Proficiency. Lambert Academic Publishing, 2010.
9. Karamāli, Hamza, Sunnipath Academy, ARB201 and ARB202: Introductory Arabic 1 and 2, Fall 2007 to Spring 2008.
10. Khān, 'Abdul Sattar. Arabic Tutor – Part 1, Translated by Moulāna Ebrāhīm Muḥammad, 1st Edition, 2007. Darul-Ishaat, Karachi, Pakistan.
11. Khān, 'Abdul Sattar. Arabic Tutor – Part 2, Translated by Moulāna Ebrāhīm Muḥammad, 1st Edition, 2007. Darul-Ishaat, Karachi, Pakistan.
12. Khān, 'Abdul Sattar. Arabic Tutor – Part 3, Translated by Moulāna Ebrāhīm Muḥammad, 1st Edition, 2007. Darul-Ishaat, Karachi, Pakistan.
13. Khān, 'Abdul Sattar. Arabic Tutor – Part 4, Translated by Moulāna Ebrāhīm Muḥammad, 1st Edition, 2007. Darul-Ishaat, Karachi, Pakistan.
14. Khān, Farooq Sarar. Open Burhān. January 2007. **http://www.openburhan.net/**.
15. Lane, Edward William An Arabic- English Lexicon , 1968, Libraire Beirut, Lebanon.
16. Muḥammad, Ebrāhīm, From the Treasures of Arabic Morphology, Zam Zam Publishers, 2nd Edition, 2008.
17. Ranginwala, Masood, Essentials of Quranic Arabic – Intermediate Level, Volume 2, 2013, ILF-NY Publications: New York, 1st Edition.
18. Ṣaḥīḥ International. Translation of the Meaning of the Glorious Qur'ān, AbulQāsim Publishing House (1997), Riyāḍh.
19. Wehr, Hans and Milton J. Cowan (Editor). Hans Wehr: A Dictionary of Modern Written Arabic. 3rd Edition. Ithica, NY: Spoken Language Services, Inc., 1976.
20. Ziyād, MM. *Dr. Mosād.* Website: **http://www.drmosad.com**.

About the Author

Masood Aḥmed Ranginwala has studied Arabic with various teachers and institutions. He has been teaching basic Qur'ānic Arabic over the past few years at the Islāmic Learning Foundation, an institution of Islāmic Circle of North America (ICNA). He earned the Sībawayh Degree in Arabic Studies from the Qibla Institute. He obtained a Diploma in Islāmic Studies from the Islāmic Online University (IOU) where he serves as the Arabic Studies Coordinator for the Diploma Series since 2012. At IOU, he is the instructor for the Diploma Course Series "Introduction to Qur'anic Arabic". He is a member of ICNA, and a founding member of its youth organization, Young Muslims. He is a practicing emergency physician and resides with his wife and three children in New Jersey.

وَ الصَّلاةُ وَ السَّلامُ عَلى مُحَمَّدٍ وَ عَلى آلِهِ وَ أَصْحابِهِ أَجْمَعين

اللهُ سُبْحانَهُ و تَعالى حَسْبُنا و نِعْمَ الْوَكيل

20414969R00124

Made in the USA
San Bernardino, CA
09 April 2015